Annual Review of Addictions and Offender Counseling, Volume IV

Best Practices

Annual Review of Addictions and Offender Counseling, Volume IV

Best Practices

Edited by
Trevor J. Buser,
Pamela S. Lassiter,
and Kathleen Brown-Rice

RESOURCE *Publications* • Eugene, Oregon

ANNUAL REVIEW OF ADDICTIONS AND OFFENDER COUNSELING, VOLUME IV
Best Practices

Resource Publications
An Imprint of Wipf and Stock Publishers
199 W. 8th Ave., Suite 3
Eugene, OR 97401

www.wipfandstock.com

PAPERBACK ISBN: 978-1-5326-4139-8
HARDCOVER ISBN: 978-1-5326-4140-4
EBOOK ISBN: 978-1-5326-4141-1

Manufactured in the U.S.A. 01/07/19

Contents

1 Editorial 1

2 *DSM-5* Diagnostic Considerations for Behavioral or Process Addictions 7
Leigh Falls Holman and Kristy Carlisle

3 Mindfulness- and Acceptance-Based Intervention for Opioid Dependence in Groups with Open Enrollment 29
Christie Nelson and Daniel Gutierrez

4 *Add-Wellness*: A Humanistic Model to Conceptualize Addiction 46
James E. McDonald and Jennifer M. Cook

5 Psychedelic Therapy and Microdosing: An Overview for Counselors 68
Peter Eischens

6 Using a Group Counseling Intervention to Treat Inmates' Symptoms of Mental Illness 83
Robert m Cox, Richard K. James, Rebecca J. Grady, and Michael S. Skirius

7 Person Centered Therapy with Adult Male Prisoners Diagnosed with Gender Dysphoria 106
Amanda Hinds and Melinda M. Gibbons

8 Professional Counselors' and Students' Current Knowledge, Training, and Experience with Process Addictions 124
Angie D. Cartwright, Leigh Falls Holman, Judith A. Nelson, Kristy Carlisle, Christine Baker, Regina Moro, Sarah Monakes Whitmire, Stephanie Carroll, and LaTasha Y. Hicks Becton

9 The Systematic Influence of Past and Current Traumas: Understanding Substance Use in Native American Adolescent Populations 152
Kathleen Brown-Rice and Andrew Gerodias

10 The Utility and Practical Aspects of the Cognitive Assessment System for Professionals Working with Young Offenders with LD and ADHD: From Theory to Practice 171
Louise Anderson-Pawlina and Denise Ledi

11 Spiritual Transcendence, Religious Affiliation, and Anorexia Symptoms 202
Juleen K. Buser and Terry L. Pertuit

1

Editorial

We are delighted to introduce *The Annual Review of Addictions and Offender Counseling, Volume IV: Best Practices.* This volume represents outstanding contributions from a wide range of authors. Together, they describe innovative practices and cutting-edge research in addictions and offender counseling. The chapters are brimming with clinical wisdom, thoughtful analysis, and evidence-based practice recommendations. The authors also canvas a variety of timely issues in our field, including: cultural considerations in addictions and offender counseling (e.g., experiences of gender dysphoria, learning disabilities, and trauma associated with racial/ethnic identity); novel extensions of available treatments (e.g., diagnostic recommendations for process addictions, mindfulness-based interventions for addictions, cost- and resource-effective approaches to group counseling for offenders with mental illness, new frontiers in addiction conceptualization, and potential therapeutic benefits associated with psychedelics); and recommendations for counselor training (particularly in process addictions) and instrumentation in research on addictions and related constructs (e.g., spirituality).

We wish to express our appreciation to the International Association of Addiction and Offender Counselors (IAAOC), an organization that sponsored this edited book. IAAOC is a division of the American Counseling Association. All of the chapters in this book have been peer reviewed by the Editorial Board of the *Journal of Addictions and Offender Counseling* (*JAOC*). We are honored to support IAAOC's ongoing commitment to creating resources that help counselors serve clients to the best of their abilities. This volume fits squarely within this value orientation, with its emphasis on best practices and innovations in our field.

In the following section, we are pleased to present a description of each ensuing chapter.

DSM-5 Diagnostic Considerations for Behavioral or Process Addictions

Leigh Falls Holman and Kristy Carlisle

This article provides guidance on evaluating behavioral/process addictions (BPAs), which do not have diagnostic codes in the DSM-5 (sex addiction, Internet gaming disorder, Internet addiction, and nonsuicidal self-injury). The article evaluates several potential diagnostic strategies for these disorders utilizing existing codes, including Other Specified Obsessive Compulsive Disorders.

Mindfulness- and Acceptance-Based Intervention for Opioid Dependence in Groups with Open Enrollment

Christie Nelson and Daniel Gutierrez

Mindfulness- and acceptance-based approaches yield promise in the treatment of opioid addiction. However, there are no established guidelines for implementing these approaches within groups utilizing open enrollment. A conceptual model is presented incorporating evidence-based strategies to accommodate groups using open enrollment.

Add-Wellness: A Humanistic Model to Conceptualize Addiction

James E. McDonald and Jennifer M. Cook

The Add-Wellness *model is a humanistic addiction conceptualization approach that combines clients' phenomenology, diathesis-stress, and wellness factors. Common addiction models are assessed using humanism, the model is presented, and a case example is provided with discussion.*

Psychedelic Therapy and Microdosing: An Overview for Counselors

Peter Eischens

Psychedelic therapy and microdosing are reemerging as potential treatments for addiction. This paper will acquaint addiction counselors to the clinical efficacy of psychedelics and review pertinent research. Implications for counseling will be discussed.

Using a Group Counseling Intervention to Treat Inmates' Symptoms of Mental Illness

Robert m Cox, Richard K. James, Rebecca J. Grady, and Michael S. Skirius

Offenders with Mental Illness report anxiety, depression, PTSD, and self-esteem symptoms differently than their non-mentally ill peers. This pilot research evaluates the ARRAY group counseling program, which shows promise for the reduction of mentally ill inmates' symptoms. Implications for program development and future research are included.

Person Centered Therapy with Adult Male Prisoners Diagnosed with Gender Dysphoria

Amanda Hinds and Melinda M. Gibbons

Inmates with Gender Dysphoria face numerous individual and systemic factors that may warrant counseling. We propose person-centered counseling as an effective way to counsel inmates diagnosed with Gender Dysphoria and offer a hypothetical case study to demonstrate its application.

Professional Counselors' and Students' Current Knowledge, Training, and Experience with Process Addictions

Angie D. Cartwright, Leigh Falls Holman, Judith A. Nelson, Kristy Carlisle, Christine Baker, Regina Moro, Sarah Monakes Whitmire, Stephanie Carroll, and LaTasha Y. Hicks Becton

Counselor educators, students, and professional counselors were surveyed concerning their perceptions and experiences regarding training and exposure to process addiction cases in clinical settings. Results reveal limited formal training among professionals, despite a recognized need observed within their clinical work.

The Systematic Influence of Past and Current Traumas: Understanding Substance Use in Native American Adolescent Populations

Kathleen Brown-Rice and Andrew Gerodias

Native American adolescents are at greater risk to develop substance use disorders. The theory of historical trauma has been established to explain these disparities. This article will examine the relevant literature and provide an example case study to gain an understanding to refine prevention/treatment strategies.

The Utility and Practical Aspects of the Cognitive Assessment System for Professionals Working with Young Offenders with LD and ADHD: From Theory to Practice

Louise Anderson-Pawlina and Denise Ledi

The Cognitive Assessment System can assist professionals working with young offenders (YOs) with learning disabilities and/or attention deficit hyperactivity disorder by providing a means of going beyond theory to practice, through enhanced understanding of YOs cognitive/executive processes and associated behaviors.

Spiritual Transcendence, Religious Affiliation, and Anorexia Symptoms

Juleen K. Buser and Terry L. Pertuit

In the present study, we discuss findings of a nonsignificant relationship between spiritual transcendence and the process/behavioral addiction of anorexia symptoms. We explain how these findings contribute to the literature by clarifying types of spiritual and/or religious beliefs relevant to anorexia symptoms. Additionally, we discuss an association between Catholic religious affiliation and anorexia symptoms.

Acknowledgements

We wish to recognize the investment of time and expertise provided by the Editorial Board for *JAOC*. Board members were gracious to serve as the Editorial Board for this volume of the *Annual Review of Addictions and Offender Counseling*, as well. Their careful attention to quality and detail enhanced the chapters in this volume immensely. We are grateful for their work. The *JAOC* Editorial Board includes the following members:

Editorial Board

Kate Lamberson, *University of North Georgia*
Gabriel I. Lomas, *Western Connecticut State University*
Regina Moro, *Boise State University*
Samir Patel, *Murray State University*
Dilani Perera-Diltz, *Cleveland State University*
John Ryals, *Jefferson Parish Department of Juvenile Services*
Ganella M. Smith, *Liberty University*
Edward Wahesh, *Villanova University*
Joshua Watson, *Texas A&M University Corpus Christi*

We also offer special thanks to the editorial assistants who supported this volume with their time, thoughtful feedback, and commitment. These graduate students truly exceeded our expectations with their passion for the material and willingness to assist authors and editors in myriad ways. Specifically, we express our gratitude to Alanna D'Avanzo from Rider University and Marie Huggins from the University of North Carolina at Charlotte.

Trevor J. Buser
Graduate School of Counseling and Psychology
Naropa University
Boulder, Colorado

Pamela S. Lassiter
Department of Counseling
The University of North Carolina at Charlotte
Charlotte, North Carolina

Kathleen Rice
Department of Counselor Education
Sam Houston State University
Huntsville, Texas

2

DSM-5 Diagnostic Considerations for Behavioral or Process Addictions

Leigh Falls Holman *and* Kristy Carlisle[1]

By changing the category of Substance-Related Disorders in the *Diagnostic and Statistical Manual of Mental Disorders-IV-Text Revision (DSM-IV-TR;* American Psychiatric Association [APA], 2000) to Substance-Related and Addictive Disorders in the *Diagnostic and Statistical Manual of Mental* Disorders (5th edition; *DSM*-5; APA, 2013a), the American Psychiatric Association acknowledged the existence of Behavioral/Process Addictions (BPAs). The first of these diagnoses included is Gambling Disorder (GD). However, there are other BPAs with which clients present in treatment, including eating disorders, compulsive spending, Internet gaming disorder, Internet addiction, and sex addiction (Crozier & Agius, 2012; Nelson, Wilson, & Holman, 2015; Wilson & Johnson, 2013; Wilson, A., Holman, L., & Nelson, in press). Clients challenged with BPAs experience symptoms generally accepted as consistent with substance use disorders (SUDs). These include increased tolerance, withdrawal, obsessive thoughts, and compulsive behaviors, resulting in

1. Leigh Falls Holman, Department of Counseling, Educational Psychology and Research, The University of Memphis. Kristy Carlisle, Department of Counseling & Human Services, Old Dominion University. Correspondence concerning this article should be addressed to Leigh Falls Holman, 101A Ball Hall, University of Memphis, Memphis, TN 38152. E-mail: lfalls@memphis.edu.

clinically significant distress or functional impairment (Coombs, 2004; Freimuth, 2005; Grant, 2008; Zhang, Tian, von Deneen, Liu, & Gold, 2012). However, without specific diagnostic codes for many BPAs, a counselor's ability to diagnose these clients and provide treatment is limited.

Currently, when clients present with BPAs, counselors find no codes to use in classifying these disorders. The *DSM-5* (APA, 2013a) does not provide guidance on how to address diagnosis of most BPAs. Therefore, the purpose of this article is to discuss diagnostic issues related to BPAs, with emphasis on those which do not have current diagnostic codes. We will briefly identify BPAs that are in the *DSM-5*, but these will not be the focus of this article. Then we will examine ethical concerns related to diagnosing or refraining from diagnosing BPAs. Finally, we will discuss several common BPAs, which do not have diagnostic codes; however, they do have a research base for evaluating whether the disorder(s) exists for a particular client. Using the literature as guidance, we will make an argument for using the diagnostic code for Other Specified Obsessive Compulsive Disorders and specifying the specific BPA.

BPAs in the *DSM-5*

Although not included in the *DSM-5* (APA, 2013a) chapter on Substance-Related and Addictive Disorders, there are several BPAs with clear diagnostic criteria and codes, including eating disorders, hording with compulsive spending, and paraphilias. In fact, a review of the *DSM-5* demonstrates an acknowledgement by the APA of similarities between substance use disorders and some eating disorders, including reported symptoms and underlying neural impacts, such as those implicated in "regulatory self-control and reward" (APA, 2013a, p. 329). Additionally, although hoarding and compulsive spending are not the same, the *DSM-5* cites research indicating strong comorbidity for these behaviors, which is why one type of hoarding behavior diagnosable in the *DSM-5* is "with excessive acquisition" (APA, 2013a, p. 247; Frost, 2011; Frost, Tolin, Steketee, Fitch, & Selbo-Burns, 2009; McElroy, Keck, Pope, Smith, & Strabowski, 1994; Mueller et al., 2007). In fact, according to the *DSM-5*, "80–90% of individuals with hoarding disorder" also exhibit excessive acquisition (p. 248). The *DSM-5* goes on to note that the most common type of excessive acquisition is "excessive buying" (p. 248). Finally, paraphilias have long had a place in the *DSM-5*. These disorders are Level 2 or Level 3 sexually addictive behaviors under the Carnes' (1989) typology, although there are no diagnostic criteria in the *DSM-5* for the disorder commonly known as hypersexual disorder, which includes Level 1 sexually addictive behaviors (Kafka & Hennen, 1999; Kafka, 2002).

Additionally, the Feeding and Eating Disorder chapter of the *DSM-5* now includes Binge Eating Disorder (BED), which arguably is consistent with the literature on food addiction (APA, 2013a; APA, 2013b; Avena, Rada, & Hoebel, 2008; Blundell, Coe, & Hooper, 2013; Gearhardt, Corbin, & Brownell, 2016; Rogers, 2017; Volkow, Wang, Fowlder, & Telang, 2008; Volkow, Wang, Tomasi, & Baleer, 2013; Zhang et al., 2012). It is important to note that APA added BED to the *DSM-5* only after researchers studied large numbers of cases with Eating Disorder NOS diagnoses and found the cases had common characteristics, which became the BED diagnosis. This example of the evolution of the *DSM-5* is a good illustration of why it is crucial to have a consistent method of diagnosing BPAs. By consistently identifying these disorders, it will provide evidence to support further research on prevalence, development, and course of BPAs, which will help establish a place for those BPAs not currently in the *DSM-5*.

Given that some BPAs exist in the *DSM-5* (APA, 2013a) currently, counselors have a method for diagnosing them, even if the *DSM-5* does not explicitly identify them as addictive behaviors (e.g., eating disorders). Therefore, we will focus on those BPAs that do not have specific diagnostic codes and make suggestions as to how to best diagnose, using an existing diagnostic code allowed by the *DSM-5*. This is similar to how clinicians and researchers utilized Eating Disorder NOS to support the evolution and inclusion of the diagnosis Binge Eating Disorder. We will focus our discussion on the following four BPAs: Hypersexual Disorder or Level 1 Sex Addiction (SA; Carnes, 1989), Internet Gaming Disorder (IGD), Internet Addiction (IA), and Nonsuicidal Self-Injury (NSSI). Some of these BPAs are currently in Section III of the *DSM-5* and thus require further research before inclusion in the main section of the manual; others are the next likely disorders for Section III.

Ethical Issues in Choosing To (or Not to) Diagnose BPAs

We know that counselors report they have increasing numbers of clients presenting with mental health and relational issues associated with hypersexuality, Internet use, and Internet Gaming (Nelson, Wilson, & Holman, 2015; Wilson, Holman, & Nelson, in press). Additionally, we know that a significant number of these counselors report assessing, diagnosing, and treating BPAs with little to no training or guidance on these disorders (Nelson, Wilson, & Holman, 2015; Wilson, Holman, & Nelson, in press). This results in ethical concerns related to counselors treating in new practice areas without adequate training. The *ACA Code of Ethics* (American Counseling Association [ACA], 2014) discusses this as a matter of competence. Given that any counselor in addiction or general clinical settings is likely to have clients present with a variety of clinical issues, it is impossible to pre-determine whether a person coming for treatment is at risk of having a BPA and then refer them to a specialist. Therefore, we would argue that a basic level of competency regarding diagnosing potential BPAs is important for all counselors to have, even if ultimately counselors refer these clients elsewhere for specialized treatment.

A counter argument may be that we should not diagnose any disorder, which is not in the *DSM*. However, we need to consider that addictive disorders, which, of course, needed treatment, existed before there were diagnostic categories. In fact, the first edition of the *DSM* (1952) was the first time Alcoholism and Drug Addiction received mention as a mental health disorder, rather than a moral failing. At that time, clinicians considered substance use disorders (SUDs) as symptoms of a sociopathic personality disturbance (Robinson & Adinoff, 2016). It was 1980 before the *DSM III* (1980) published SUDs as a primary mental health disorder. Given that the mental health community did not acknowledge SUDs as mental health disorders, many people did not receive needed treatment, or they received ineffective treatment (Robinson & Adinoff, 2016). We hold that this history should act as a warning to mental health professionals about the potential damage of withholding diagnostic classification and appropriate treatment for clients suffering with BPAs.

Some clinicians may argue that providing a diagnostic label unnecessarily pathologizes BPAs. There is concern that this pathology may result in a negative stigma suffered by those who struggle with these disorders. According to the National Alliance on Mental Illness (NAMI; Greenstein,

2017), there are nine ways to fight mental health stigma. The first two of these are to talk openly about mental health and educate oneself and others about the practical struggles of living with mental health and relational issues. We would argue that it is virtually impossible to discuss mental illness, like BPAs, without having a label to clearly identify that the behavior discussed is not simply a bad choice, moral failing, or bad habit. In fact, one can argue that by choosing not to label these mental health issues, we are colluding with those who perceive addictive behaviors as shameful, thus intensifying the likelihood that clients experience stigma around mental illness.

However, if we diagnose a client with a mental health disorder, our ethical guidelines state, "Counselors take special care to provide proper diagnosis" (ACA, 2014, p. 11). Additionally, the guidelines suggest that, "Counselors may refrain from making and/or reporting a diagnosis if they believe that it would cause harm to the client or others. Counselors carefully consider both the positive and negative implications of a diagnosis" (ACA, 2014, p.11). This can become problematic in practice because it is an open secret that some mental health professionals provide secondary diagnoses (e.g., depression, bipolar disorder) as the primary diagnosis, so that clients can use insurance benefits to obtain treatment for BPAs. They rationalize that clients are then able to get some treatment for their presenting issues, rather than the mental health treatment community neglecting them.

Compounding the ethical issues related to providing an inaccurate (or incomplete) diagnosis is that treatment builds on the foundation that a diagnosis provides. With less than accurate diagnoses, we do not provide a clear picture of the client's treatment needs to future providers, the client him/herself, or to third party payers. If we inaccurately assess treatment needs, then will the client gain the necessary treatment to ameliorate his/her mental health distress? The *ACA Code of Ethics* (ACA, 2014) states that, "Counselors do not misuse assessment results, and they take reasonable steps to prevent others from misusing the information provided" (p. 11). This suggests that providing as accurate a diagnosis as possible is important for client welfare.

However, how do we go about accurately diagnosing one of these disorders when no diagnostic codes currently exist in the *DSM-5* (APA, 2013a)? We will discuss our analysis of potential diagnostic coding options for BPAs, which fall into this category. Then, we will review four

BPAs, which are increasingly common issues in practice but which have no diagnostic codes, and discuss our recommendations for diagnosing these disorders in an accurate, honest manner. The literature supporting each diagnosis is extensive; however, a comprehensive review of this literature is outside the purpose of this article, and there are extensive literature reviews available for each, which the reader may pursue (Carnes & Adams, 2002; Freimuth, 2005; McCown & Howatt, 2007; Rosenberg & Feder, 2014; Wallace, 1999).

Diagnosing BPAs not in the DSM-5

In our analysis, there are three diagnostic options for BPAs, including impulse control disorders, addictive disorders, and obsessive-compulsive disorders. We will discuss each of these options in relationship to diagnosing BPAs that do not have a diagnostic code. First, we would argue that impulse-control disorders do not adequately account for the addictive qualities involved in obsessive preoccupation with the activities, evidence of increased tolerance over time, or evidence of withdrawal symptoms. Therefore, we would eliminate Other Specified Disruptive, Impulse-Control, and Conduct Disorder as a potential option for diagnosing BPAs.

Interestingly, the *DSM-5* (APA, 2013a) chapter on Substance-Related and Addictive Disorders offers diagnostic options for disorders not otherwise specified which are substance-related. However, in the section of the chapter on non-substance related addictive disorders, only GD is listed with its criteria and supporting information. Currently, there is not an option to specify an addictive behavior, such as a BPA, which does not have diagnostic criteria in this section. If there were such an option, we would recommend classifying BPAs using that designation. We hypothesize the workgroup developing this chapter likely was intentional in leaving this option out of the chapter, given the already controversial nature of adding addictive behaviors beyond SUDs for the first time in the *DSM-5*. Regardless of our speculation, this potential diagnostic category does not exist and, therefore, we cannot use such a category for documentation and billing purposes.

Finally, we consider obsessive-compulsive disorders. As we argue under each BPA, we believe it is possible to conceptualize the thoughts, fantasies, and urges associated with addictive behaviors as obsessions, consistent with the OCD criteria (APA, 2013a). We also believe the increased urge clients experience to act out on these thoughts are evidence of compulsions, consistent with the OCD criteria. Further, clients demonstrating these behaviors to the point of needing increasing amounts of the activity (e.g., increasing risk in sexual activities in SA, more challenging games in IGD, or increasing severity of self-injurious behaviors in NSSI) are evidence of building tolerance, similar to what is observed in GD and SUDs. Over time, it is relatively easy to identify a loss of control and withdrawal symptoms when the client is unable to engage in the behavior, similar to that demonstrated by people with GD or SUDs.

Therefore, we believe it is reasonable to use OCD as an appropriate diagnostic choice. However, if a counselor chooses this diagnostic route, we must acknowledge that APA did not intend BPAs to be the focus of the OCD diagnosis. Therefore, we would further suggest that the best practice for counselors choosing OCD to categorize BPAs is to specify these behaviors by choosing to diagnose them as 300.3 Other Specified Obsessive-Compulsive Disorder, and then specify which disorder it is (e.g., SA, IGD, IA, or NSSI).

Sexual Addiction (SA)

The first BPA we will consider is Sexual Addiction (SA), also called hypersexual disorder. In the ground-breaking book *Contrary to Love: Helping the Sexual Addict* (1989), Dr. Patrick Carnes was the first to propose a typology of sexually addictive behavior still used to conceptualize SA. There are three levels discussed. Level 1 includes victimless behaviors, such as masturbation and pornography. Society generally considers these behaviors normal sexual behaviors until obsessive thoughts and compulsions become so frequent or destructive that distress or functional impairment occurs. These are perhaps the most difficult for counselors diagnostically because the APA rejected diagnostic criteria used to diagnose these behaviors under the diagnosis of hypersexual disorder, for inclusion in Section III of the *DSM-5* (APA, 2013a), due to the need for more research to support its inclusion (Kafka, 2010; Krueger, 2016; Reid et al., 2012). Carnes' Level 2 behaviors include exhibitionistic, voyeuristic behaviors, and similar activities. The *DSM-5* includes these behaviors in the paraphilias chapter. Similarly, Carnes' Level 3 behaviors, involving pedophilia and rape (Sadism), continue to have well-established criteria published in the *DSM-5* as paraphilias.

Therefore, the dilemma diagnostically is the lack of consistent direction regarding the appropriate diagnosis for someone who falls within the Level 1 behaviors of sexual addiction. Kafka (2010) outlined the diagnostic criteria for hypersexual disorder (HD), describing these behaviors through a review of the literature on SA. Further, in 2012 a group of researchers conducted field trials on the diagnosis, which provided support for the criteria (Reid et al., 2012). The evidence demonstrated good interrater reliability when using the criteria to diagnose with stability over time. In addition, the diagnosis accurately reflected clients' presenting problems, as indicated by indices on sensitivity and specificity of the criteria. Additionally, they found that the criteria demonstrated good validity when measuring hypersexuality, impulsivity, emotional dysregulation, and stress proneness, and good internal consistency (Reid et al., 2012).

These criteria indicate that an individual must demonstrate repeated or even ritualized sexual thoughts or behaviors related to at least four of the following:

- excessive time spent on sexual fantasies and planning for and engaging in sexual thoughts or behaviors (Kafka & Hennen, 1999; Kafka, 2002; Kalichman & Cain, 2004),
- using sexual thoughts or behaviors to regulate negative affective states (Bancroft et al., 2004; Bancroft et al., 2003),
- demonstrating stress-triggered sexual thoughts or behaviors (Nelson & Oehlert, 2008),
- loss of control and inability to stop engaging in sexual thoughts or behaviors when trying to do so (Kalichman & Cain, 2004; Kalichman & Rompa, 1995, 2001; Nelson & Oehlert, 2008),
- disregarding risk to oneself or others related to the sexual behavior (Bancroft et al., 2004; Janssen, Goodrich, Petrocelli, & Bancroft, 2009; Kalichman & Cain, 2004; Kalichman & Ropa, 1995, 2001).

Additionally, the impact of engaging in excessive sexual fantasizing, planning, and acting out should result in clinically significant distress or functional impairment in social, emotional, or occupational functioning (Bancroft & Vukadinovic, 2004; Briken, Habermann, Berner, & Hill, 2007; Cooper, Delmonico, & Burg, 2000, Kafka & Hennen, 1999).

We first considered using a paraphilia diagnosis for SA, since this is how we classify other sexually addictive behaviors. Specifically, we would utilize the diagnosis Other Specified Sexual Problems or Paraphilia, Sexual Addiction (or hypersexual disorder). However, we believe SA does not fit under this diagnosis because the examples listed for other specified diagnoses include commonly accepted paraphilic activity, such as necrophilia and zoophilia, which are level 2 SA behaviors on Carnes' typology. Similarly, although the Unspecified Paraphilic Disorder is a diagnostic coding option for SA, it seems inconsistent with the intent of the paraphilic disorders category because Level 1 behaviors do not involve non-human objects, humiliation or suffering, or non-consenting partners typical of paraphilias.

In our analysis, we observed that the *DSM*-5 (2013a) Obsessive-Compulsive Disorder category (OCD) includes diagnostic criteria consistent with the Hypersexual Disorder (SA) criteria. These include obsessions that conceptually account for sexual fantasies and compulsions conceptually consistent with sexual urges or behaviors. The OCD diagnosis also provides for the client involving him/herself in this activity for excessive periods of time and causing distress and/or functional impairment. These diagnostic criteria are consistent with those proposed for Hypersexual Disorder. Although OCD may not be the best fit for diagnosing HD/SA, we suggest counselors consider 300.3 "Other Specified Obsessive-Compulsive and Related Disorder," Hypersexual Disorder (or Sexual Addiction; APA, 2013a, p. 263). This diagnosis provides integrity in the OCD diagnostic intent while allowing for a more specific manifestation of OCD through sexual behavior. We recommend utilizing the Kafka (2010) diagnostic criteria discussed above to diagnose, as the literature supported these criteria; however, we suggest counselors use the *DSM*-5 diagnostic code 300.3 when completing documentation of need for services.

Internet Gaming Disorder (IGD)

Internet gaming disorder (IGD) is another increasingly common presenting issue, particularly for adolescents and young adults (Anderson, Steen,

& Stavropoulos, 2016). We need to be careful, however, not to over-pathologize gaming behavior. Enthusiastic, or even professional, gamers may devote large amounts of time to gaming or to discussing gaming strategy, but other addiction criteria may not be present beyond the apparent preoccupation. In addition, gaming is a highly popular activity among adolescents. Therefore, clinicians must consider how gaming may be part of developmentally and culturally appropriate (e.g., youth culture) exploration, in contrast with behavior exhibited by a gamer who excludes other interests, thus resulting in functional impairment.

According to the *DSM-5* (2013a), there is sufficient research to establish the diagnostic criteria for IGD under Section III of the manual, which is the section for disorders needing further research. However, the research used for inclusion in the *DSM-5* is primarily from China and South Korea, which may not be culturally consistent with the United States (U.S.) cultural norms. Definitions vary, but they provide a good construct of IGD for the reader. Although there are recent advances in establishing prevalence rates for IGD (.7–15.6%), at the time of publication there were no established prevalence rates in the U.S., a necessary step for inclusion as a diagnosis in the *DSM-5* (Feng, Ramo, Chan & Bourgeois, 2017). The lack of consistency in defining IGD is the primary reason researchers cannot establish prevalence rates from current literature. Inconsistencies in the literature include variations in population, criteria, and assessment instrumentation. For these reasons, IGD is included in Section III of the *DSM-5* as a diagnosis needing further study before consideration as a diagnosable condition with an assigned diagnostic code.

Additionally, Griffiths (2016) noted over 20 different assessment tools used to evaluate IGD in existing studies. An examination of these tools revealed discrepancies in diagnostic criteria, problems with cutoff scores, and reliability and validity issues (King, Haagsma, Delfabbro, Gradisar, & Griffiths, 2013). Therefore, using these studies is problematic. The research also remains unclear about whether there are sub-types of the disorder based on the types of games (massively multiplayer online, simulations, adventure, real-time strategy, combat, stealth shooter, action, puzzle, etc.) in which clients are involved and whether different games may result in different levels of severity. Another element of a *DSM-5* (APA, 2013a) diagnosis is establishment of clinical course, which is how the disorder manifests over time and long-term outcomes of IGD. Additionally, the research does not consistently demonstrate potential neurological, physiological or genetic factors involved, as are implicated in other addictive disorders in the *DSM-5*. However, IGD's inclusion in Section III of the *DSM-5* should encourage the epidemiological and brain mapping studies necessary to provide the data needed to determine whether this disorder classification is clinically useful.

Although the *DSM-5* (APA, 2013a) provides diagnostic criteria for IGD based on existing research, the disorder does not have a diagnostic code to use for official diagnoses or billing purposes. In reviewing the criteria, we find that in order to meet the nine criteria for IGD, an individual must spend significant time on Internet gaming, and the commonly accepted threshold is thirty hours a week (APA, 2013a; Chappell, Eatough, Davies, & Griffiths, 2006). Upon assessment, a counselor should be able to identify symptoms consistent with other addictions: loss of control, tolerance, withdrawal, and resulting clinically significant functional impairment or distress. Of the nine criteria, a client must meet five within the previous year to diagnose him/her with IGD. The criteria represent a progression in the severity of the disorder, as illustrated below.

First, the client may obsessively think about gaming experiences, whether past or future, to the point that it becomes an organizing feature of the client's life. Second, the client exhibits negative affective states in response to not being able to participate in the activity, indicating withdrawal symptoms. Third, the client's behavior or self-report indicates that s/he feels the need to spend more and more time on Internet games in order to have the same high or satisfaction, indicating tolerance and potential engagement of the reward path and neural circuitry commonly involved in addictive behaviors. Over time, the fourth criterion may become an issue in that, whether self-imposed or other-imposed, the client is unable to cut down or stop Internet gaming, thus indicating a loss of control similar to the experiences of people with SUDs or GD. Due to the amount of time the client spends thinking about or engaging in Internet games, s/he may demonstrate a fifth criterion, loss of interest in things that s/he previously enjoyed. This often leads to the sixth criterion, continued use although there is clear evidence of distress or functional impairment.

Next, the client may become deceptive about the amount of time spent on gaming. This may contribute to further functional impairment due to damaging relationships with significant others or negative impact on the client's work or educational endeavors, also a criterion to consider.

Finally, a client needs to be assessed to determine whether his/her use of Internet games is functioning as a way to regulate emotion, also consistent with other addictions. In terms of differential diagnosis, it is important to identify whether the Internet games are strictly gambling in nature. If so, then GD is likely the better diagnosis. Given that these criteria are grounded in the literature and are now established in the *DSM-5* (APA, 2013a) as consistent diagnostic criteria for IGD, we suggest counselors use these criteria to determine whether clients presenting with these behaviors correspond with IGD.

Again, we recommend coding the disorder as 300.3 OCD, Other Specified, Internet Gaming Disorder. The IGD criteria allow for obsessive thoughts and compulsive behaviors related to Internet gaming, and the criteria specify the manifestation of functional impairments, consistent with OCD, other specified diagnosis. Additionally, using this diagnosis  provides consistency across BPA diagnoses, which may help track these disorders, establish prevalence rates, and help researchers show the utility of the criteria as currently written.

Internet Addiction (IA)

Internet addiction (IA) is commonly confused with IGD. Additionally, much like other BPAs, professionals continue to debate the existence of IA or whether some people simply use the Internet more than others, which might be considered excessive by someone with a different standard of normal. However, the literature indicates that there is a qualitative difference between excessive Internet use and IA (Wallace, 1999). IA is "characterized by either irresistible preoccupations with the Internet or excessive use of the Internet for longer periods of time than planned" (Young, 2011, p.21). We would argue that "irresistible preoccupations" are consistent with obsessive thoughts, and "excessive use" is consistent with compulsive behaviors, both related to the diagnostic group of OCD, other specified.

Further, Freimuth (2005) differentiates excessive use from addiction as "a loss of control over the behavior and an onset of negative consequences" (p. 85). Some common consequences include significant functional impairment in personal relationships, work, and finances (Grant, 2008). Individuals suffering with IA, similar to other addictions, demonstrate a loss of control or ability to cut down on Internet use. "Tolerance is indicated if a patient reports spending more time or money on the computer to get a similar level of pleasure" (Freimuth, 2005, p. 85). Clinicians can evaluate withdrawal when the client reports or demonstrates negative affect and irritability resulting when s/he cannot use the Internet. With these descriptions, we see how the obsessive thoughts and compulsive behaviors related to Internet use ultimately result in functional deficits, consistent with OCD.

Orzack and Ross (2000) identified specific criteria for classifying whether a client has IA, including five or more of the following criteria:

- The client experiences a "high" or a release when using the Internet. The client becomes preoccupied with thoughts of surfing the web.
- The client demonstrates evidence of tolerance, as described previously.
- The client demonstrates loss of control over Internet use.
- The client demonstrates signs of withdrawal.
- There is evidence of functional impairment in social, interpersonal, school, or work activities.
- The client lies to the counselor or significant others about the amount of time he/she is spending on Internet use.
- The client may experience loss of a significant relationship, educational opportunity, job, or financial hardship because of their Internet use.

Similar to IGD, there is a need for further research to identify prevalence rates, development, and course of the disorder, among other aspects of the condition. However, existing literature indicates the disorder is more common in men, employed individuals, and those with some college education (Shapira et al., 2003).

There are limitations to these criteria discussed in the literature, as well. Addictive activities for which the Internet is the medium include gambling (Lee, Choi, Shin, Lee, Jung, & Kwon, 2012), gaming (Potenza, 2014), sex (Jones & Hertlein, 2012), auctions (Tonioni et al., 2012), shopping and social networking (Murali & Onuba, 2009). Thus, different people who use the Internet to engage in various activities may experience IA differently and with different sets of consequences

(Potenza, 2014). Potential diagnostic criteria should reflect the many possibilities and combinations. Given these complications, Nelson, Wilson, and Holman (2015) highlighted the need to agree on how to conceptualize IA: either as an umbrella addiction with a stand-alone diagnosis (Luo, Brennan, & Wittenauer, 2015) or simply as the medium that allows users to engage in the specific activity to which they are addicted.

In spite of these limitations, counselors have clients presenting in treatment with functional impairments related to excessive Internet use, and we believe that we need to have a consistent way to diagnose them and begin to identify effective treatments. Our suggestion is to utilize the Orzack and Ross (2000) criteria listed above as a guide for determining whether clients meet the definition of someone with IA. However, we recommend coding the diagnosis as 300.3 Other Specified Obsessive Compulsive and Related Disorder, Internet Addiction. Similar to the other BPAs discussed, using a consistent diagnosis, while allowing for identification of specific BPAs, can help researchers begin to establish prevalence rates and encourage future research.

Nonsuicidal Self-Injury (NSSI)

Finally, similar to other BPAs discussed, the *DSM-5* (APA, 2013a) identifies criteria for NSSI consistent with addictive processes and can be found in Section III of the manual as a condition for further study. These criteria include utilizing NSSI to regulate emotion, obsessive thoughts or preoccupation with thoughts about engaging in NSSI, and demonstrated difficulty or reported difficulty in controlling the behavior (APA, 2013a). Conterio and Lader (1998) also reported that NSSI shares addictive qualities such as "the need to engage in the behavior as uncontrollable and necessary in larger and larger quantities to achieve the desired effect. . . . It seems to provide relief from tension" (pp. 24–25). This description demonstrates addictive characteristics of NSSI including a loss of control, building tolerance, and using NSSI as an effective way for emotionally dysregulated clients to address their discomfort. Further, the diagnostic criteria for NSSI listed in Section III of the *DSM-5* include a discussion of urgency or craving and use of multiple methods of NSSI as indication of increased severity, which is conceptually similar to increasing tolerance and craving following withdrawal in SUDs.

To meet the proposed diagnostic criteria in the *DSM-5* (APA, 2013a), the client would have intentionally harmed him/herself five or more days in the previous year, not including behaviors intended to result in death. Evaluating whether there was suicidal intent can be inferred due to the client engaging in the behaviors frequently and because objective evaluation reveals the behaviors are not likely to result in death. Therefore, counselors must consider differential diagnosis with Borderline Personality Disorder (BPD) or Suicidal Behavior Disorder (SBD), which also manifest in self-harm. Additionally, there are other disorders that counselors need to rule out, including Trichotillomania, Stereotypic self-injury, and Excoriation Disorder. If the context in which the behavior manifests is consistent with the client's culture or religion or is socially sanctioned, such as tattooing or body piercing, this would prevent the client from meeting the diagnostic criteria. Finally, the client must either experience distress around the behavior or have functional impairment involving school, work, or relationships attributable to NSSI.

Although the NSSI criteria are listed in Section III of the *DSM-5* (APA, 2013a), like IGD, it does not have a diagnostic code. The criteria published in the manual build upon a significant foundation of literature, and they provide a consistent, accurate, description of the disorder. Therefore, we recommend counselors utilize these criteria to determine if a client presenting for treatment with similar behaviors is suffering with NSSI. If the client is determined to meet the criteria, as outlined in the *DSM-5*, then, once again, we suggest the counselor use the 300.3 Other Specified Obsessive Compulsive and Related Disorder, NSSI diagnostic code.

Summary of Diagnostic Recommendations

Changes in the *DSM-5* (APA, 2013a) acknowledge addictive behaviors beyond SUDs with the inclusion of gambling as the first BPA. This is a significant step forward for the counseling profession and our ability to meet clients' needs who present with these issues. Additionally, the diagnostic manual acknowledges similarities in neurobiological structures, processes and behavioral manifestations of SUDs and GDs with some other BPA diagnoses, which appear in chapters other than the addictive behaviors chapter. These include eating disorders, hoarding with excessive acquisition (compulsive spending), and paraphilias. These additions demonstrate a significant evolution of the concept of addiction beyond SUDs. This is consistent with the American Society of Addictive Medicine's (ASAM) longstanding inclusion of BPAs in its definition of addiction (2011). Additionally, the Council for Accreditation of Counseling and Related Educational Programs (CACREP, 2016) standards further support this evolution by requiring accredited programs to include BPAs in the educational curriculum for addictions.

However, when a client presents with behaviors that indicate one of the BPAs which do not have a designated diagnostic code, the counselor may still believe it is in the client's best interest and welfare to provide therapeutic intervention. This presents an ethical challenge between client welfare and diagnostic standards. Previous research has demonstrated that counselors are screening, diagnosing, and treating clients with BPAs without proper knowledge and skills to do so (Nelson, Wilson, & Holman, 2015; Wilson, Holman, & Nelson, in press). Therefore, it is a concern for ethical professional development that we provide some guidance for counselors on how to diagnose BPAs lacking clear diagnostic codes in the *DSM*-5 (APA, 2013a).

As a foundational point, we know that several BPAs have generally accepted criteria grounded in the literature, which clinicians use to diagnose or categorize clients' presenting issues. As described previously, we propose counselors first use these criteria to determine whether clients fit within diagnostic categories supported by the literature. However, if there is no diagnostic code to use for documentation and billing purposes, there are limited options for counselors who want to meet the client's need for treatment.

At this point, some counselors choose to give a secondary diagnosis (e.g., depression or bipolar disorder), in order to facilitate the client's ability to obtain treatment. We argued that diagnosing in this manner is deceptive at worst and incomplete at best. Providing a diagnosis that does not truly reflect the disorder may result in the client receiving inappropriate or ineffective treatment. Additionally, misdiagnosis results in difficulties identifying the actual prevalence of these disorders and hinders research efforts.

Therefore, we evaluated the possible use of three other diagnostic strategies. First, we considered Other Specified Impulse Control Disorders and dismissed this option due to the lack of inclusion of addictive qualities, such as preoccupation with the activities, increased tolerance over time, and withdrawal symptoms. Next, we identified that although classification within the Substance-Related and Addictive Disorders seems ideal, the *DSM-5* (APA, 2013a) does not currently offer this option for additional BPAs. Finally, we considered Obsessive Compulsive Disorder and determined that this diagnosis best allows for consideration of obsessive thinking, compulsive behaviors, loss of control, use of the behavior to regulate dysregulated affect, and functional impairment related to increasing tolerance and withdrawal symptoms. Therefore, we recommend utilizing the 300.3 Other Specified Obsessive compulsive and Related Disorders diagnosis, and specifying the specific BPA (SA, IGD, IA, or NSSI). We hope this provides well-supported and logical guidance for diagnostic coding for BPAs, which currently do not have unique diagnostic codes as addictive behaviors.

Limitations

As stated, this article is limited to providing initial guidance for diagnostic coding of BPAs lacking *DSM-5* (APA, 2013a) diagnostic codes, so that counselors can pursue appropriate treatment or referral for clients in need. We did not intend this article be an exhaustive discussion on the existence of BPAs or a detailed discussion of the literature published about any of these specific disorders. Additionally, we limited this paper to discussing only those BPAs that have established criteria supported by literature. However, we acknowledge that there are additional behaviors conceptualized as BPAs, which we did not cover in this article. Some disorders were left out because there are established diagnostic codes in the *DSM-5* (e.g., BED), which can be used to diagnose. For others, such as relationship addiction and work addiction, we were unable to find research-supported criteria for these behaviors from which to diagnose. Future research should address these limitations.

Future Research

We acknowledge that there is a clear need for a variety of studies intended to add to our understanding of the diagnostic characteristics of each of these BPAs. Future research needs to include epidemiological, brain-scan, neuro-psychological, and clinical studies in order to establish a firm research base and treatment protocols for individual BPAs. Specifically, research needs to use consistent instrumentation to establish prevalence rates for individual BPAs. Additionally, we need longitudinal studies to understand the development and course of the disorders. Additional research should also be devoted to examining the appropriateness of proposed diagnostic criteria, so that each BPA diagnosis has unique and contextualized criteria. Finally, randomized controlled studies can contribute to determining the efficacy of any proposed interventions.

Clearly, there are many opportunities for future research related to BPAs. However, if the profession uses a consistent diagnostic scheme, then it will be easier to compare findings across studies. Specifically, with regard to diagnosis of BPAs, research targeting each criterion proposed by existing literature can provide more support for a diagnostic framework, or alternatively, provide an argument for removing a criterion from consideration in diagnosing. Additionally, prevalence rates of these disorders are crucial to identifying whether there are significant portions of the population who suffer with BPAs. Therefore, a consistent manner of diagnosing may help researchers conduct multiple studies, which together provide evidence of the prevalence of each disorder.

Finally, by providing a consistent diagnostic scheme, researchers examining efficacy of treatment interventions are able to replicate existing studies and/or provide alternative treatments, which we can compare against existing modalities. As noted, for each area of research, it is crucial to have a consistent manner of defining or diagnosing these disorders. Doing so allows us to engage in systematic examination through the scientific method. This research allows us to build our knowledge base about who suffers from these disorders, how the disorders develop, the course they are likely to take, potential differential diagnoses to consider, and potential treatment interventions.

References

American Counseling Association. (2014). *ACA Code of Ethics*. Alexandria, VA: Author.

American Psychiatric Association. (1952). *Diagnostic and statistical manual of mental disorders*. Washington, DC: Author.

American Psychiatric Association. (1980). *Diagnostic and statistical manual of mental disorders* (3rd ed.). Washington, DC: Author.

American Psychiatric Association. (2000). *Diagnostic and statistical manual of mental disorders* (4th ed., text rev.). Washington, DC: Author.

American Psychiatric Association. (2013a). *Diagnostic and statistical manual of mental disorders* (5th ed.). Arlington, VA: Author.

American Psychiatric Association. (2013b). *Feeding and eating disorders fact sheet.* Retrieved from: http://www.dsm5.org/Pages/Default.aspx.

American Society of Addictive Medicine. (ASAM, 2011). *Public policy statement: Definition of addiction.* Retrieved March 26, 2018 from https://www.asam.org/resources/definition-of-addiction.

Anderson, E. L., Steen, E., & Stavropoulos, V. (2016). Internet use and problematic Internet use: A systematic review of longitudinal research trends in adolescence and emergent adulthood. *International Journal of Adolescence and Youth, 22*(4), 430–454. doi:10.1080/02673843.2016.1227716

Avena, N. M., Rada, P., & Hoebel, B. G. (2008). Evidence for sugar addiction: Behavioral and neurochemical effects of intermittent, excessive sugar intake. *Neuroscience and Biobehavioral Reviews, 32*, 20–39. doi:10.1016/j.neubiorev.2007.04.019

Bancroft, J., Janssen, E., Carnes, L., Strong, D. A., Goodrich, D., & Long, J. S.(2004). Sexual activity and risk taking in young heterosexual men: The relevanceof sexual arousal, mood and sensation seeking. *Journal of Sex Research, 41*,181–192.

Bancroft, J., Janssen, E., Strong, D., Carnes, L., Vukadinovic, Z., & Long, S. L. (2003). The relation between mood and sexuality in heterosexual men. *Archives ofSexual Behavior*, 32, 217–230. doi:10.1023/A:1023409516739

Bancroft, J., & Vukadinovic, Z. (2004). Sexual addiction, sexual compulsivity, sexual impulsivity or what? Toward a theoretical model. *Journal of Sex Research, 41*,225–234. doi: 10.1080/00224490409552230

Batthyány, D., Müller, K. W., Benker, F., & Wölfling, K. (2009) Computer game playing: clinical characteristics of dependence and abuse among adolescents. *The Central European Journal of Medicine, 121*, 502–509. doi:10.1007/s00508-009-1198-3

Blundell, J., Coe, S., & Hooper, B. (2013). Food addiction: What is the evidence? *British Nutrition Bulletin, 39*, 218–222. doi:10.1111/nbu.12092

Briken, P., Habermann, N., Berner, W., & Hill, A. (2007). Diagnosis and treatmentof sexual addiction: a survey among German sex therapists. *Sexual Addiction& Compulsivity, 14*, 131–143.doi: 10.1080/10720160701310450

Council for Accreditation of Counseling and Related Educational Programs. (2016). *2016 CACREP Standards.* Retrieved from http://www.cacrep.org/wp-content/uploads/2018/05/2016-Standards-with-Glossary-5.3.2018.pdf.

Carnes, P. J., & Adams, K. M. (Eds.) (2002). *Clinical management of sex addiction.* New York: Taylor & Francis.

Carnes, P. (1989). *Contrary to love: Helping the sexual addict.* Minneapolis, MN: CompCare Publishers.

Chappell, D., Eatough, V., Davies, M. N. O., & Griffiths, M. D. (2006). Everquest—It's just a computer game right? An interpretative phenomenological analysis of online gaming addiction. *International Journal of Mental Health and Addiction, 4*, 205–216. doi:10.1007/s11469-006-9028-6

Conterio, K., & Lader, W. (1998). *Bodily harm: The breakthrough healing program for self-injurers.* New York: Hyperion.

Coombs, R. H. (Ed.). (2004). *Handbook of addictive disorders: A practical guide to diagnosis and treatment.* Hoboken, NJ: John Wiley & Sons.

Cooper, A., Delmonico, D. D., & Burg, R. (2000). Cybersex users, abusers, and compulsives: New findings and implications. *Sexual Addiction & Compulsivity,7,* 5–29.doi: 10.1080/10720160008400205

Crozier, M., & Agius, M. (2012). Counselor educators & process addictions: How we know what we know. *NC Perspectives, 7,* 32–40.

Feng, W., Ramo, D. E., Chan, S. R., & Bourgeois, J. A. (2017). Internet gaming disorder: Trends in prevalence 1998–2016. *Addictive Behaviors, 75,* 17–24.doi: 10.1016/j.addbeh.2017.06.010

Freimuth, M. (2005). *Hidden addictions.* Lanaham, MD: Jason Aronson.

Frost, R. O. (2011). Assessment of hoarding. *Journal of Clinical Psychology, 67,* 5, 456–466. doi:10.1002/jclp.20790

Frost, R. O., Tolin, D. F., Steketee, G., Fitch, K. E., Selbo-Burns, A. (2009). Excessive acquisition in hoarding. *Journal of Anxiety Disorders, 23,* 5, 632–639. doi:10.1016/j.janxdis.2009.01.013

Gearhardt, A. N., Corbin, W. R., & Brownell, K. D. (2016). Development of the Yale Food Addiction Scale Version 2.0. *Psychology of Addictive Behaviors, 30*(1), 113–121. doi:10.1037/adb0000136

Grant, J. E. (2008). *Impulse control disorders: A clinician's guide to understanding and treating behavioral addictions.* New York: W.W. Norton & Company.

Greenstein, L. (2017). 9 ways to fight mental health stigma. *National Alliance on Mental Illness.* Retrieved March 23, 2018 from https://www.nami.org/blogs/nami-blog/october-2017/9-ways-to-fight-mental-health-stigma.

Griffiths, M. D. (2016). Playing the field: Another look at Internet gaming disorder. Retrieved from http://www.gamasutra.com/blogs/MarkGriffiths/20160211/265709/Playing_the_field_Another_look_at_Internet_Gaming_Disorder.php

Janssen, E., Goodrich, D., Petrocelli, J. V., & Bancroft, J. (2009). Psychophysiological response patterns and risky sexual behavior in heterosexual and homosexual men. *Archives of Sexual Behavior, 38,* 538–550. doi:10.1007/s10508-008-9432-z

Jones, K., & Hertlein, K. (2012). Four key dimensions for distinguishing Internet infidelity from Internet and sex addiction: Concepts and clinical application. *American Journal of Family Therapy, 40,* 115–125. doi:10.1080/01926187.2011.600677

Kafka, M. P. (2010). Hypersexual disorder: A proposed diagnosis for DSM-V. *Archives of Sexual Behavior, 39*(2), 377–400. doi:10.1007/s10508-009-9574-7

Kafka, M. P. (2002). The paraphilia-related disorders: A proposal for a unified classification of nonparaphilic hypersexuality disorders. *Sexual Addiction & Compulsivity: Journal of Treatment and Prevention, 8,* 227–240.doi: 10.1080/107201601753459937

Kafka, M. P. & Hennen, J. (1999). The paraphilia-related disorders: An empirical investigation of nonparaphilic hypersexuality disorders in outpatient males. *Journal of Sex and Marital Therapy, 25,* 305–319.doi: 10.1080/00926239908404008

Kalichman, S. C., & Cain, D. (2004). The relationship between indicators of sexual compulsivity and high risk sexual practices among men and women receiving services from a sexually transmitted infection clinic. *Journal of Sex Research, 41,* 235–241.doi: 10.1080/00224490409552231

Kalichman, S. C., & Rompa, D. (1995). Sexual sensation seeking and sexual compulsivity scales: Reliability, validity, and predicting HIV risk behavior. *Journal of Personality Assessment, 65*(3), 586–601.doi: 10.1207/s15327752jpa6503_16

Kalichman, S. C., & Rompa, D. (2001). The Sexual Compulsivity Scale: Further development and use with HIV-positive persons. *Journal of Personality Assessment, 76*(3), 379–395.

King, D. L., Haagsma, M. C., Delfabbro, P. H., Gradisar, M., & Griffiths, M. D. (2013). Toward a consensus definition of pathological video-gaming: a systematic review of psychometric assessment tools. *Clinical Psychology Review, 33*, 331–342. doi:10.1016/j.cpr.2013.01.002

Krueger, R. B. (2016). Diagnosis of hypersexual or compulsive sexual behavior can be made using ICD-10 and DSM-5 despite rejection of this diagnosis by the American Psychiatric Association. *Addiction, 111*(12), 2110–2111. doi:10.1111/add.13366

Lee, H., Choi, J., Shin, Y., Lee, J., Jung, H., & Kwon, J. (2012). Impulsivity in Internet addiction: A comparison with pathological gambling. *Cyberpsychology, Behavior and Social Networking, 15*, 373–377. doi:10.1089/cyber.2012.0063

Luo, S. X., Brennan, T. K., & Wittenauer, J. (2015). Internet Addiction: The case of Henry, the "Reluctant Hermit." In M. S. Ascher & P. Levounis (Eds.), *The behavioral addictions* (pp. 81–99). Washington, DC: American Psychiatric Publishing.

McCown, W. G., & Howatt, W. A. (2007). *Treating gambling problems*. Hoboken, NJ: John Wiley and Sons.

McElroy, S. L., Keck, P. E., Pope, H. G., Smith, J. M. R., & Strakowski, S. M. (1994). Compulsive buying: A report of 20 cases. *Journal of Clinical Psychiatry, 55*, 242–248.

Mueller, A., Mueller, U., Albert, P., Mertens, C., Silbermann, A., Mitchell, J. E., de Zwaan, M. (2007). Hoarding in a compulsive buying sample. *Behaviour Research & Therapy, 45*, 11, 2754–2763. Doi:10.1016/j.brat.2007.07.012

Murali, V., & Onuba, I. (2009). Management of Internet addiction. *General Practice Update, 2*, 32–35.

Nelson, K. G., & Oehlert, M. E. (2008). Psychometric exploration of the Sexual Addiction Screening Test in veterans. *Sexual Addiction & Compulsivity, 15*, 39–58. doi:10.1080/10720160701876609

Nelson, J. Wilson, A., & Holman, L. (2015). Training students in counselor education programs in process addictions: A pilot study. *Annual Review of Best Practices in Addictions and Offender Counseling.*

Orzack, M. H., & Ross, C. J. (2000). *Should virtual sex be treated like other addictions? In Cybersex: The dark side of the force* (Ed. A. Cooper). Philadelphia, PA: Brunner-Routledge.

Potenza, M. N. (2014). Non-substance addictive behaviors in the context of the DSM-5. *Addictive Behaviors, 39*(1), 1–2. doi:10.1016/j.addbeh.2013.09.004

Rogers, P. J. (2017). Food and drug addictions: Similarities and differences. *Pharmacology, Biochemistry, and Behavior, 153*, 182–190. doi:10.1016/j.pbb.2017.01.001

Reid, R. C., Carpenter, B. N., Hook, J. N., Garos, S., Manning, J. C., Gilliland, R., et al., (2012). Report of findings in a DSM-5 Field Trial for Hypersexual Disorder. *The Journal of Sexual Medicine, 9*(11), 2868–2877. doi:10.1016/j.eururo.2013.07.019

Robinson, S. M., & Adinoff, B. (2016). The classification of substance use disorders: Historical, contextual, and conceptual considerations. *Behavioral Science, 6*(18). Retrieved March 23, 2018 from https://www.ncbi.nlm.nih.gov/pmc/articles/PMC5039518/pdf/behavsci-06-00018.pdf.

Rosenberg, K. P., & Feder, L. C. (Eds.). (2014). *Behavioral addictions: Criteria, evidence, and treatment*. London, UK: Elsevier.

Shapira, N. A., Lessig, M. C., Goldsmith, T. D., Szabo, S. T., Martin, L., Gold, M. S., et al. (2003). Problematic internet use: Proposed classification and diagnostic criteria. *Depression and Anxiety, 17*(4), 207–216.

Tonioni, F., D'Alessandris, L., Lai, C., Martinelli, D., Corvino, S., Vasale, M. Bria, P. (2012). Internet addiction: Hours spent online, behaviors and psychological symptoms. *General Hospital Psychiatry, 34*, 80–87. doi:10.1016/j.genhosppsych.2011.09.013

Volkow, N. D., Wang, G. J., Fowler, J. S., & Telang, F. (2008). Overlapping neuronal circuits in addiction and obesity: Evidence of systems pathology. *Philosophical Transactions of The Royal Society B Biological Sciences, 363*(1507), 3191–3200. doi:10.1098/rstb.2008.0107

Volkow, N. D., Wang, G. J., Tomasi, D., & Baler, R. D. (2013). Obesity and addiction: Neurobiological overlaps. *Obesity Reviews, 14*, 2–18. doi:10.1111/j.1467-789X.2012.01031.x

Wallace, P. (1999). *The psychology of the Internet*. Cambridge, UK: Cambridge University Press.

Wilson, A., & Johnson, P. (2013) Counselors understanding of process addictions: A blind spot in the counseling field. *The Professional Counselor, 3*, 16–22. Retrieved from http://tpcjournal.nbcc.org/counselors-understanding-of-process-addiction-a-blind-spot-in-the-counseling-field/

Wilson, A., Holman, L., & Nelson. (in press). Professional counselors' and students' current knowledge, training, and experience with process addictions. *Annual Review of Addictions & Offender Counseling (Vol. 4).*

Young, K. S. (2011). Clinical assessment of Internet-addicted clients. In K. S. Young & C. N. de Abreu (Eds.). *Internet addiction: A handbook and guide to evaluation and treatment*. Hoboken, NJ: John Wiley & Sons.

Zhang, Y., Tian, J., von Deneen, K. M., Liu, Y., & Gold, M. S. (2012). Process addictions in 2012: Food, internet and gambling. *Neuropsychiatry, 2*(2), 155–161.

3

Mindfulness- and Acceptance-Based Intervention for Opioid Dependence in Groups with Open Enrollment

Christie Nelson *and* Daniel Gutierrez[2]

Opioids include any illicit or licit drugs such as heroin or prescription pain killers that act upon the opiate receptors in the brain and body to reduce pain and produce pleasure (National Institute on Drug Abuse [NIDA], 2017). About 30% of patients prescribed opiates for pain misuse them, and about 80% of those that misuse opiates transition to heroin (NIDA, 2017). According to the American Society of Addiction Medicine (ASAM; Mee-Lee, 2013), most drug overdoses in the United States are related to opioid addiction, and opioid overdoses have more than quadrupled since 1999. This significant increase in opioid related deaths has alerted federal agencies to declare an opioid epidemic (United States Senate, 2006), which has led to several states calling a state of emergency (e.g., Virginia, West Virginia, Florida; Baker-White, 2017).

Given the public crisis and the continually increasing overdose statistics (Rudd, Aleshire, Zibbell, & Gladden, 2016), addictions counselors

2. Christie Nelson, Department of Counseling, University of North Carolina at Charlotte; Daniel Gutierrez, Department of School Psychology and Counselor Education, College of William and Mary. Correspondence concerning this article should be addressed to Christie Nelson, Department of Counseling, University of North Carolina, Charlotte, 9201 University City Blvd., Charlotte NC, 28223. E-mail: cnelso38@uncc.edu.

must have effective strategies for treating clients struggling with opioid addiction to manage cravings, cope with chronic pain, attend to the distress that often triggers relapse, and reduce compulsivity. Current evidence suggests that mindfulness- and acceptance-based treatments can significantly reduce addiction to substances including alcohol, cocaine, amphetamines, marijuana, cigarettes, and opiates compared to waitlist controls and psychoeducational groups (Chiesa & Serretti, 2014). Mindfulness-based Relapse Prevention (MBRP; Bowen, Chawla, & Marlatt, 2011), Acceptance and Commitment Therapy (ACT; Hayes, Strosahl, & Wilson, 1999), and Mindfulness-Oriented Recovery Enhancement (MORE; Garland, 2013) offer clinicians manualized, evidenced-based approaches for working with clients struggling with addiction using a closed-enrollment format. However, using a manualized approach with a predetermined course of treatment and closed group structure is challenging when its implementation is within groups utilizing open enrollment and for individuals attending for different lengths of stay.

The use of open-enrollment groups, rather than closed-enrollment groups, is more common in community-based substance abuse treatment settings (Morgan-Lopez & Fals-Stewart, 2008). Additionally, because addictions treatment is provided in group settings with open enrollment, resulting in different lengths of stay based on personal resources, such as insurance and available funding (Morgan-Lopez & Fals-Stewart, 2008), treatment strategies must also be flexible enough to fit into real-world settings. Many treatment facilities share this structure in addiction counseling groups and it creates a complex pattern of interrelatedness among clients' needs (Paddock, Hunter, Watkins, & McCaffrey, 2011), presenting unique challenges for clinicians.

It is our assertion that mindfulness- and acceptance-based interventions can accommodate open enrollment group structure and offer effective treatment for those addicted to opioids. However, there are no established guidelines on how to provide mindfulness- and acceptance-based group treatments for opioid dependence within formats utilizing open enrollment. The aim of this paper is to distill what appears to be the most effective and empirically informed mindfulness- and acceptance-based elements from the extant treatment literature, as found in MBRP, ACT, and MORE, into a conceptual model fostering recovery from opioid dependence delivered in groups utilizing open enrollment.

Clinical Use of Mindfulness

The practice of mindfulness involves cultivating one's inborn ability to pay attention, moment-to-moment with a nonjudgmental and curious attitude, thereby making space for greater self-awareness and insight into the nature of one's suffering (Kabat-Zinn, 1990). Kabat-Zinn (1990) pioneered the use of mindfulness in clinical settings. Since then, mindfulness has been incorporated into clinical programs to treat an array of behavioral health issues (Chisea & Malinowski, 2011). Positive outcomes of mindfulness meditation in counseling can be categorized along the dimensions of affective benefits including emotional regulation, such as decreased reactivity and increased response flexibility; interpersonal benefits such as greater relationship satisfaction; and intrapersonal benefits pertaining to lifestyle, health, and well-being (Davis & Hayes, 2011). Mindfulness and acceptance-based interventions are particularly effective in treating and reducing anxiety, depression, and stress-related issues (Khoury et al., 2013) and an array of medical issues (see Carlson, 2012, for a review).

In addictions treatment, interventions focus on cultivating mindfulness and acceptance to decrease the impact of internal triggers by altering their context and function, so that cravings and other patterned cues to use substances are less likely to lead to substance use behavior (Lee et al., 2015). Acceptance has been noted as a significant factor in the recovery from addictions (Gifford et al., 2004), mediating engagement in recovery behaviors (Gifford et al., 2011). In a recent meta-analysis, Li, Howard, Garland, McGovern, and Lazar (2017) found significant small-to-large effects of mindfulness treatments in reducing the frequency and severity of substance misuse, intensity of craving for substances, and severity of stress. In particular, MBRP (Bowen et al., 2011), ACT (Hayes et al., 1999), and MORE (Garland, 2013) each offer evidenced-based interventions that, when taken collectively, may provide a method of delivering the most empirically informed mindfulness- and acceptance-based elements to individuals in groups using open enrollment.

Mindfulness- and Acceptance-Based Approaches in Substance Abuse Treatment

MBRP was developed as an aftercare program designed to reduce the risk and severity of relapse, incorporating cognitive behavioral relapse prevention and mindfulness meditation (Witkiewitz, Marlatt, & Walker, 2005) with the understanding that craving and addiction can be targeted by mindfulness, but that many individuals need additional cognitive and behavioral skills to cope with high-risk situations associated with relapse (Witkiewitz, Bowen, Douglas, & Hsu, 2013). MBRP is manualized and delivered in eight, 2-hour weekly group sessions (Bowen et al., 2011). Each session is structured and designed to be experiential in nature incorporating cognitive skills training and meditation practices, and group discussion of experiences (Bowen et al., 2009).

Research has shown that MBRP reduces the use of substances (Bowen et al., 2009; Bowen et al., 2014; Witkiewitz et al., 2014; Witkiewitz & Bowen, 2010) such as stimulants (Glasner et al., 2017) and heavy drinking (Bowen et al., 2014) and substance use among ethnic minority women (Witkiewitz, Greenfield, & Bowen, 2013). MBRP decreases substance craving (Bowen et al., 2009; Witkiewitz & Bowen, 2010; Zemestani, & Ottaviani, 2016) and mood symptoms such as anxiety and depression in people with co-occurring substance use disorders (Glasner et al., 2017; Zemestani, & Ottaviani, 2016). MBRP has also yielded beneficial results to clients in a therapeutic community detoxifying from methadone (Harris, 2015).

ACT (Hayes et al., 1999) is also used as a treatment for addictions. The cultivation of mindfulness and acceptance is used to foster psychological flexibility to promote engagement in a more purposeful, values-consistent life that is incompatible with a life encumbered by substance use (Heffner et al., 2003). ACT for the treatment of addictions has been delivered in groups with varying lengths of time, such as 90 minutes per session over a 7-week period (Gifford et al., 2004), with positive outcomes.

Research has demonstrated that ACT can reduce the use of substances such as cigarettes (Bricker et al., 2010, 2014a, 2014b, 2017; Bricker, Wyszynski, Comstock, & Heffner, 2013; Gifford et al., 2004, 2011; Hernandez-Lopez et al., 2009; Minami et al., 2015), alcohol (Heffner et al., 2003; Petersen & Zettle, 2009), marijuana (Twohig, Shoenberger, & Hayes, 2007) amphetamines (Smout et al., 2010), polysubstances (Hayes et al., 2004; Luoma et al., 2012; Menéndez et al., 2014) and co-occurring PTSD and substance use (Hermann et al., 2016). ACT has also been used as an effective treatment for opioid misuse (Hayes et al., 2004; Smallwood, Potter, & Robin, 2016; Stotts, Masuda, & Wilson, 2009; Stotts et al., 2012).

MORE integrates mindfulness, third-wave cognitive behavioral therapy, and aspects of positive psychology designed to simultaneously target mechanisms underpinning chronic pain and opioid misuse (Garland, 2013). Mindfulness training is used to target automatic behavior and foster non-reactivity; cognitive reappraisal training is applied to regulate negative emotions; and training in savoring pleasant events is implemented to improve deficits in natural reward processing with the goal of modifying the feedback loop between chronic pain and opioid misuse behaviors (Garland et al., 2014c). MORE is manualized and delivered in 2-hour weekly group sessions over an 8-week course of treatment (Garland, 2013).

Positive outcomes of MORE include reductions in perceived stress and thought-suppression in alcohol-dependent adults (Garland, Gaylord, Boettiger & Howard, 2010) and reductions in cigarette smoking (Froeliger et al., 2017). Among individuals with co-occurring substance dependence, traumatic stress, and psychiatric disorders, MORE has provided decreases in negative affect and greater increases in positive affect (Garland et al., 2016). Among chronic pain patients using opioids, MORE has shown reduced impairment in daily functioning including general activity, walking ability, sleep, work, relationships, mood, and overall enjoyment of life (Garland, Thomas, & Howard, 2014). In those who misuse opioids, MORE has evidenced decreases in stress arousal and perceived pain (Garland et al., 2014c), reductions in craving (Garland, Froeliger, & Howard, 2014b, 2015; Garland et al., 2014), and in opioid use (Garland et al., 2014b; Garland et al., 2014c). Research demonstrates MORE fosters less opioid cue-reactivity (Garland et al., 2014b), greater response to natural reward cues (Garland et al., 2014b, 2015), and increases in positive affect in those with chronic pain and opioid misuse (Garland et al., 2015).

Individually, these three evidenced-based approaches have much to offer clinicians working in addiction treatment settings and, in particular, those working with opioid-dependent clients. Taken collectively and drawing from these evidenced-based approaches, key elements and core processes associated with positive treatment outcomes have been distilled and condensed into a daily treatment protocol that is deliverable to and supports the provision of treatment of clients with opioid addiction in groups with open enrollment.

Treatment Model for Outpatient Groups with Open Enrollment

This model is intended to be suitable for groups lasting approximately 3 hours in length following the guidelines set forth by the American Society of Addictive Medicine (ASAM criteria 2.1) for intensive outpatient treatment (Mee-Lee et al., 2013). A primary function of the group is to accommodate a rolling admission; therefore, each group will follow a daily routine consisting of the same skills development and basic flow day-to-day, so that all members can benefit from the interventions regardless of admission point. An added benefit of each group following the same daily structure is the repetition of core skills rehearsal.

An overview of the daily schedule including a breakdown of tasks with suggested time frames is provided. The daily group schedule includes: (a) reading of group mission statement, 5 minutes; (b) body scan, 10 minutes; (c) automatic pilot and psychological flexibility, 10 minutes; (d) formulating relapse prevention plan and identifying triggers and high-risk situations, 20 minutes; (e) mindfulness core skills practice (5 minutes each) and group process, 45 minutes; (f) values and committed action, 20 minutes; (g) homework review and assignments, 20 minutes; (h) urge-surfing, 10 minutes; (i) savoring, 10 minutes; (j) closing the group with metta, 10 minutes.

Mission Statement

Each group begins with a reading of the group mission statement which serves as the intention for the group and a reminder of the way in which treatment is delivered using mindfulness- and acceptance-based modalities. This sets the daily agenda, while orienting new group members to the format and simultaneously serves as a mindful reminder to established members of the mission and vision of the group. A sample mission statement is provided here:

Today we come together to support one another in our recovery from addictions. We are going to use the processes of mindfulness and self-acceptance to foster a greater sense of awareness and compassion toward our experiences. By paying attention, moment-to-moment with a nonjudgmental and curious attitude, we allow space for greater self-awareness and self-compassion. This will help us to begin to see ourselves from a new perspective, which includes possibilities for healing and growth.

Today we will practice various brief meditative exercises that will promote a sense of relaxation and help to quiet the mind and calm our emotions. Mindfulness meditation allows us to slow down so that we can begin to notice some things about ourselves that will help us in our recovery. We become more aware of the situations—people, places, and things—that lead to our use and addictive behaviors. This self-awareness will be used to stop the old habits involved in our addictions and interrupt the automatic nature of our behaviors. We become more aware of our patterns so that we can make better choices. Mindfulness fosters an awareness of our bodies which helps to relieve tension, stress, and pain. This helps us to manage withdrawal symptoms and assists in learning how to ride the wave of cravings without needing to take part in the addictive behaviors.

Today we give ourselves permission to heal. We will use mindfulness to help us set goals for a more positive future that includes not only recovery, but a life filled with purposeful activity and simple pleasures. We will learn to focus on the pleasant things we have long forgotten or may not be aware of because we have been too busy trying to cope with addiction. We practice doing this with a sense of kindness towards ourselves. Along the way we will share our thoughts and feelings with the group to receive feedback and support. We will take notes, complete homework assignments, and work towards developing a relapse prevention plan for ourselves.

Body Scan and Core Mindfulness Practice

The first intervention is the guided body scan meditation which is intended to assist clients in developing awareness of bodily sensations and forms the basis of all subsequent meditation practices (Kabat-Zinn, 1990). The body scan technique can relieve bodily tension, stress, and pain and has yielded positive results as an intervention in reducing craving and withdrawal symptoms (Cropley, Ussher, & Charitou, 2007). Core mindfulness practices include mindfulness of the breath, mindfulness of sound, mindfulness of thought, and mindfulness of emotions/sensation, respectively. For a detailed description of mindfulness practice see Gunaratana (1991) and Kabat-Zinn (1990). Depending on the counselor's level of comfort, individual meditations, such as the body scan and core mindfulness exercises, can be facilitated by the counselor by memorizing the contents of each meditation and guiding the group through the steps, by playing an audio recording, or by streaming a particular meditation from the Internet.

Automatic Pilot

After the mindfulness meditations, participants are encouraged to share their experiences, which are processed by the counselor. Processing the meditations should include the introduction of automatic pilot. Automatic pilot can be thought of as functioning mechanically without full awareness of one's own behavior (Kabat-Zinn, 1990), which correlates to addiction (Bowan et al., 2011). In the treatment of addictions, mindfulness affords the practitioner an alternative to a habitual mode of existence, creating space between stimulus and response (Bowen et al., 2011), and resulting in an opportunity to choose an alternative to addictive behavior.

Addictive automaticity or, in other words, automatic pilot, has been linked to low levels of mindfulness and increases in self-medication via drug use (Garland et al., 2015). Automatic pilot can be thought of as a state of psychological inflexibility, which predicts a host of psychological problems including substance use disorders (Lee, An, Levin, & Twohig, 2015). Conversely, psychological flexibility involves the ability to adapt to various situational demands and to choose behavior consciously that is in line with value-based goals (Hayes et al., 1999), such as overcoming addiction. The following is an example of a discussion that follows the body scan and core mindfulness exercises and includes the integration of automatic pilot:

Counselor: What did people notice in doing the body scan meditation?

Client A: I noticed that the chair felt kind of uncomfortable and my stomach was grumbling and then I realized I forgot to eat breakfast. Then I started thinking about other things and it was hard for me to focus.

Counselor: So thoughts arose about your experience of sitting in the chair in response to noticing a sensation of being uncomfortable and hungry. You also noticed how the mind can jump from one topic to the next.

Client A: I got really caught up in all these things I have to do once I leave here, but then I heard the prompt to focus on the present moment and it was like all of a sudden, I was back in the room.

Counselor: Sounds like you were able to recognize the difference between being caught in a stream of thoughts and being aware of the present moment. You also noticed you were able to shift your attention from one to the other pretty easily.

Client B: I noticed my feet pressed against the floor and how they felt in my shoes. I tried to wiggle my toes and my shoes felt kind of tight. I was surprised.

Counselor: You noticed several different sensations. You reacted to this with surprise. How is this different from the way you normally experience yourself?

Client B: I don't pay much attention to my feet. I'm realizing how much I use them and never think about it.

Counselor: How do you think this practice and your experiences here might be related to relapse or recovering from addiction?

Client C: It's like using is so automatic. I never stopped to think about it. At first I started taking pills to help with the pain and I just kept going because I didn't want the pain to come back.

Client A: I didn't realize that I could interrupt my thoughts just by changing how I looked at them instead of being so overwhelmed all the time by what's going on in my head.

Counselor: So this shows us how slowing down and becoming aware of ourselves—our bodies, our feelings, and our thoughts in the present moment—can lead to making more informed choices, instead of acting in automatic pilot mode.

Relapse Prevention Plan

Clients are instructed to take notes of their experience and the information learned about themselves, which is incorporated into their relapse prevention plan over the course of treatment. Relapse prevention is a cognitive behavioral approach that sees relapse as a multidimensional, complex system focused on the interrelationships between client dispositions, contexts, and past and current experiences (Witkiewitz & Marlatt, 2004). The discussion of automatic pilot sets the stage for the work of developing a relapse prevention plan, as participants are beginning to become familiar with their thoughts, emotional reactions, and behavioral patterns (Bowen et al., 2011). Developing a detailed relapse prevention plan includes a functional analysis of triggers and high-risk situations (Marlatt & Donovan, 2007) and is created as a living document that can be added to and addended as clients learn about their addictive patterns. Clients are assisted in creating a recovery reminder card (Bowen et al., 2011) using an index card wherein one side contains the names and phone numbers of individuals that can provide support in times of crisis and the other side lists several activities the client can engage in when triggered and/or when cravings become intense, such as practicing mindfulness, physical activity, attending a recovery meeting, etc.

Values and Homework

Values exercises guide group members in naming values underlying the overarching goal of overcoming opioid dependence (e.g., I want to stop using because I love my partner). There are nine suggested life domains pertaining to values which include intimate relationships, family, friends, spirituality, health, career, education, leisure, and community (for details, see Hayes et al., 1999). For example, clients can be asked how they would behave differently if they were not struggling with opioid dependence. To further facilitate this inquiry, clients can be given the task of imaging themselves at their 80th birthday party (Harris, 2009) and to envision several people who they would want to give a speech on their behalf. Clients are encouraged to imagine what would be said about what they have stood for and the impact they have had on others. Responses can include a wide range of possibilities, such as being a loyal friend, a successful business owner, or a leader in the community. These values are processed within the group from which goals and objectives are constructed to facilitate actions that will move clients toward their chosen values.

Setting goals to move members along the path to valued directions can be linked with homework assignments. For the client who wants to be seen as a loyal friend, a homework assignment can be created to facilitate the goal of building a social network by reaching out to others who they may have been avoiding due to their addiction. Several possible objectives toward reaching that goal include: (a) developing a list of positive support persons, (b) identifying a person they would like to contact, (c) practicing what they might say to this person, (d) committing to and contacting this person, and (e) reporting back to the group what this process was like and the ways in which this action may have triggered urges to use.

Additional homework assignments can be facilitated through handouts aimed at targeting a specific area of need, such as the Noticing Triggers Worksheet (Bowen et al., 2011) or by assigning specific behavioral tasks like walking 30 minutes, 3 times per week, to address goals related to the value of improved health. The use of in-session assessments during group can pinpoint areas of client concern that can lead to targeted interventions and personalized homework experiences. Assessing for such things as detox fear, pain, and depressed feelings, for example, can lead to a more tailored experience within the group format.

Targeted Meditations: Urge Surfing, Savoring, and Metta

Urge surfing is a guided meditation used to assist with craving, wherein one learns how to ride an urge, like an ocean wave, through fluctuations in its intensity, rather than fighting the urge or giving in to it (Bowen & Marlatt, 2009). This practice helps clients build the inner resources needed to resist giving in to urges that may provide immediate relief but likely lead to problematic longer-term outcomes (Witkiewitz et al., 2013). Even brief mindfulness-based practice of observing negative affect and urges without reacting, helps participants learn alternative responses to these unpleasant experiences (Bowen & Marlatt, 2009). Urge surfing meditation can be led by the counselor, pre-recorded, or streamed from the Internet during in-session training.

Savoring involves the use of the senses to sustain awareness on objects or events such as nature scenes or past pleasant experiences while metacognitively reflecting on and absorbing any positive emotions arising in response to the experience (Garland et al., 2015). Through mindful savoring, positive feelings are intensified and prolonged to offset the negative affect and anhedonia often found within clients struggling with opioid use disorders (Garland et al., 2016). Strengthening attention to natural rewards and positive emotional states without clinging to them through mindful savoring may remediate faulty reward processing implicated in addictive behavior (Garland et al., 2015). Savoring exercises can be carried out by the group facilitator, prerecorded, or found on the Internet and played during session.

Metta, or Loving Kindness Meditation (LKM), has been used in the treatment of addictions (Bowen et al., 2011) through the development of unconditional love and kindness toward self and others. Studies have shown that LKM is linked with greater levels of overall happiness and reductions in avoidance motivation, depression, anxiety, and stress (Alba, 2013); reductions in anger and psychological distress (Carson et al., 2016); increases in positive emotions (Fredrickson et al., 2008); increased feelings of social connectedness (Hutcherson, Seppala, & Gross, 2008); and improvements in self-compassion (Pidgeon, Ford, & Klaassen, 2014). Metta meditation can be led by the counselor, pre-recorded, or streamed from the Internet during in-session training.

Conclusion

The goal of this manuscript is to offer addiction counselors a conceptual process for including elements of evidence-based mindfulness and acceptance strategies into the treatment of opioid addiction. The model presented is designed to fit into a group treatment setting with open enrollment. The interventions outlined are provided from a review of the literature that demonstrates their use in helping individuals addicted to opioids. Given the significant need for opioid addiction treatment strategies, mindfulness- and acceptance-based approaches may provide significant benefits to the field of addiction counseling.

References

Alba, B. (2013). Loving-kindness meditation: A field study. *Contemporary Buddhism, 14*(2), 187–203. doi: 10.1080/14639947.2013.832494

American Society of Addiction Medicine. (2016). *National Practice Guideline for the Use of Medications in the Treatment of Addiction Involving Opioid Use*

Baker-White, A. (2017, June 8) Emergency declarations and opioid overdose prevention. Retrieved from http://www.astho.org/StatePublicHealth/Emergency-Declarations-and-Opioid-Overdose-Prevention/6-8-17/

Bowen, S. & Marlatt, G. A. (2009). Surfing the urge: Brief mindfulness-based intervention for college student smokers. *Psychology of Addictive Behaviors, 23*, 666–671.

Bowen, S., Chawla, N., Collins, S. E., Witkiewitz, K., Hsu, S., Grow, J., . . . & Marlatt, A. (2009).

Mindfulness-based relapse prevention for substance use disorders: A pilot efficacy trial. *Substance Abuse, 30*(4), 295–305. doi:10.1080/08897070903250084

Bowen, S., Chawla, N., & Marlatt, G. A. (2011). *Mindfulness-based relapse prevention for addictive behaviors: a clinician's guide.* New York, NY: The Guilford Press

Bowen, S., Witkiewitz, K., Clifasefi, S. L., Grow, J., Chawla, N., Hsu, S. H., Carroll, H. A., Harrop, E., Collins, S. E., Lustyk, M. K., & Larimer, M. E. (2014). Relative efficacy of mindfulness-based relapse prevention, standard relapse prevention, and treatment as usual for substance use disorders: A randomized trial. *JAMA Psychiatry, 71*(5), 547–556.

Bricker, J.B., Bush, T., Zbikowski, S.M., Mercer, L.D., Heffner, J.L., (2014a). Randomized trial of telephone-delivered acceptance and commitment therapy versus cognitive behavioral therapy for smoking cessation: A pilot study. *Nicotine Tobacco Research, 16*, 1446–1454.

Bricker, J. B., Copeland, W., Mull, K. E., Zeng, E. Y., Watson, N. L., Akioka, K. J., & Heffner, J. L. (2017). Single-arm trial of the second version of an acceptance & commitment therapy smartphone application for smoking cessation. *Drug and Alcohol Dependence, 170*, 37–42. doi:10.1016/j.drugalcdep.2016.10.029

Bricker, J. B., Mann, S. L., Marek, P. M., Liu, J., & Peterson, A. V. (2010). Telephone-delivered acceptance and commitment therapy for adult smoking cessation: A feasibility study. *Nicotine & Tobacco Research, 12*(4), 454–458. doi:10.1093/ntr/ntq002

Bricker, J.B., Mull, K.E., Kientz, J.A., Vilardaga, R., Mercer, L.D., Akioka, K.J., Heffner, J.L., (2014b). Randomized, controlled pilot trial of a smartphone app for smoking cessation using acceptance and commitment therapy. *Drug and Alcohol Dependence, 143*, 87–94.

Bricker, J., Wyszynski, C., Comstock, B., Heffner, J.L., (2013). Pilot randomized controlled trial of web-based acceptance and commitment therapy for smoking cessation. *Nicotine Tobacco Research, 15*, 1756–1764. doi:10.1093/ntr/ntt056

Carlson, L. E. (2012). Mindfulness-based interventions for physical conditions: A narrative review evaluating levels of evidence. *ISRN Psychiatry*. doi:10.5402/2012/651583

Carson, J. W., Keefe, F. J., Lynch, T. R., Carson, K. M., Goli, V., Fras, A. M., & Thorp, S. R. (2016). Loving-kindness meditation for chronic low back pain. *Journal of Holistic Nursing, 23*(3), 287–304. doi:10.1177/0898010105277651

Chiesa, A., & Malinowski, P. (2011). Mindfulness-based approaches: Are they all the same? *Journal of Clinical Psychology, 67*, 404–424. doi:10.1002/jclp.20776

Chiesa, A., & Serretti, A. (2014). Are mindfulness-based interventions effective for substance use disorders? A systematic review of the evidence. *Substance Use and Misuse, 49*(5), 492–512. doi:10.3109/10826084.2013.770027

Cropley, M., Ussher, M., & Charitou, E. (2007). Acute effects of a guided relaxation routine (body scan) on tobacco withdrawal symptoms and cravings in abstinent smokers. *Addiction, 102*, 6, 989–993. doi:10.1111/j.1360-0443.2007.01832.x

Davis, D. M., & Hayes, J. A. (2011). What are the benefits of mindfulness? A practice review of psychotherapy-related research. *Psychotherapy, 48*(2), 198–208.

Fredrickson, B., Cohn, M., Coffey, K., Pek, J., & Finkel, S. (2008). Open hearts build lives: Positive emotions, induced through loving-kindness meditation, build consequential personal resources. *Journal of Personality and Social Psychology, 95*(5), 1045. doi:10.1037/a0013262

Froeliger, B., Mathew, A. R., McConnell, P. A., Eichberg, C., Saladin, M. E., Carpenter, M. J., & Garland, E. L. (2017). Restructuring reward mechanisms in nicotine addiction: A pilot fMRI study of mindfulness-oriented recovery enhancement for cigarette smokers. *Evidence-based Complementary and Alternative Medicine: Ecam,* Retrieved from https://www.hindawi.com/journals/ecam/2017/7018014/abs/

Garland, E. L. (2013). *Mindfulness-oriented recovery enhancement for addiction, stress, and pain.* Washington, DC: NASW Press.

Garland, E. L. (2014a). Disrupting the downward spiral of chronic pain and opioid addiction with mindfulness-oriented recovery enhancement: A review of clinical outcomes and neurocognitive targets. *Journal of Pain and Palliative Care Pharmacotherapy, 28*(2), 122–129. doi:10.3109/15360288.2014.911791

Garland, E.L., Froeliger, B., & Howard, M.O. (2014b). Effects of mindfulness-oriented recovery enhancement on reward responsiveness and opioid cue-reactivity. *Psychopharmacology, 231*(16), 3229–3238. doi:10.1007/s00213-014-3504-7

Garland, E.L., Froeliger, B.E., & Howard, M.O. (2015). Neurophysiological evidence for remediation of reward processing deficits in chronic pain and opioid misuse following treatment with mindfulness-oriented recovery enhancement: Exploratory ERP findings from a pilot RCT. *Journal of Behavioral Medicine, 38*(2), 327–336.

Garland, E.L., Gaylord, S.A., Boettiger, C.A., & Howard, M.O. (2010). Mindfulness training modifies cognitive, affective, and physiological mechanisms implicated in alcohol dependence: Results of a randomized controlled pilot trial. *Journal of Psychoactive Drugs 42*, 177–192.

Garland, E. L., Manusov, E. G., Froeliger, B., Kelly, A., Williams, J. M., & Howard, M. O. (2014c). Mindfulness-oriented recovery enhancement for chronic pain and prescription opioid misuse: Results from an early-stage randomized controlled trial. *Journal of Consulting and Clinical Psychology, 82*(3), 448–459. doi:10.1037/a0035798

Garland, E.L., Roberts-Lewis, A., Tronnier, C., Kelley, K., & Graves, R. (2016). Mindfulness-oriented recovery enhancement versus CBT for co-occurring substance dependence, traumatic stress, and psychiatric disorders: Proximal outcomes from a pragmatic randomized trial. *Behaviour Research and Therapy, 77*, 7–16.

Garland, E. L., Thomas, E. A., Hanley, A. W., Knoll, P., & Ferraro, J. (2015). Low dispositional mindfulness predicts self-medication of negative emotion with prescription opioids. *Journal of Addiction Medicine, 9*(1), 61–67.

Garland, E.L., Thomas, E.A., & Howard, M.O. (2014d). Mindfulness-oriented recovery enhancement ameliorates the impact of pain on self-reported psychological and physical function among opioid-using chronic pain patients. *Journal of Pain and Symptom Management, 48*(6), 1091–1099.

Gifford, E., Kohlenberg, B., Hayes, S. C., Antonuccio, D., Piasecki, M., Rasmussen-Hall, M. (2004). Acceptance-based treatment for smoking cessation. *Behaviour Therapy, 35*, 689–705. doi:10.1016/S0005-7894(04)80015-7

Gifford, E. V., Kohlenberg, B. S., Hayes, S. C., Pierson, H. M., Piasecki, M. P., Antonuccio, D. O., & Palm, K. M. (2011). Does acceptance and relationship focused behavior therapy contribute to bupropion outcomes? A randomized controlled trial of functional analytic psychotherapy and acceptance and commitment therapy for smoking cessation. *Behavior Therapy, 42*, 700 –715. doi:10.1016/j.beth.2011.03.002

Glasner, S., Mooney, L. J., Ang, A., Garneau, H. C., Hartwell, E., Brecht, M., & Rawson, R. A. (2017). Mindfulness-based relapse prevention for stimulant dependent adults: A pilot randomized clinical trial. *Mindfulness, 8*(1), 126–135.

Gunaratana, V. H. (1991). *Mindfulness in plain English*. MA: Wisdom Publications.Harris, A. H. (2015). A qualitative study on the introduction of mindfulness based relapse prevention (MBRP) into a therapeutic community for substance abusers. *Therapeutic Communities, 36*(2), 111–123. 123. doi:10.1108/TC-04-2014-0015

Harris, R. (2009). *ACT with love: Stop struggling, reconcile differences, and strengthen your relationship with acceptance and commitment therapy*. Oakland, CA: New Harbinger Publications.

Hayes, S. C., Strosahl, K., & Wilson, K. G. (1999). *Acceptance and commitment therapy: An experiential approach to behavior change*. New York, NY: Guilford Press.

Hayes, S. C., Wilson, K., Gifford, E., Bisset, R., Piasecki, M., Batten, S., et al. (2004). A preliminary trial of twelve step facilitation and acceptance and commitment therapy withpolysubstance-abusing methadone maintained opiate addicts. *Behaviour Therapy, 35*, 667–688. doi.10.1016/S0005-7894(04)80014-5

Heffner, M., Eifert, G. H., Parker, B. T., & Hernandez, H. S., & Sperry, J.A. (2003). Valued directions: Acceptance and commitment therapy in the treatment of alcohol dependence. *Cognitive & Behavioral Practice, 10*, 378–383.

Hermann, B. A., Meyer, E. C., Schnurr, P. P., Batten, S. V., & Walser, R. D. (2016). Acceptance and commitment therapy for co-occurring PTSD and substance use: A manual development study. *Journal of Contextual Behavioral Science, 5*(4), 225–234. doi:10.1016/j.jcbs.2016.07.001

Hernandez-Lopez, M., Luciano, M. C., Bricker, J. B., Roales-Nieto, J. G., & Montesinos, F. (2009). Acceptance and commitment therapy for smoking cessation: A preliminary study of its effectiveness in comparison with cognitive behavioral therapy. *Psychology of Addictive Behaviours, 23*(4), 723–730.

Hutcherson, C. A., Seppala, E. M., & Gross, J. J. (2008). Loving-kindness meditation increases social connectedness. *Emotion, 8*(5), 720–724. doi: 10.1037/a0013237

Kabat-Zinn, J. (1990). *Full catastrophe living*. New York, NY: Delacorte.

Khoury, B., Lecomte, T., Fortin, G., Masse, M., Therien, P., Bouchard, V., Chapleau, M.-A., . . . Hofmann, S. G. (2013). Mindfulness-based therapy: A comprehensive meta-analysis. *Clinical Psychology Review, 33*(6), 763–771. doi: 10.1016/j.cpr.2013.05.005

Lee, E. B., An, W., Levin, M. E., & Twohig, M. P. (2015). An initial meta-analysis of Acceptance and Commitment Therapy for treating substance use disorders. *Drug & Alcohol Dependence, 155*. doi: 10.1016/j.drugalcdep.2015.08.004

Li, W., Howard, M. O., Garland, E. L., McGovern, P., & Lazar, M. (2017). Mindfulness treatment for substance misuse: A systematic review and meta-analysis. *Journal of Substance Abuse Treatment, 75*(1), 62–96.

Luoma, J.B., Kohlenberg, B.S., Hayes, S.C., & Fletcher, L. (2012). Slow and steady wins the race: A randomized clinical trial of acceptance and commitment therapy targeting shame in substance use disorders. *Journal of Consulting Clinical Psychology, 80*, 43–53.

Marlatt, G. A., & Donovan, D. M. (2007). *Relapse prevention: Maintenance strategies in the treatment of addictive behaviors.* New York, NY: Guilford Press.

Mee-Lee, D., Shulman, G. D., Fishman, M., Gastfriend, D. R., Miller, M. M., Provence, S. M. (2013). *The ASAM criteria: Treatment for addictive, substance-related, and co-occurring conditions.* Chevy Chase, MD: American Society of Addiction Medicine.

Menéndez, A.G., García, P.F., Lamelas, F.R., Lanza, P.V. (2014). Long-term outcomes of acceptance and commitment therapy in drug-dependent female inmates: a randomized controlled trial. *Int. Journal of Clinical Health Psychology, 14*, 18–27.

Minami, H., Bloom, E. L., Reed, K. M., Hayes, S. C., & Brown, R. A. (2015). The moderating role of experiential avoidance in the relationships between internal distress and smoking behavior during a quit attempt. *Psychology of Addictive Behaviors, 29*, 400–407. doi:10.1037/adb0000030

Morgan-Lopez, A. A., & Fals-Stewart, W. (2008). Analyzing data from open enrollment groups: Current considerations and future directions. *Journal of Substance Abuse Treatment, 35*(1), 36–40.

National Institute on Drug Abuse (2017, July). *Opioids.* Retrieved from https://www.drugabuse.gov/drugs-abuse/opioids

Paddock, S. M., Hunter, S. B., Watkins, K. E., & McCaffrey, D. F. (2011). Analysis of rolling group therapy data using conditionally autoregressive priors. *Annals of Applied Statistics, 5*, 605–627. doi: 10.1214/10-AOAS434

Petersen, C. L., & Zettle, R. D. (2009). Treating inpatients with comorbid depression and alcohol use disorders: A comparison of acceptance and commitment therapy. *Psychological Record, 59*(4), 521–536.

Pidgeon, A. M., Ford, L., & Klaassen, F. (2014). Evaluating the effectiveness of enhancing resilience in human service professionals using a retreat-based mindfulness with metta training program: A randomised control trial. *Psychology, Health and Medicine, 19*(3), 355–364.

Rudd, R. A., Aleshire, N., Zibbell, J. E., & Gladden, R. M. (2016). Increases in drug and opioid overdose deaths—United States, 2000–2014. *MMWR: Morbidity & Mortality Weekly Report, 64(50/51)*, 1378–1382. doi:10.15585/mmwr.mm6450a3

Smallwood, R. F., Potter, J. S., & Robin, D. A. (2016). Neurophysiological mechanisms in acceptance and commitment therapy in opioid-addicted patients with chronic pain. *Psychiatry Research: Neuroimaging, 250*, 12–14.

Smout, M. F., Longo, M., Harrison, S., Minniti, R., Wickes, W., & White, J. M. (2010). Psychosocial treatment for methamphetamine use disorders: A preliminary randomized controlled trial of cognitive behavior therapy and acceptance and commitment therapy. *Substance Abuse, 31*(2), 98–107.

Stotts, A.L., Green, C., Masuda, A., Grabowski, J., Wilson, K., Northrup, T.F., Moeller, F.G.,

Schmitz, J.M., (2012). A stage I pilot study of acceptance and commitment therapy for methadone detoxification. *Drug and Alcohol Dependence, 125*, 215–222.

Stotts, A. L., Masuda, A., & Wilson, K. (2009). Using acceptance and commitment therapy during methadone dose reduction: Rationale, treatment description, and a case report. *Cognitive and Behavioral Practice, 16*(2), 205–213.

Twohig, M. P., Shoenberger, D., & Hayes, S. C. (2007). A preliminary investigation of acceptance and commitment therapy as a treatment for marijuana dependence in adults. *Journal of Applied Behavioural Analysis, 40*(4), 619–632.

United States Congress (2016). *Examining the Opioid Epidemic Challenges and Opportunities.* https://www.finance.senate.gov/imo/media/doc/23291.pdf

Witkiewitz, K. & Bowen, S. (2010). Depression, craving and substance use following a randomized trial of mindfulness-based relapse prevention. *Journal of Consulting and Clinical Psychology, 78*, 362–374.

Witkiewitz, K., Bowen, S., Douglas, H., & Hsu, S. H. (2013). Mindfulness-based relapse prevention for substance craving. *Addictive Behaviors, 38*(2), 1563–1571.

Witkiewitz, K., Greenfield, B. L., & Bowen, S. (2013). Mindfulness-based relapse prevention with racial and ethnic minority women. *Addictive Behaviors, 38*(12), 2821–2824.

Witkiewitz, K., & Marlatt, G. A. (2004). Relapse prevention for alcohol and drug problems: That was Zen, this is Tao. *American Psychologist, 59*(4), 224–235. doi:10.1037/0003-066X.59.4.224

Witkiewitz, K., Marlatt, G. A., & Walker, D. (2005). Mindfulness-based relapse prevention for alcohol and substance use disorders. *Journal of Cognitive Psychotherapy: An International Quarterly, 19*, 211–228.

Witkiewitz, K., Warner, K., Sully, B., Barricks, A., Stauffer, C., Thompson, B. L., & Luoma, J. B. (2014). Randomized trial comparing mindfulness-based relapse prevention with relapse prevention for women offenders at a residential addiction treatment center. *Substance Use & Misuse, 49*(5), 536–546.

Zemestani, M., & Ottaviani, C. (2016). Effectiveness of mindfulness-based relapse prevention for co-occurring substance use and depression disorders. *Mindfulness, 7*(6), 1347–1355.

4

Add-Wellness

A Humanistic Model to Conceptualize Addiction

James E. McDonald *and* Jennifer M. Cook[3]

Since 2000, drug overdose deaths have increased in the US by 137%, including a 200% increase in opioid-related overdose deaths, creating an epidemic and adding a heightened sense of urgency to addiction counseling (Rudd, Aleshire, Zibbell, & Gladden, 2016). Addiction is one of the most pressing mental health concerns for counselors today, yet the complexity and intricacy of addiction are as unique to each individual as they are a shared human phenomenon. While addiction counseling approaches have become stronger and medical advances have occurred, counselors and healthcare professionals alike still struggle to conceptualize and treat addiction. There are many influential models to understanding addiction, yet our knowledge and perspectives remain incomplete.

Perhaps the most influential model of the last several decades is the brain disease model, which described addiction as a "chronic, relapsing brain disorder" (Leshner, 1997, p. 45). Conceptualizing addiction as a brain disease has served to destigmatize treatment and bolster preven-

3. James E. McDonald and Jennifer M. Cook, Counselor Education and Counseling Psychology, Marquette University. Correspondence concerning this article should be addressed to James E. McDonald, 4480 N. Oakland Ave., #107, Shorewood, WI 53211. E-mail: james.mcdonald@bastyr.edu.

tion efforts, as well as shift public policy conversations to increase treatment (Leshner, 1997; Volkow, Koob, & McLellan, 2016). Increasingly, sophisticated research into the neurological mechanisms of addiction has provided a richly detailed picture of how the brain changes in response to prolonged substance use (Volkow et al., 2016). Yet, while the brain disease model offers a detailed picture of the neurological mechanisms of addiction, it has done little to explain why some individuals become addicted to substances while others do not. Nor does it explain the variety of individual differences in seeking and responding to substance use treatment. Recently, researchers have begun to call the brain disease model into question, not with the intent to discount the effects addiction has on the brain, but rather to pinpoint the effects and to depict more accurately how the brain responds (Lewis, 2017; Volkow et al., 2016).

Although many addiction models exist in addition to neurobiological explanations, most professionals recognize individual client differences, and they do not uncritically support one addiction model over another, often holding several views simultaneously (Bell et al., 2014; Shaffer, 1987; Thombs & Osborn, 2001). This results in selecting conceptualization models and treatment approaches that make sense to counselors and resonate for clients, often offering a destigmatizing, empowering framework to engage clients with treatment (Bell et al., 2014). The ability to hold several perspectives in tension is an essential skill for counselors practicing in an increasingly complex multicultural world (Sue & Sue, 2013). This is particularly important when clinicians conceptualize clients' addiction, because clients' addiction, or any struggles they experience, rarely have a single etiology. A thorough case conceptualization from multiple perspectives allows counselors to understand and treat clients holistically (Zubernis, Snyder, & Neale-McFall, 2017).

Diagnosis is one key process in case conceptualization. Diagnostically, addiction has been defined as "a cluster of cognitive, behavioral, and physiological symptoms indicating that the individual continues using the substance despite significant substance-related problems" (American Psychiatric Association, 2013, p. 483). Notably, this definition is limited to substance use and does not include process addictions. Although this definition outlines some common addiction symptoms necessary for diagnosis, it does not inform counselors about who a person is or what her experiences have been, a critical step in case conceptualization (Zubernis et al., 2017). This crucial information is grounded in the humanistic perspective foundational to the counseling profession. Without it, counselors run the risk of identifying individuals as their addiction only and can account for some of the shame and stigma persons with addictions experience (van Boekel, Brouwers, van Weeghel, & Garretsen, 2013).

Humanism emphasizes a positive, self-actualizing, holistic view of individuals experiencing addiction, and conceptualizing addiction from this perspective may reduce stigma and treatment barriers (Scholl, 2008). To this end, we offer a model that emphasizes understanding clients who are struggling with substance use that aligns with humanistic principles and allows counselors to conceptualize fully each client's holistic uniqueness. This model was not designed with specific treatment goals or outcomes in mind (i.e., abstinence or harm-reduction). This model was developed as a tool for counselors to integrate critical humanistic factors influencing their clients' addictions, so they can collaboratively set treatment goals. Concurrently, this model is meant to be used in conjunction with other theoretical perspectives that inform case conceptualization, not as a stand-alone approach. In this article, we outline the strengths and liabilities of current addiction models, provide a humanistic evaluation of these models, present the *Add-Wellness Model* for conceptualizing addiction, and provide a case example and discussion using the model.

Current Addiction Models

Currently, there are seven major models commonly used to conceptualize addiction: the moral, developmental, brain disease, behavioral, psychological, adaptive, and the sociocultural models. Each of these models has made important contributions to our current understanding of addiction. In this section, we summarize these approaches and, in the subsequent section, provide a humanistic evaluation of each model.

Moral and Developmental Models of Addiction

In the moral model of addiction, addiction is viewed as a character flaw, a symptom of moral failing, and a personal weakness (Moyers & Miller, 1993). Further, the moral model emphasizes self-responsibility, a concept central to addiction literature and many recovery programs (Butler, Meloy, & Call, 2015; Peele, 1987). The developmental model places similar emphasis on self-responsibility and understands addiction as the result of immaturity or incomplete cognitive development (Windle et al., 2008). Notably, the developmental model applies to individuals without acquired or congenital disabilities. Self-responsibility is a central feature of both models and was most popular prior to the rise of the disease model in the early 1950's (Jellinek, 1952; Levine, 1978).

Brain Disease Model of Addiction

Neurobiological research on addicted animals' brains gave rise to the widely adopted brain disease model of addiction (Leshner, 1997; McLellan, Lewis, O'Brien, & Kleber, 2000; Volkow & Fowler, 2000). In this model, addiction is understood to manifest through long-lasting changes in the structure and function of various parts of the brain responsible for habituation and reward (Everitt, Dickinson, & Robbins, 2001; Leshner, 1997; Newlin & Strubler, 2007). Currently, this view is held by both the American Medical Association and the American Society of Addiction Medicine, which have a large cultural impact on the way addiction is conceptualized and treated in the US (The National Center on Addiction and Substance Abuse, 2017). Researchers have begun to question the brain disease model, offering that addiction is not a *brain disease* per se, but rather a dramatic brain change that occurs in response to substance abuse; this is in accord with what the brain is designed to do—to change in response to differing stimuli and situations—and therefore should not be viewed as a *disease* (Lewis, 2017). Further, researchers offer that substance abuse can trigger higher levels of dopamine, the brain chemical responsible for activating neuroplasticity, which is indicative of the brain *changing*, not developing a *disease* (Volkow et al., 2016).

Behavioral and Psychological Models of Addiction

The behavioral model of addiction understands addiction as a combination of classical and operant conditioning (Butler, Call, Meloy, & Zitzman, 2014). In effect, learned associations become conditioned triggers, which lead to the habituation of repetitive behaviors that can become entrenched and ritualized behavior patterns (Butler et al., 2014). Addiction becomes an unconscious process that continues to reinforce associations and neurobiological pathways. This entrenched, ritualized behavior pattern can become activated when one encounters a conditioned trigger, culminating in relapse, and result in a trance-like state many people describe during relapse (Butler et al., 2014). The psychological model of addiction incorporates the behavioral perspective and adds to it by positing that the motivation to continue to use substances, despite damaging consequences, results from expectations, beliefs, self-efficacy, coping, and other internal schemas, in addition to reinforcement and neurobiology (Gifford & Humphreys, 2007).

Adaptive and Sociocultural Models of Addiction

The adaptive model of addiction views addiction as the result of an individual's attempts to reduce distress through substance use (Alexander, 1990). In this model, the temporal causality of events is important and distinguishes between the original motivation to use a substance and the resulting addiction (Alexander & Hadaway, 1982). From this perspective, addiction is conceptualized as the result of individuals using maladaptive coping tools to manage distress (Alexander & Hadaway, 1982; Hunt, 2014); several studies have confirmed addiction can result from such attempts to alleviate stress and trauma (Debnam, Milam, Furr-Holden, & Bradshaw, 2016; Ford & Russo, 2006). Relatedly, this model has been used with clients who struggle with co-occurring substance use and posttraumatic stress disorders (PTSD), as it provides a unique framework to conceptualize addiction as a symptom of unresolved trauma (Ford & Russo, 2006). Similarly, the sociocultural model accounts for distress individuals experience and explains addiction as the result of cultural context and systemic inequality. The model purports that some cultures may encourage substance use and lead to addiction. Additionally, the model notes that systemic inequality, which often results in lack of opportunity, discrimination, and poor quality of life, may encourage substance use to alleviate pain and distress, and lead to the development of addiction (Gifford & Humphreys, 2007).

A Humanistic Evaluation of Current Models

Humanism emphasizes a growth-producing perspective of clients, including a positive view of individuals as self-actualizing and that a sense of purpose, rather than cause, is the motivation for human behavior (Scholl, 2008). In turn, counseling must be based on a strong relationship, and holistic approaches are more effective than reductionist ones (Scholl, 2008), which includes integrating clients' cultural and contextual experiences to understand their realities more fully. Broadly, the goals of humanism are to identify and remove an individual's barriers to self-actualization. These goals are accomplished through the counselor striving to empower clients and encourage their personal growth, while displaying empathy and unconditional positive regard. The existing humanistic model of addiction integrates humanistic techniques into substance use counseling to aid clients in their personal growth (Barry & Panel, 1999). Core treatment components include empathy, encouragement of affect, reflective listening, and acceptance of the client's subjective experience (Barry & Panel, 1999). However, this model focuses almost exclusively on treatment rather than conceptualization. It provides little direction on how to *understand* a human being's unique addiction experience, which is an essential component of effective case conceptualization. Responsibility, shame, stigma, purpose, and motivation are key concepts to a humanistic perspective of addiction. Therefore, we utilize these concepts to explore and evaluate the aforementioned models.

Responsibility

Responsibility is fundamental to many addiction models and appears to fall on a continuum. Proponents of the brain disease model assign little responsibility to the individual, proponents of the moral model assign full responsibility to the individual, while behavioral, psychological, developmental, and adaptive models fall closer toward the middle of the continuum (Butler et al., 2014; Hammer et al., 2013; Peele, 1987). Connectedly, the sociocultural model adds an additional layer by considering how society assigns responsibility vis-à-vis criminalization. In the US, legal ramifications connected to drug possession vary widely based on race and socioeconomic status (Kushner, 2006). For example, sentencing is stricter for less expensive crack cocaine than more expensive white powder cocaine, and people of color make up 85% of the sentences for cocaine violations, yet only constitute 15% of people who use crack (Mauer, 2004). Debate continues about the usefulness of assigning responsibility. While some scientists and counselors report that models which assign little individual responsibility reduce stigma, shame, and guilt, others argue that conceptualizing addiction in this way alleviates individuals' responsibility for their addiction (Hammer et al., 2013). Humanism holds a different perspective on self-responsibility, recognizing it as a difficult and courageous process of personal growth. Instead of assigning responsibility, humanism seeks to empower individuals to identify and take ownership for their choices.

Shame and Stigma

Despite neuroscientific advances about the physiologically addictive nature of some substances, many scientists and counselors maintain the perspective that addiction is a symptom of moral failing (Hammer et al., 2013), and shame should be used to motivate change. Due to its repetitive nature, addiction is often viewed as failure to have self-control over one's behavior, and feelings of shame are a normative reaction to this sense of failure (Flanagan, 2013). This view is paramount to the moral and developmental models of addiction. Unfortunately, this perspective can deter people from seeking help, and research indicates that people who view addiction as a moral failing or character flaw are less likely to seek treatment (Cunningham, Sobell, & Chow, 1993; Varney et al., 1995). Similarly, stigma and shame seem to be used as societal prevention tools to discourage substance use (Flanagan, 2013). Consequently, if individuals become addicted, they may not seek treatment because of the very stigma and shame they learned would befall them if they used substances.

Although many clinicians have shifted away from the moral model as their only view, many have combined it with the brain disease model (Bell et al., 2014; Moyers & Miller, 1993), with shame continuing to be the primary change motivator. A natural result is stigma for individuals who struggle with addiction, their loved ones, healthcare providers, and the general population's beliefs about those who struggle with addiction. Indeed, when healthcare providers have negative attitudes towards people using substances, it may result in shorter visits, reduced empathy, and diminished personal engagement, reducing the quality and quantity of care (van Boekel et al., 2013), which may be similar with counseling professionals.

Supporters of behavioral, psychological, adaptive, and sociocultural models tout their usefulness in promoting clients' self-efficacy (Miller & Rollnick, 2012) and encouraging individuals to create new patterns, which may serve to reduce shame and stigma (Butler et al., 2014). Stigma and shame are linked; shame is counterproductive to empowerment and the antithesis of a humanistic perspective, because it deters clients from their ability to recognize and actualize their strengths. From a humanistic viewpoint, shame and stigma function as barriers to self-actualization. Counselors strive to empower clients, to view them with dignity, and to meet them with empathy based on their lived experience, rather than lessen their sense of agency with stigma, shame, and powerlessness.

Purpose and Motivation

Motivation is an essential component of the experience of addiction and therapeutic intervention, so it is imperative to consider what purpose an addiction is serving when conceptualizing client cases. Apart from the adaptive and psychological models of addiction, which consider how addiction can function as a maladaptive coping mechanism, the other models are founded on the notion of seemingly unwitting cause and effect. That is, addiction is the effect of moral weakness, behavioral learning, environmental stressors, or neurobiological changes that causes uncontrollable, entrenched, compulsive patterns (Butler et al., 2014; McLellan, Lewis, O'Brien, & Kleber, 2000; Moyers & Miller, 1993). In contrast, a humanistic perspective emphasizes a fuller understanding of the purpose addictions serve *from clients' perspectives*. Rather than viewing clients as unwilling participants in their addiction, humanism recognizes that individuals construct meaning and engage in behaviors with purpose (Scholl, 2008). Actively creating meaning and purpose is a central tenet of humanism, deeply linked to an individual's experience and their striving towards growth and self-actualization. In the context of addiction, the motivation to continue, reduce, or cease an addiction lies within the individual; this motivation can be explored but not judged by the counselor. It is essential to expanding how a counselor understands a person's addiction.

A Purposeful, Integrated, Humanistic Approach

As we develop a more sophisticated understanding of neuroscience and counseling, how counselors conceptualize addiction must become more integrated and nuanced. Furthermore, we must achieve this integration without departing from the humanistic roots of our profession. For example, the adaptive model utilizes research from both the brain disease and behavioral models to explain the physiological and psychological mechanisms of addiction and provides an alternate view to the moral model regarding addiction causality. Instead of emphasizing addiction etiology as moral weakness, the adaptive model views it as distress. Similarly, the behavioral model of addiction makes use of interdisciplinary research from the brain disease model to explain the neurological pathways that are formed and reinforced in the process of addiction (Newlin & Strubler, 2007). As our understanding of addiction continues to progress toward a fuller biopsychosocial conceptualization of addiction, counselors must strive to integrate scientific progress in their work while simultaneously honoring their humanistic roots.

The seven aforementioned addiction models are useful to understand certain components of addiction, yet each is fundamentally reductionist, viewing addiction from a single perspective. Further, each model offers detailed explanations of the mechanisms of addiction. However, they do little to enable counselors to understand and value the holistic experience of addiction for each individual. While each of these models has worth for conceptualizing addiction, a holistic approach may offer a more complete understanding of the factors that influence addiction and the *human being* who is experiencing the addiction. The strength of these models is in their specificity, yet this is where they fall short as well, as they are not designed to offer a paradigm to capture an individual's holistic uniqueness. Counseling professionals could benefit from an additional model to conceptualize addiction that aligns with the fundamental humanistic principles of the counseling profession and allows them to empower individuals to understand their motivation, purpose, and choices so they can direct their lives intentionally.

A Humanistic Model to Conceptualize Factors Influencing Addiction

We brought together phenomenology, the diathesis-stress model, and the addiction-to-wellness continuum to develop *Add-Wellness* (see figure 1), a humanistic conceptualization of factors influencing addiction. The model has two interlocking circles: (a) the desire to change one's lived experience, and (b) diathesis-stress. The desire to change one's lived experience is rooted in the belief that many people use substances because they want their lives to be different (Schlimme, 2010). The desire to escape one's lived experience provides a useful theoretical convergence of subjective client experiences, biological changes, and environmental predispositional vulnerabilities. This incorporates neuroscientific research from the brain disease model and other salient models to understand the client's holistic addiction experience. Diathesis-stress pertains to the interaction between inherited genetic vulnerabilities and environmental stressors, a theory which may explain why some individuals develop addictive disorders and others do not (Ingram & Luxton, 2005). Phenomenology is closely linked to diathesis-stress because many people experience genetic and environmental stressors outside their control (Zuckerman, 1999), which can influence their desire to change their lived experiences. Beneath the interlocking circles is the addiction-to-wellness continuum. The continuum is bidirectional to account for individuals' ability to move to new places on the continuum. The dotted box with arrows surrounding the model represents movement, and the non-linear process most individuals experience related to substance use. The *Add-Wellness* title was selected in order to recognize the humanistic and wellness perspectiveser to emphasize both the humanis foundational to the model and to emphasize the continuum from addiction to wellness, as opposed to dichotomous states. Further, it encapsulates a strength-based perspective in that clinicians *add wellness* when they conceptualize cases from this perspective. *Add-Wellness* is intended as a flexible guide for case conceptualization. Each model factor is discussed below.

Phenomenology

To understand addiction, it is useful to begin at the source: the lived experience of the person who is experiencing addiction. From this perspective, the fundamental purpose addiction serves is the desire to change one's lived experience (Schlimme, 2010). This perspective is influenced by the psychological, sociocultural, and adaptive models, because one's lived experience is comprised of the individual's internal and external experiences. To escape an internal state of suffering, a mood or mind-altering substance can be a highly effective method to change one's reality (Reith, 1999; Schlimme, 2010). Put simply, the desire to change one's lived experience is the motivation to engage in substance use, as the adaptive and sociocultural models indicate. This motivation to change can come from innumerable sources, both positive and negative, including trauma, emotional pain, spiritual emptiness, spiritual seeking, to lower inhibitions, and peer groups (Brooks & McHenry, 2009; Levers, 2012; van Wormer & Davis, 2013). Additionally, the sociocultural model calls attention to how one's cultural identities, context, and social location can influence the types of substances one chooses to use, and which substance one might consider *acceptable* (van Wormer & Davis, 2013).

In this conceptualization, the choice to use substances is unique to the individual, based on their life experiences. This perspective aligns closely with humanism, which emphasizes the need for counselors to deeply understand clients' subjective experience (Scholl, 2008). As counselors come to understand the richness of each individual's feelings, values, and experiences, they are better able to empower clients with specific insights and strategies to promote self-actualization. Therefore, a deep understanding of the phenomenological world of each person is an essential beginning point from which to conceptualize clients' motivation to use a substance.

Diathesis-Stress

Phenomenology provides a framework for understanding the motivation to use a substance, a perspective on addiction influenced by the psychological, adaptive, and sociocultural models. Substance use can vary between being a part of the person's wellness and a hindrance in her/his life as an addiction. The relationship between one's desire to change lived experience and the extent to which substance use is problematic in a person's life (that is, placement on the addiction-to-wellness continuum, which is further discussed in the next section), is explained by the diathesis-stress model. Ingram and Luxton (2005) stated diathesis-stress is grounded in the idea "that all people have some level of predisposing factors (diatheses) for any given mental disorder" (p. 36). Further, "individuals have their own point at which they will develop a given disorder, a point that depends on the interaction between the degree to which these risk factors exist and the degree of stress experienced by the individual" (p. 36), which can account for why some develop an addiction while others do not. The strength of the diathesis-stress model is that it seeks to explain the interaction between genetics and environmental stressors. Research continues to emerge documenting evidence of an integrated relationship between genetics and environmental stressors on the development of substance use disorders (Wickens, 2009; Zuckerman, 1999). This integrated understanding combines the usefulness of the intrapersonal explanation for addiction from the psychological model with the environmental explanation from the sociocultural and adaptive models.

Conceptualizing addiction from a diathesis-stress perspective can account for the desire to change one's lived experience and the genetic and environmental stressors that may influence individuals' substance use. For example, diathesis-stress is stronger for a person who comes from a family with a history of addiction, who is a person of color from low social class, and who has less access to resources (van Wormer & Davis, 2013; Zuckerman, 1999). The result of this combination of predispositional vulnerabilities and environmental stressors can be stronger diathesis-stress. This experience of strong diathesis-stress can influence the person's desire to change their lived experience and turn to substance use as a coping mechanism of choice, particularly if they have experienced discrimination, prejudice, fewer opportunities due to race and social class, and a family history of addiction (van Wormer & Davis, 2013). It is important to note the contribution from the sociocultural model that includes society as part of environment in this example, as society plays a crucial role in the experience of environmental stress. Discrimination, structural inequality, and systemic oppression are embedded in the US social structure and impact individuals with nondominant cultural identities, particularly in terms of race and social class (Hancock, Waites, & Kledaras, 2012; van Wormer & Davis, 2013). When individuals experience these atrocities, they may be inclined to escape their lived experience through substances. This, combined with strong diathesis-stress, creates barriers to wellness and promotes addiction. Furthermore, the experience of strong-diathesis stress has been linked to the development of mental disorders that commonly co-occur with addiction, including anxiety and depression (Zuckerman, 1999). By understanding the lived experience of the individual and the barriers to wellness strong diathesis-stress creates, counselors can more fully conceptualize the integrated relationship between mental health and substance use disorders.

Addiction-to-Wellness Continuum

Travis and Ryan (2004), strong proponents of the wellness movement, view illness and wellness as a continuum, with illness representing one end and wellness representing the other.

This is a departure from the medical model, which has traditionally viewed illness in dichotomous terms, that is, it is either present or not (Travis & Ryan, 2004). For the purposes of our model, the illness-to-wellness continuum has been adapted as the *addiction*-to-wellness continuum to depart from language that stigmatizes individuals with addictions as being *sick*.

The addiction-to-wellness continuum proves useful because it acknowledges the nuances particular to the individual. For example, it is possible for a person, who is towards the addiction end of the continuum, to be implementing wellness practices in their life, and thereby be oriented towards wellness, yet still experiencing addiction. In contrast, a person toward the wellness end may be engaging in many behaviors that orient them towards addiction, yet they have not developed an addiction. Viewing addiction and wellness as a continuum provides an excellent grounding for the *Add-Wellness* model. The *Add-Wellness* model acknowledges there is no clear distinction between substance use and addiction. That is, there is no objective boundary where substance use becomes addiction; it is relative to the individual. This can be helpful both for individuals who may benefit from self-labeling as a person who has an addiction, and those who benefit more from self-labeling as a person who is experiencing addictive symptoms.

Responsibility, Shame and Stigma, and Purpose and Motivation in Add-Wellness

The *Add-Wellness* model components seek to offer a flexible and integrated approach to conceptualize addiction from a humanistic perspective. Previous models have sought to assign responsibility for an individual's substance use to one of several factors (e.g., society, moral failing, a brain disease). In contrast, *Add-Wellness* understands addiction as a combination of phenomenology and diathesis-stress, so counselors expand their conceptualization to include the complex multitude of factors influencing individuals' addiction, not just one. Instead of perseverating on responsibility, counselors can choose to collaborate with clients to discover the salient influences on their substance use. When assigning responsibility is no longer essential to understanding addiction, clients can be freed from shame and stigma that stem from this concept. By alleviating these burdens, the counselor and client can begin their work together unhampered by rigid, predetermined explanations for an individual's substance use. Similarly, by deeply understanding individuals' lived experience and the context of environmental stressors and genetic predispositions, the *Add-Wellness* model recognizes that individuals engage in substance use for a purpose, and they are actively creating meaning in their lives both when using and not using substances. By combining phenomenology, diathesis-stress, and the addiction-to-wellness continuum, the *Add-Wellness* model integrates scientific progress, the strengths of current addiction models, and the humanistic principles that underlie the counseling profession.

Case Study

Karina stated she came to counseling in order to "check it out. . .and because my mom and friends thought it might be a good idea." Karina is a 22-year-old African American who identifies as bisexual, spiritual but not religious, and who expresses her gender fluidly and prefers the pronoun, *she*. Currently, Karina is completing her senior year at a local university. She is in a "semi-serious" three-year relationship with her partner, Taylor, a 23-year-old, White, lesbian, female. Karina reported that her partner's family often comments on her race and gender expression, and this has become a source of tension in Karina and Taylor's relationship.

Karina reported she was raised by her mother in a single-parent home, and they struggled financially. Karina's mother rarely talks about her father, who left when Karina was young, except to say, "He's a drunk." Her uncles on both sides of her family struggle with depression and alcohol abuse, and Karina reported her grandmother often smells of alcohol when she visits her, and her mood is "real up and down." Karina works part-time and has taken on sizeable student loans through the course of her education. She shared her job impacts her sleep because she has to get up early for work, yet it is one of the only places where she feels comfortable because past employers made comments and appeared to be uncomfortable with her gender expression. Karina stated she is passionate about organic foods, eats a nutritious diet, and regularly practices yoga and meditation. She described a strong sense of spirituality that connects these wellness practices and serves as a source of strength and support in her life.

Karina reported using marijuana and drinking alcohol socially, in order to "unwind" and "have a good time." She stated she has been using more than she used to, including using outside of social situations. In fact, for the past eight months, Karina has been smoking pot and taking vodka shots every night before bed in order to sleep without nightmares. Karina reported she was sexually assaulted as a freshman but chose not to report the assault to the authorities; she only told her partner when she woke up crying from a nightmare about the experience. The nightmares have increased in the past year since the man who assaulted her began frequenting the café where she works. Karina stated her grades have fallen and work performance decreased. She feels ambivalent about completing her education and described, "just going through the motions day to day" and "feeling empty." She stated she does not feel her classmates understand her perspective, and she often hears comments about how "different" she is. When asked about her future goals, Karina shrugged her shoulders and stated she is unsure. When asked about her desire to decrease her substance use, Karina offered, "The only reason I would do that is to get my mom and Taylor off my back."

Case Analysis Using the Add-Wellness Model

Using the *Add-Wellness* model, we analyze the interaction between Karina's lived experience and diathesis-stress point by point, beginning with demographics. Karina identifies as a member of the LGBTQIA+ community and a person of color, and she described feeling that others do not understand her perspective and there are few places where she feels comfortable. This lived experience interacts with environmental stressors affecting Karina in the form of prejudice from former employers, her partner's family, and microaggressions from classmates. Research indicates that people with multiple minority statuses are at an increased risk for multiple mental health symptoms due to stigma-related stress (Hatzenbuehler, 2009). Furthermore, as a first-generation college student from low social class, Karina has the added environmental stresses of stereotype threat and financial insecurity (Blascovich, Spencer, Quinn, & Steele, 2001; Williams, Yu, Jackson, & Anderson, 1997). Karina's lived experience includes multiple influences that may be profound sources of stress and account partly for her substance use.

Next, Karina's family has a history of alcoholism, depression, and possible bipolar disorder on both sides of her family, creating a genetic predisposition (Zuckerman, 1999). Zuckerman (1999) noted genetics and environment each account for about 50% of predisposition for substance use and inherited brain structure vulnerabilities, and sensitized mesolimbic reward pathways may prime Karina to have a particularly strong physiological reaction to the effects of substances (Brady & Sinha, 2007). Further compounding the genetic vulnerability to these disorders is limited family support. Because Karina has never known her father, and Karina's grandmother and uncles struggle with mental illness and substance use, Karina's family support is limited. Although it appears her mother is an engaged parent, her financial and interpersonal resources are limited, and research shows that individuals from single-parent homes engage in higher rates of substance use (Griffin, Botvin, Scheier, Diaz, & Miller, 2000).

From a phenomenological perspective, Karina described feelings of meaninglessness and ambivalence about her education and future, manifesting as a feeling of emptiness. She reported using substances to "unwind" and "have a good time," which could stem from peer group expectations and a desire for social belonging (van Wormer & Davis,

2013). Social use is culturally accepted, and social belonging is a deep human need; however, Karina's substance use habits changed in the past eight months since she encountered the man who assaulted her. She has begun to use substances each evening, which may be fueled by potential symptoms of PTSD (e.g., nightmares) related to the sexual assault she experienced (Levers, 2009).

At the same time, Karina has many positive environmental influences and strengths, including the relationship with her mother and partner, stable employment, higher education, a nutritious diet, and a regular yoga and meditation practice (Hawkins, Catalano, & Miller, 1992). Although Karina expressed some ambivalence about change, stating that she would only reduce her substance use to "get my mom and Taylor off my back," research indicates that, in emerging adulthood, encouragement from peers and romantic partners can be an important predictor of intrinsic motivation to reduce substance use (Goodman, Peterson-Badali, & Henderson, 2011). Finally, Karina cited her spirituality connected to her wellness practices, and research affirms spirituality as central to wellness (Myers & Williard, 2003).

Considering the interaction of phenomenology and diathesis-stress, we conceptualized Karina toward the addiction end of the continuum. The addiction-to-wellness continuum allows counselors to understand the complex interaction of factors that may push clients toward wellness or addiction and can help empower clients to understand the totality of their experiences in order to take steps toward wellness. For Karina, there are clear areas of diathesis-stress (e.g., family history, minority stress, financial insecurity), and numerous strengths, even though her substance use has increased to everyday. From a phenomenological perspective, we conceptualized Karina's substance use to be motivated initially by the desire to relax and unwind and for social belonging, and recently by the desire to reduce symptoms of unprocessed trauma. This conceptualization may allow counselors to acknowledge the complexity of Karina's motivations to use and could validate Karina's experiences and allow her to explore how prejudice, stigma, and genetics, combined with potential symptoms of depression and sub-clinical PTSD, may be contributing to her desire for change and substance use. Conceptualizing Karina's substance use with the *Add-Wellness* model allows for a more complete, humanistic conceptualization of addiction to reduce treatment barriers. Furthermore, this model could allow her counselor to focus treatment on specific stress areas, while also reinforcing and building on her strengths. Indeed, by understanding Karina's substance use as a combination of her lived experience and diathesis-stress on an addiction-to-wellness continuum, her counselor can offer her tailored, person-centered treatment that allows her to discover meaning and purpose.

Conclusion

The experience of addiction is multifaceted and complex. We contend prior addiction conceptualization models are more reductionist and static, and they fail to incorporate individuals' lived experience and diathesis-stress that contribute to addiction. We proposed the *Add-Wellness* model to conceptualize addiction and address the need for a more complete, humanistic addiction conceptualization to reduce treatment barriers. We believe this approach allows counselors to account more fully for clients' experiences, both those that lead to addictive behaviors and the addiction experience, while recognizing clients' strengths and the ways they are oriented toward wellness. The *Add-Wellness* model offers clients hope, may reduce stigma, and could increase clients' treatment participation because it orients counselors toward clients' full experience, not solely their addiction. Finally, the *Add-Wellness* model offers counselors and clients an integrative and empowering framework to understand each person's full and unique experience of addiction.

Figure 1

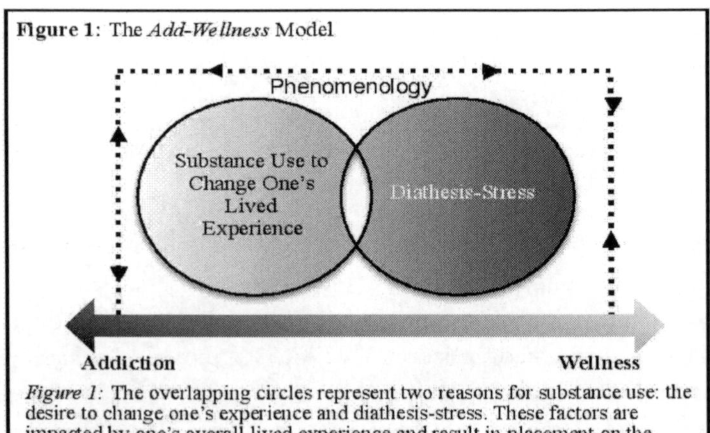

Figure 1: The overlapping circles represent two reasons for substance use: the desire to change one's experience and diathesis-stress. These factors are impacted by one's overall lived experience and result in placement on the addiction to wellness continuum. The dotted box represents the ability to move and change one's place on the continuum.

References

Alexander, B. K. (1990). The empirical and theoretical bases for an adaptive model of addiction. *Journal of Drug Issues, 20*(1), 37–65. doi:10.1177/002204269002000103.

Alexander, B. K., & Hadaway, P. F. (1982). Opiate addiction: The case for an adaptive orientation. *Psychological Bulletin, 92*(2), 367–381. doi:10.1037/0033-2909.92.2.367.

American Psychiatric Association. (2013). *Diagnostic and statistical manual of mental disorders: DSM-5*. Arlington, VA: Author.

Barry, K. L., & Panel, C. (1999). *Treatment improvement protocol (TIP) series 34: Brief interventions and brief therapies for substance abuse*. Rockwell, MD: Substance Abuse and Mental Health Services Administration Center for Substance Abuse Treatment.

Bell, S., Carter, A., Mathews, R., Gartner, C., Lucke, J., & Hall, W. (2014). Views of addiction neuroscientists and clinicians on the clinical impact of a 'brain disease model of addiction.' *Neuroethics, 7*(1), 19–27. doi:10.1007/s12152-013-9177-9.

Blascovich, J., Spencer, S. J., Quinn, D., & Steele, C. (2001). African Americans and high blood pressure: The role of stereotype threat. *Psychological Science, 12*(3), 225–229. doi:10.1111/1467-9280.00340.

Brady, K. T., & Sinha, R. (2007). Co-occurring mental and substance use disorders: the neurobiological effects of chronic stress. *Focus, 5*(2), 229–239. doi:10.1176/foc.5.2.foc229.

Brooks, F., & McHenry, B. (2009). *A contemporary approach to substance abuse and addiction counseling*. Alexandria, VA: American Counseling Association.

Butler, M. H., Meloy, K. C., & Call, M. L. (2015). Dismantling powerlessness in addiction: Empowering recovery through rehabilitating behavioral learning. *Sexual Addiction & Compulsivity, 22*(1), 26–58. doi:10.1080/10720162.2014.993778

Butler, M. H., Call, M. L., Meloy, K. C., & Zitzman, S. T. (2014). Deconstructing mechanisms of powerlessness for clients seeking recovery: Learning to be powerless over addiction. *Sexual Addiction & Compulsivity, 21*(2), 92–113. doi:10.1080/10720162.2014.895461.

Cunningham, J. A., Sobell, L. C., & Chow, V. M. (1993). What's in a label? The effects of substance types and labels on treatment considerations and stigma. *Journal of Studies on Alcohol, 54*, 693–699. doi:10.15288/jsa.1993.54.693.

Debnam, K., Milam, A. J., Furr-Holden, C., & Bradshaw, C. (2016). The role of stress and spirituality in adolescent substance use. *Substance Use & Misuse, 51*(6), 733–741. doi:10.3109/10826084.2016.1155224

Everitt, B. J., Dickinson, A., & Robbins, T. W. (2001). The neuropsychological basis of addictive behaviour. *Brain Research Reviews, 36*(2), 129–138. doi:10.1016/s0165-0173(01)00088-1.

Flanagan, O. (2013). The shame of addiction. *Frontiers in Psychiatry, 4*(120), 1–11. doi:10.3389/fpsyt.2013.00120.

Ford, J. D., & Russo, E. (2006). Trauma-focused, present-centered, emotional self-regulation approach to integrated treatment for posttraumatic stress and addiction: Trauma adaptive recovery group education and therapy (TARGET). *American Journal of Psychotherapy, 60*(4), 335–55.

Gifford, E., & Humphreys, K. (2007). The psychological science of addiction. *Addiction, 102*(3), 352–361. doi:10.1111/j.1360-0443.2006.01706.x.

Goodman, I., Peterson-Badali, M., & Henderson, J. (2011). Understanding motivation for substance use treatment: The role of social pressure during the transition to adulthood. *Addictive Behaviors, 36*(6), 660–668. doi:10.1016/j.addbeh.2011.01.011.

Griffin, K. W., Botvin, G. J., Scheier, L. M., Diaz, T., & Miller, N. L. (2000). Parenting practices as predictors of substance use, delinquency, and aggression among urban minority youth: Moderating effects of family structure and gender. *Psychology of Addictive Behaviors: Journal of the Society of Psychologists in Addictive Behaviors, 14*(2), 174–184. doi:10.1037/0893-164X.14.2.174.

Hammer, R., Dingel, M., Ostergren, J., Partridge, B., McCormick, J., & Koenig, B. A. (2013). Addiction: Current criticism of the brain disease paradigm. *American Journal of Bioethics Neuroscience, 4*(3), 27–32. doi:10.1080/21507740.2013.796328.

Hancock, T. U., Waites, C., & Kledaras, C. G. (2012). Facing structure inequality: Students' orientation to oppression and practice with oppressed groups. *Journal of Social Work Education, 48*, 5–25. doi:10.5175/JSWE.2012.201000078.

Hatzenbuehler, M. L. (2009). How does sexual minority stigma 'get under the skin'? A psychological mediation framework. *Psychological Bulletin, 135*(5), 707–730. doi:10.1037/a0016441.

Hawkins, J. D., Catalano, R. F., & Miller, J. Y. (1992). Risk and protective factors for alcohol and other drug problems in adolescence and early adulthood: Implications for substance abuse prevention. *Psychological Bulletin, 112*(1), 64–105. doi:10.1037//0033-2909.112.1.64.

Hunt, A. (2014). Expanding the biopsychosocial model: The active reinforcement model of addiction. *Graduate Student Journal of Psychology, 15*, 57–69

Ingram, R. E., & Luxton, D. D. (2005). Vulnerability-stress models. In B. L. Hankin & J. R. Z. Abela (Eds.), *Development of psychopathology: A vulnerability stress perspective* (pp. 32–46). Thousand Oaks, CA: Sage Publications Inc.

Jellinek, E. M. (1952). Phases of alcohol addiction. *Quarterly Journal of Studies on Alcohol, 13*(4), 673–684. doi:10.15288/qjsa.1952.13.673.

Kushner, H. I. (2006). Taking biology seriously: The next task for historians of addiction?. *Bulletin of the History of Medicine, 80*(1), 115–143. doi:10.1353/bhm.2006.0025

Levine, H. G. (1978). The discovery of addiction. Changing conceptions of habitual drunkenness in America. *Journal of Studies on Alcohol, 39*(1), 143–174. doi:10.15288/jsa.1978.39.143.

Leshner, A. I. (1997). Addiction is a brain disease, and it matters. *Science,* 278, 45–47. doi:10.1126/science.278.5335.45.

Levers, L. L. (2012). *Trauma counseling: Theories and interventions.* New York, NY: Springer Publishing Company.

Lewis, M. (2017). Addiction and the brain: Development, not disease. *Neuroethics, 10*(1), 7–18. doi:10.1007/s12152-016-9293-4

Mauer, M. (2004). Race, class, and the development of criminal justice policy. *Review of Policy Research 21*(1), 79–92. doi:10.1111/j.1541-1338.2004.00059.x

McLellan, A. T., Lewis, D. C., O'Brien C. P., & Kleber, H. D. (2000). Drug dependence, a chronic medical illness: implications for treatment, insurance, and outcomes evaluation. *Journal of the American Medical Association, 284*(13), 1689–1695. doi:10.1001/jama.284.13.1689

Miller, W. R., & Rollnick, S. (2012). *Motivational interviewing: Preparing people for change* (3rd ed.). New York, NY: Guilford.

Moyers, T. B., & Miller, W. R. (1993). Therapists' conceptualizations of alcoholism: Measurement and implications for treatment decisions. *Psychology of Addictive Behaviors, 7*(4), 238–245. doi:10.1037/0893-164X.7.4.238.

Myers, J. E., & Williard, K. (2003). Integrating spirituality into counselor preparation: A developmental, wellness approach. *Counseling and Values, 47*(2), 142–155. doi:10.1002/j.2161-007x.2003.tb00231.x.

The National Center on Addiction and Substance Abuse. (2017). Addiction as a disease. Retrieved from https://www.centeronaddiction.org/what-addiction/addiction-disease.

Newlin, D. B., & Strubler, K. A. (2007). The habitual brain: An "adapted habit" theory of substance use disorders. *Substance Use & Misuse, 42*(2–3), 503–526. doi:10.1080/10826080601144606.

Peele, S. (1987). A moral vision of addiction: How people's values determine whether they become and remain addicts. *Journal of Drug Issues, 17*(2), 187–215. doi:10.1177/002204268701700205.

Reith, G. (1999). In search of lost time recall, projection and the phenomenology of addiction. *Time & Society, 8*(1), 99–117. doi:10.1177/0961463x99008001005.

Rudd, R. A., Aleshire, N., Zibbell, J. E., & Gladden, R. (2016). Increases in drug and opioid overdose deaths—United States, 2000–2014. *American Journal of Transplantation, 16*(4), 1323–1327. doi:10.1111/ajt.13776.

Schlimme, J. E. (2010). Addiction and self-determination: A phenomenological approach. *Theoretical Medicine and Bioethics, 31*(1), 49–62. doi:10.1007/s11017-010-9134-0.

Scholl, M. B. (2008). Preparing manuscripts with central and salient humanistic content. *Journal of Humanistic Counseling Education and Development, 47*(1), 3–8. doi:10.1002/j.2161-1939.2008.tb00043.x.

Shaffer, H. J. (1987). The epistemology of "addictive disease": The Lincoln-Douglas debate. *Journal of Substance Abuse Treatment, 4*(2), 103–113. doi:10.1016/0740-5472(87)90021-3.

Sue, D.W. & Sue, D. (2013). *Counseling the culturally diverse: Theory and practice (6th ed.).* New York: John Wiley & Sons, Inc.

Thombs, D. L., & Osborn, C. J. (2001). A cluster analytic study of clinical orientations among chemical dependency counselors. *Journal of Counseling & Development, 79*(4), 450–458. doi:10.1002/j.1556-6676.2001.tb01992.x.

Travis, J. W., & Ryan, R. S. (2004). *Wellness workbook: How to achieve enduring health and vitality.* New York, NY: Random House Inc.

van Boekel, L. C., Brouwers, E. P., van Weeghel, J., & Garretsen, H. F. (2013). Stigma among health professionals towards patients with substance use disorders and its consequences for healthcare delivery: Systematic review. *Drug and Alcohol Dependence, 131*(1), 23–35. doi:10.1016/j.drugalcdep.2013.02.018.

van Wormer, K., & Davis, D. R. (2013). *Addiction treatment: A strengths perspective* (3rd ed.). Belmont, CA: Brooks/Cole.

Varney, S. M., Rohsenow, D. J., Dey, A. N., Myers, M. G., Zwick, W. R., & Monti, P. M. (1995). Factors associated with help seeking and perceived dependence among cocaine users. *The American Journal of Drug and Alcohol Abuse, 21*(1), 81–91. doi:10.3109/00952999509095231.

Volkow, N. D., & Fowler, J. S. (2000). Addiction, a disease of compulsion and drive: Involvement of the orbitofrontal cortex. *Cerebral Cortex, 10*(3), 318–325. doi:10.1093/cercor/10.3.318.

Volkow, N. D., Koob, G. F., & McLellan, A. T. (2016). Neurobiologic advances from the disease model of addiction. *New England Journal of Medicine, 374*(4), 363–371. doi: 10.1056/NEJMra1511480.

Wickens, A. (2009). *Introduction to biopsychology* (3rd ed.). Harlow, England: Pearson Education Limited.

Williams, D. R., Yu, Y., Jackson, J. S., & Anderson, N. B. (1997). Racial differences in physical and mental health: Socio-economic status, stress and discrimination. *Journal of Health Psychology, 2*(3), 335–351. doi:10.1037/t13463-000.

Windle, M., Spear, L. P., Fuligni, A. J., Angold, A., Brown, J. D., Pine, D., . . . & Dahl, R. E. (2008). Transitions into underage and problem drinking: Developmental processes and mechanisms between 10 and 15 years of age. *Pediatrics, 121*(Supplement 4), S273-S289. doi:10.1542/peds.2007-2243c.

Zubernis, L., Snyder, M., & Neale-McFall, C. (2017). Case conceptualization: Improving understanding and treatment with the Temporal/Contextual model. *Journal of Mental Health Counseling, 39*(3), 181–194. http://dx.doi.org/10.17744/mehc.39.3.01

Zuckerman, M. (1999). *Vulnerability to psychopathology: A biosocial model.* Washington, DC: American Psychological Association.

5

Psychedelic Therapy and Microdosing

An Overview for Counselors

Peter Eischens[4]

After decades of prohibition (Courtwright, 2004), psychedelics are experiencing a renaissance in both popular culture (Leonard, 2015; Levy, 2016; Malone, 2016) and medical research (Bogenshutz et al., 2015; Fantegrossi, Woods, & Winger, 2004; Grob et al., 2011; Hasler, Grimberg, Benz, Huber, & Vollenwieder, 2004; Johnson, Garcia-Romeau, Cosimano, & Griffiths, 2014; Moreno, Wiegand, Taitano, & Delgado, 2006) as treatment for a myriad of mental illnesses and disorders (Tupper, Wood, Yensen & Johnson, 2015). Psychedelics are a class of compounds found in a variety of plants, fungi, and animals across the planet (Grinspoon & Bakalar, 1979). These compounds have been described using a variety of labels, all of which have different meanings dependent on context (Ott, 1996; Strassman, 1995). The purpose for use may dictate the label assigned to the substance. Some common labels include classic hallucinogen, which denotes scientific or anthropological use, and entheogen, which may signify the facilitation of a religious experience. Humphry

4. Peter Eischens, Department of Addiction and Rehabilitation Studies, East Carolina University. Correspondence concerning this article should be addressed to Peter Eischens, Department of Addiction and Rehabilitation Studies, Health Sciences Building, 4425, Mail Stop 668, Greenville, NC 27834. E-mail: eischensp16@students.ecu.edu.

Osmond is credited with coining the term *psychedelic*, which translates from Greek as meaning "mind-manifesting" (Dyck, 2008, p. 2).

Fadiman (2011) described two camps of social psychedelic advocacy: the human right for personal exploration and the therapeutic or medical use of psychedelics. Thus, the most apt label in the context of therapeutic work would be psychedelic in reference to the mind. For therapeutic purposes, psychedelics may be used to invoke cognitive, psychodynamic, and peak experiences which facilitate the exploration of inner relationships, emergence of unconscious material, and stimulation of deep psychological or philosophical insight (Pahnke et al., 1970). Aftereffects of increased self-reflection and introspection have been reported to continue beyond therapeutic psychedelic sessions and lead to meaningful behavioral change (Zamaria, 2016). Psychedelics that have been used for therapeutic purposes include lysergic acid diethylamide (LSD), dipropyltryptamine (DPT), psilocybin, psilocin, *N,N*-Dimethyltryptamine (*N,N*-DMT), Ayahuasca (containing DMT), and peyote (mescaline; Bogenschutz & Johnson, 2016; Bogenschutz & Pommy, 2012). The primary psychedelics described in this paper include LSD and psilocybin.

A Brief History

The history of humans using psychedelics for spiritual development and medicinal purposes has spanned across continents, cultures and time (Grinspoon & Bakalar, 1979; Schultes, Hoffman, & Rätsch, 2001; Tupper, 2008). Traditional psychedelic use was highly ritualized (Johnson et al., 2008; Tupper, 2008; Tylš, Páleníček, & Horáček, 2014) and designed to facilitate religious and healing experiences (Doblin, 1991; Grinspoon & Bakalar, 1979: Tupper, 2008). The consumption of these plants was considered transcendental and sacred (McKenna, 1991, 1992). Despite the heterogeneity between the diverse societies that engaged in psychedelic use (Grinspoon & Bakalar, 1979), many developed practices and procedures simultaneously analogous of the others (Johnson, Richards & Griffiths, 2008), implying universal effects related to the ingestion of these alkaloids.

After centuries of colonization and Western misrepresentation of indigenous practices (Johansen & Krebs, 2015; Taussig, 1986), psychedelics experienced a brief renaissance in the 1940's when LSD was accidentally ingested by the Swiss chemist Albert Hofmann (Hofmann, 1979; Sessa, 2005). Shortly thereafter, Robert G. Wasson would introduce science to psilocybin mushrooms after participating in a traditional religious ceremony during a trip to Mexico (Tylš et al., 2014). The research and medical community were not far behind. Throughout the next decade, psychedelics were clinically administered by researchers to approximately 40,000 patients (Bogenshutz & Johnson, 2016; Grinspoon & Bakalar, 1979; Nutt, King, & Nichols, 2013) and quickly became recognized as therapeutic tools (Hollister, Shelton & Krieger, 1969; Pahnke, Kurland, Unger, Savage & Grof, 1970).

Psychedelics were introduced into the cultural Western lexicon through authors such as Huxley and Keens (Dyck, 2008; Huxley, 1954), and academics such as Timothy Leary and Richard Alpert (Leary, Metzner & Alpert, 1966), igniting the counterculture of the 1960s and ultimately leading to its demise (Dyck, 2008; Grinspoon & Baklar, 1979; Nichols, 2004). As psychedelics disseminated into mainstream society (Johnson et al., 2008), the substances were sensationalized and eventually outlawed (Nichols, 2004; Nutt et al., 2013). Decades of misinformation regarding psychedelics (Grinspoon & Bakalar, 1979; Ott, 1996; Weil, 2004) and their classification as a Schedule I drug, as described in the Controlled Substances Act of 1970 (Ross, 2012), has hindered modern research into the potential therapeutic benefits of these substances (Nutt et al., 2013) and has associated them with physically addicting narcotics, stimulants, and barbiturates (Pahnke et al., 1970). As Schedule I drugs, psychedelics are defined as having a high potential for abuse, no currently accepted medical use, and are considered unsafe for use under medical supervision (Nutt et al., 2013). Yet almost a half-century since the federal prohibition of LSD, psilocybin and other psychedelics (Sessa, 2005), interest in the potential therapeutic benefits of these unique alkaloids and compounds persists (Grob et al., 2011; Sessa, 2005; Strassman, 1995; Tupper et al., 2015).

Dozens of articles have been written about the benefits of psychedelic use in mainstream publications such as the *Rolling Stone* (Leonard, 2015) and *Vogue* (Mechling, 2017) magazines. The growing trend of ayahuasca tourism (Prayag, Mura, Hall & Fontaine, 2016) and the acknowledgment of LSD as a catalyst in the life of influential public figures, such as Steve Jobs (Markoff, 2005), indicate that psychedelics are once again being reintroduced into Western dialogue at a critical time. As the

United States renegotiates previously held policies and laws regarding the use and health benefits of cannabis (Mead, 2017), psychedelics should also be reconsidered.

Research

Research on psychedelics in the U.S. has been restricted and highly regulated due to the Controlled Substances Act of 1970 which classified most psychedelics as Schedule I drugs (Ross, 2012). Thousands of papers have been published (Grinspoon & Bakalar, 1979) on research which had taken place prior to psychedelics becoming classified as a Schedule I drug, and the results from those studies indicated both medical safety and efficacy for the treatment of substance use disorders (Abuzzahab & Anderson, 1971). However, the research from this period cannot be substantially generalized due to weak methodological designs and a lack of standardization. To reconcile past deficiencies, current researchers have employed standardized protocol (Johnson et al., 2008) and more robust methodological design.

In a meta-analysis of randomized controlled trials featuring LSD to treat substance use disorders, Krebs and Johansen (2012) found promising results. To mediate discrepancies of past research procedures, six double-blind clinical trials were selected through a strict inclusion process. Dose, patients, and outcome measure variables were standardized. The eligible trials included 536 adults, with 325 receiving psychedelic therapy and 211 adults in the control group (Krebs & Johansen, 2012). One of the predominant challenges of performing double-blind trials with LSD is that effects become obvious to the patient once ingested. In an attempt to correct for this, some researchers used physiologically reactive substances within the control groups, such as ephedrine sulfate (Smart, Storm, Baker & Solursh, 1966) and d-amphetamine (Hollister et al., 1969). Other studies used very low doses of LSD (25—50 mcg compared to 450—500 mcg) within the control group to create minimal physiological reaction (Pahnke et al., 1970; Bowen, Soskin & Chotlos, 1970). According to this meta-analysis, Krebs and Johansen (2012) determined that a single dose of LSD produced a significant positive effect on alcohol misuse at follow-up assessments ranging from 1 to 12 months. However, statistically significant benefits were no longer present at 12 months.

Recent investigations have explored the use of psychedelics to treat addiction (Bogenshutz et al., 2015; Bogenshutz & Johnson, 2016; Halpern, 1996; Johnson et al., 2014; Ross, 2012) in response to a need for novel treatment (Johnson et al., 2014; Tupper et al., 2015). Though restricted through federal regulation (Nutt et al., 2013), more current studies on psychedelics in therapeutic settings have become highly standardized (Johnson et al., 2008) to better align with modern research criteria (Sessa, 2005) and ensure clinical safety (Johnson et al., 2008; Johnson et al., 2014; Strassman, 1984). Results from these studies have demonstrated some positive outcomes.

Findings from a recent study on the effects of psilocybin in alcohol dependent adults reported a significant decrease in alcohol consumption, decreased cravings, and increased self-efficacy (Bogenshutz et al., 2015). The single-group proof-of-concept study sought to determine whether two psilocybin sessions could induce a mystical-type experience to reduce alcohol consumption in ten alcohol dependent adults. All ten participants ingested 0.3 mg/kg of psilocybin in session one, and six participants ingested an increased dose of 0.4 mg/kg during a second session. One participant voluntarily left after session one and was excluded from data analysis. In addition to being administered psilocybin, participants underwent 12 weeks of therapeutic interventions, preparatory sessions, and debriefing sessions. Abstinence increased significantly after the initial psilocybin session, and some improvements lasted up to 36 weeks (Bogenshutz et al., 2015).

An open-label pilot study to determine the effects of psilocybin on tobacco addiction found that 80% of participants were abstinent after 1 to 3 psychedelic sessions (Johnson et al., 2014). Fifteen participants engaged in a fifteen-week smoking cessation treatment which combined cognitive behavioral therapy and psilocybin. After enrolling in treatment, all participants set a quit date which coincided with their first psilocybin session. Subsequent sessions were planned to promote long-term abstinence for those who met the target quit goal and to provide additional opportunities for those unable to quit after one session. A moderate dose of psilocybin (20 mg) was administered during Week 5, and higher doses (30 mg) were administered during Weeks 7 and 13 with the permission of the participants. Twelve of the participants were able to quit smoking after the initial psilocybin session and continued to be abstinent at the six-month follow-up (Johnson et al., 2014).

Summary of Research and Future Directions

Modern research investigating LSD (Krebs & Johansen, 2012) and psilocybin (Bogenshutz et al., 2015; Johnson et al., 2014) to treat substance abuse and addiction supports treatment efficacy and clinical safety. Data from these studies indicate overall improvements in both alcohol dependent adults and tobacco addicted adults. However, future research should include larger samples for randomized double-blind control studies.

Beyond treating substance abuse disorders directly, psychedelics have been found to produce acute and long-term effects which address several biopsychosocial issues associated with substance abuse. These include cognitive impairment (Bogenshutz & Johnson, 2016), mood and affect issues (Grob et al., 2011), thought content and processing issues (Hendricks, Johnson, & Griffiths, 2015; Johansen & Krebs, 2015), and spirituality (Griffiths, Richards, Johnson, McCann, & Jesse, 2008). Future studies should investigate these and other biopsychosocial issues related to addiction treatment and recovery.

Implications

The integration of psychedelics into substance use disorder treatment would require the assessment and adoption of treatment models designed specifically for the therapeutic use of psychedelics. Additionally, counselor educators would have to revise outdated curriculum on the use of psychedelics and promote a holistic conceptualization of psychedelic use to include potential therapeutic benefits. The following section will describe models of treatment and provide suggestions for counselor educators.

Models of Treatments

Two predominant treatment models have been developed and explored in psychedelic research: psychedelic therapy and psycholytic therapy (Fadiman, 2011; Johnson et al., 2008; Pahnke et al., 1970). Both models are conducted using a similar research protocol detailed in Johnson et al. (2008). All applications are restricted to use in research and are not currently available for clinical use. The following is a brief summary of the two models. An emerging and related model, microdosing, is also discussed.

Psychedelic therapy. The psychedelic therapy model employs high dosages (350 mcg—500 mcg) of psychedelics with the purpose of facilitating peak experiences, often characterized as mystical, spiritual or transcendental (Burdick & Adinoff, 2013; Pahnke et al., 1970; Sessa, 2005). Intense experiences or reactions to the agent are encouraged (Grinspoon & Bakalar, 1979). Individuals undergoing psychedelic therapy often have several preparatory sessions and a period of debriefing following a psychedelic session in order to psychologically integrate the experience (Johnson et al., 2008; McCabe, 1977; Grof, 1988).

Johnson et al. (2008) described in detail the clinical protocols currently being used in psychedelic therapeutic research. Sessions occur in comfortable living-room like settings, with a couch and blanket for the subject to lie on. Subjects often wear an eye-mask and listen to carefully chosen music through headphones (Richards, 2015). Supportive music is often utilized during the psychedelic session and is tailored for the individual to promote personal growth or healing (Barrett, Robbins, Smooke, Brown, & Griffiths, 2017). Establishing a supportive environment with all individuals involved throughout the process is paramount to decrease the potential for adverse effects (Johnson et al., 2008). To address the chances of challenging experiences occurring, individuals are carefully supervised throughout a session by a lead monitor who is typically a clinical psychologist, clinical social worker, or a psychiatrist who possesses knowledge of the potential adverse effects of the drugs. Two monitors are recommended per session, with at least one being the same gender as the participant. Participants may be left uninterrupted for the 6–8 hour psychedelic sessions except for occasional wellness check-ins (Carhart-Harris et al., 2016; Johnson et al., 2008).

Johnson et al. (2008) and Pahnke et al. (1970) have discussed the importance of incorporating traditional therapeutic processes with any psychedelic models of therapy. Supplemental counseling theories for psychedelic therapy can include Cognitive-Behavioral Therapy (Johnson et al., 2014), Motivational Enhancement Therapy (Bogenschutz et al., 2015), psychoanalytic psychotherapy (Ross et al., 2016) and Focusing (Danforth, 2009). Insights which arise throughout the session are typically processed the following day. More research is needed exploring the efficacy of different counseling theories with psychedelic therapy.

Psycholytic therapy. The psycholytic therapy model is a psychoanalytic therapeutic approach which involves ingesting many small doses (100 mcg—400 mcg) of psychedelics over several sessions and processing unconscious material which manifests throughout the session (Burdick & Adinoff, 2013; Metzner, 2005; Pahnke et al., 1970). Within this model, psychedelics act as a "mind-loosening" agent to facilitate the "exploration of repressed material" as it manifests (Sessa, 2005, p. 457). Psycholytic therapy occurs over an extended period of time and may not be as economically feasible as psychedelic therapy. Most clinical research currently being conducted utilizes the psychedelic therapy model.

Microdosing. Microdosing is a relatively new method being explored within the field of psychedelic research which may offer several therapeutic benefits. Fadiman (2011) has led the modern investigation into microdosing, though all results are preliminary and no peer review studies have been published. However, future research on the practice may establish microdosing as a viable complementary treatment for substance use disorders.

Microdosing psychedelics involves routinely ingesting subperceptual amounts of LSD (10 mcg) or psilocybin (0.5—2.0 g), typically every 3 to 4 days (Fadiman, 2011). Users are encouraged to continue with their daily routines and to notice any subtle changes within themselves (Fadiman & Korb, 2016). Though no clinical studies have been conducted utilizing microdosing, Fadiman and colleagues have been collecting self-reports from volunteers about their experiences of microdosing over the course of a 30-day standard protocol (Fadiman & Korb, 2017). His research team has been actively recruiting participants to accumulate information about microdosing rituals, motivation for engaging in microdosing, and changes experienced as a result of microdosing (Fadiman & Korb, 2016). The current working sample of volunteers totals over 1,300 (Fadiman & Korb, 2017). In their first sample, participants ranged in ages from 21 to 79 and represented over 12 different countries. Prior to beginning the 30-day protocol, individuals were asked to identify any prerecorded symptoms. Throughout the course of the protocol, participants completed daily check-ins regarding mood and energy. The preliminary findings from this study indicated increases in productivity and creativity, and decreases in depression, anxiety, and irritability. There have been no reports of lasting harm, however some participants reported increased anxiety. Some colorblind men experienced visual disturbances and were instructed to discontinue. Microdosing is not suggested for people with psychosis (Fadiman & Korb, 2017). This research is the first known study collecting data from individual users about their experiences with microdosing.

Unlike other models of treatment, such as psychedelic therapy and psycholytic therapy, microdosing may present a sustainable method for producing lasting effects that are comparable to traditional psychedelic treatment methods and lack the side-effects of commonly prescribed pharmaceutical medications (Kilgus, Maxmen & Ward, 2016). While psychedelic therapy and psycholytic therapy are beneficial, they require approximately 8 hour-long sessions on top of extensive pre and post-session counseling for preparation and integration (Johnson et al., 2008). Microdosing may eliminate the need for the extensive sessions and make psychedelic treatment fiscally viable.

The concept of taking subperceptual amounts of psychedelics to enhance well-being may be new to Western culture, however indigenous cultures participated in similar practices for thousands of years (Fadiman, 2011). Past and current psychedelic research has routinely demonstrated the safety of these substances (Johnson et al., 2008; Grinspoon & Bakalar, 1979; Bogenschutz & Johnson, 2016; Burdick & Adinoff, 2013; Johnson et al., 2014; Strassman, 1984), which one might consider in comparison to medications currently being prescribed for mental illness and addiction (Kilgus et al., 2016). Though current reports regarding microdosing psychedelics are anecdotal, the accounts from individuals engaging in this practice of self-medication will be valuable in advocating for further research into the potential therapeutic benefits of this treatment model.

Counselor Educators and Counselors

Counselor educators must reevaluate previously held views about psychedelics and reconsider their application to therapeutic practices. Redefining psychedelics from being illicit substances to pharmacological tools may enhance their potential to become future therapeutic agents.

Counselor educators should consider revising addiction curriculum to reflect current knowledge and research regarding psychedelics. They could also consider promoting innovative and creative research which legally investigates the behavioral, physical, and psychiatric effects of psychedelic use. Addiction counselors should advocate for the revision of prohibitive drug laws and be open to exploring rather than condemning alternative healing methods clients may present to them. Additionally, counselors may serve functionary roles in future models of psychedelic treatment. The depiction of study personnel used for recent psilocybin research at Johns Hopkins describes professionals who can build rapport, demonstrate compassion, and are able to work with the inner emotional worlds of participants (Johnson et al., 2008), which are the foundations of counseling. The counseling profession must become educated about the realities of psychedelic use, understand their role in the perpetuation of false information regarding psychedelics, and advocate for the future application of psychedelics in therapy.

Contradictions and Negative Side-Effects

Due to the prohibition of psychedelics, psychedelic therapy currently taking place outside of clinical research is considered unregulated and illegal, compromising the efficacy and safety of therapeutic psychedelic practice. Psychedelic therapy cannot currently be prescribed and will require further clinical trials. Additionally, using psychedelics to treat drug dependence could be considered paradoxical (Johnson et al., 2014). Chemical abstinence is a primary outcome measure of traditional treatment models, and practicing addiction counselors may have trepidations about incorporating Schedule I drugs into treatment (Kilgus et al., 2016). Psychedelics may also conflict with participation in abstinence-based social support groups such as AA (Rodriguez & Smith, 2014). Though psychedelics are not generally addictive (Nichols, 2004), they do have the potential to generate adverse reactions for some individuals (Barrett, Bradstreet, Leoutsakos, Johnson & Griffiths, 2016).

Psychedelics have generated challenging experiences which produce undesirable affective, cognitive, and somatic symptoms (Barrett et al., 2016). A challenging experience may induce fear, panic, depression, paranoia, and hallucinations (Barrett et al., 2016; Strassman, 1984).

Physiological symptoms could include elevated heart rate, nausea, and insomnia. Negative side-effects related to psychedelic use typically do not last longer than 48 hours (Johnson et al., 2008) and can be mediated through client screening and controlling the dose, set or intention, and setting of the use (Barrett et al., 2016). Negative consequences of psychedelic use that are typically referenced often occur through recreational experimentation outside of clinical settings (Tupper et al., 2015). Individuals with a personal or family history of psychosis should not take psychedelics, and instances of prolonged psychosis and Hallucinogen Persisting Perception Disorder (HPPD) are extremely rare, with an estimated incidence rate of only a few cases in a million (Johnson et al., 2008; Strassman 1984). Clinical protocols and models of treatment have been developed in an attempt to minimize adverse effects and standardize research (Fadiman, 2011; Johnson et al., 2008; Tupper et al., 2015).

Conclusion

Past and present research on psychedelics as therapeutic tools has demonstrated both safety and efficacy. Researchers have demonstrated their potential for improving alcohol and tobacco addiction without causing long-lasting negative side-effects. Further research is required to determine the true clinical value of psychedelics in addiction treatment. The role of psychedelics in treatment needs to be reconsidered, and the counseling profession should begin advocating for the reintroduction of psychedelics into the therapeutic paradigm.

References

Abuzzahab, F. S., & Anderson, B. J. (1971). A review of LSD treatment in alcoholism. *International Pharmacopsychiatry, 6*, 223–235.

Barrett, F. S., Bradstreet, M. P., Leoutsakos, J. M. S., Johnson, M. W., & Griffiths, R. R. (2016). The challenging experience questionnaire: Characterization of challenging experiences with psilocybin mushrooms. *Journal of Psychopharmacology, 30*(12), 1279–1295.

Barrett, F. S., Robbins, H., Smooke, D., Brown, J. L., & Griffiths, R. R. (2017). Qualitative and quantitative features of music reported to support peak mystical experiences during psychedelic therapy sessions. *Frontiers in Psychology, 8*, 1238.

Bogenschutz, M. P., & Pommy, J.A. (2012). Therapeutic mechanisms of classic hallucinogens in the treatment of addiction: From indirect evidence to testable hypotheses. *Drug Testing and Analysis, 4*, 543–555.

Bogenschutz, M. P., Forcehimes, A. A., Pommy, J. A., Wilcox, C. E., Barbosa, P. C. R., & Strassman, R. J. (2015). Psilocybin-assisted treatment for alcohol dependence: A proof-of concept study. *Journal of Psychopharmacology, 29*(3), 289–299.

Bogenschutz, M. P., & Johnson, M. W. (2016). Classic hallucinogens in the treatment of addictions. *Progress in Neuro-Psychopharmacology and Biological Psychiatry, 64*, 250–258.

Bowen, W. T., Soskin, R. A., & Chotlos, J. W. (1970). Lysergic acid diethylamide as a variable in the hospital treatment of alcoholism: A follow-up study. *Journal of Nervous and Mental Disorders, 150*, 111–118.

Burdick, B. V., & Adinoff, B. (2013). A proposal to evaluate mechanistic efficacy of hallucinogens in addiction treatment. *The American Journal of Drug and Alcohol Abuse, 39*(5), 291–297.

Carhart-Harris, R. L., Bolstridge, M., Rucker, J., Day, C. M., Erritzoe, D., Kaelen, M., . . . & Taylor, D. (2016). Psilocybin with psychological support for treatment-resistant depression: An open-label feasibility study. *The Lancet Psychiatry, 3*(7), 619–627.

Courtwright, D. T. (2004). The controlled substances act: How a "big tent" reform became a punitive drug law. *Drug and Alcohol Dependence, 76*(1), 9–15.

Danforth, A. (2009). Focusing-oriented psychotherapy as a supplement to preparation for psychedelic therapy. *The Journal of Transpersonal Psychology, 41*(2), 151–160.

Doblin, R. (1991). Pahnke's" Good Friday experiment": A long-term follow-up and methodological critique. *The Journal of Transpersonal Psychology, 23*(1), 1–28.

Dyck, E. (2008). *Psychedelic psychiatry: LSD from clinic to campus.* Baltimore, MA: John Hopkins University Press.

Fadiman, J. (2011). *The psychedelic explorer's guide: Safe, therapeutic, and sacred journeys.* Rochester, VT: Inner Traditions/Bear & Co.

Fadiman, J., & Korb, S. (2016). *Microdosing psychedelics: Self-study protocol and sign-up form.* Retrieved from https://sites.google.com/view/microdosingpsychedelics/home

Fadiman, J., & Korb, S. (2017, April). *Microdosing: The phenomenon, research results, and startling surprises.* Concurrent session at the Psychedelic Science 2017 Conference, San Francisco, CA.

Fantegrossi, W. E., Woods, J. H., & Winger, G. (2004). Transient reinforcing effects of phenylisopropylamine and indolealkylamine hallucinogens in rhesus monkeys. *Behavioural Pharmacology, 15*(2), 149–157.

Griffiths, R. R., Richards, W. A., Johnson, M. W., McCann, U. D., & Jesse, R. (2008). Mystical type experiences occasioned by psilocybin mediate the attribution of personal meaning and spiritual significance 14 months later. *Journal of Psychopharmacology, 22*(6), 621–632.

Grinspoon, L., & Bakalar, J. B. (1979). *Psychedelic drugs reconsidered.* New York, NY: Basic Books.

Grob, C. S., Danforth, A. L., Chopra, G. S., Hagerty, M., McKay, C. R., Halberstadt, A. L., & Greer, G. R. (2011). Pilot study of psilocybin treatment for anxiety in patients with advanced-stage cancer. *Archives of General Psychiatry, 68*(1), 71–78.

Grof, S. (1988). *The adventure of self-discovery: Dimensions of consciousness and new perspectives in psychotherapy and inner exploration.* Albany, NY: SUNY Press.

Halpern, J. H. (1996). The use of hallucinogens in the treatment of addiction. *Addiction Research, 4*(2), 177–189.

Hasler, F., Grimberg, U., Benz, M. A., Huber, T., & Vollenweider, F. X. (2004). Acute psychological and physiological effects of psilocybin in healthy humans: A double-blind, placebo-controlled dose–effect study. *Psychopharmacology, 172*(2), 145–156.

Hendricks, P. S., Johnson, M. W., & Griffiths, R. R. (2015). Psilocybin, psychological distress, and suicidality. *Journal of Psychopharmacology, 29*(9), 1041–1043.

Hofmann, A. (1979). How LSD originated. *Journal of Psychedelic Drugs, 11*(1–2), 53–60.

Hollister, L. E., Shelton, J., & Krieger, G. (1969). A controlled comparison of lysergic acid diethylamide (LSD) and dextroamphetamine in alcoholics. *American Journal of Psychiatry, 125*(10), 1352–1357.

Huxley, A. (1954). *The doors of perception & heaven and hell.* New York, NY: New Canadian Library.

Johansen, P. Ø., & Krebs, T. S. (2015). Psychedelics not linked to mental health problems or suicidal behavior: A population study. *Journal of Psychopharmacology, 29*(3), 270–279.

Johnson, M. W., Richards, W. A., & Griffiths, R. R. (2008). Human hallucinogen research: Guidelines for safety. *Journal of Psychopharmacology, 22*(6), 603–620.

Johnson, M. W., Garcia-Romeu, A., Cosimano, M. P., & Griffiths, R. R. (2014). Pilot study of the 5-HT2AR agonist psilocybin in the treatment of tobacco addiction. *Journal of Psychopharmacology, 28*(11), 983–992.

Kilgus, M. D., Maxmen, J. S., & Ward, N. G. (2016). *Essential psychopathology & its treatment.* New York, NY: WW Norton & Company.

Krebs, T. S., & Johansen, P. Ø. (2012) Lysergic acid diethylamide (LSD) for alcoholism: Meta -analysis of randomized controlled trials. *Journal of Psychopharmacology, 26*(7), 994–1002.

Leary, T., Metzner, R., & Alpert, R. (1966). *The psychedelic experience.* New York, NY: Smithsonian Folkways Recordings.

Leonard, A. (2015, November 20). How LSD microdosing became the hot new business trip. *Rolling Stone.* Retrieved from http://www.rollingstone.com/culture/features/how-lsd microdosing-became-the-hot-new-business-trip-20151120

Levy, A. (2016, September 12). The drug of choice for the age of kale. *The New Yorker.* Retrieved from http://www.newyorker.com/magazine/2016/09/12/the-ayahuasca-boom in-the-u-s

Malone, N. (2016, November 17). Why power women are micro-dosing LSD at work. *Marie Claire.* Retrieved from http://www.marieclaire.com/culture/news/a23669/power-women microdosing-lsd/

Markoff, J. (2005). *What the dormouse said: How the sixties counterculture shaped the personal computer industry.* Westminster, UK: Penguin Books.

McCabe, O. L. (1977). Psychedelic drug crises: Toxicity and therapeutics. *Journal of Psychedelic Drugs, 9*(2), 107–121.

McKenna, T. (1991). *The archaic revival.* San Francisco, CA: Harper San Francisco.

McKenna, T. (1992*). Food of the gods: The search for the original tree of knowledge a radical history of plants, drugs and human evolution.* New York, NY: Bantam.

Mead, A. (2017). The legal status of cannabis (marijuana) and cannabidiol (CBD) under US law. *Epilepsy & Behavior, 70*, 288–291.

Mechling, L. (2017, January 9). Here's why microdosing with LSD isn't a fringe wellness movement. *Vogue*. Retrieved from http://www.vogue.com/article/microdosing-lsd-risks benefits-mindfulness-depression-ayelet-waldman

Metzner, R. (Ed.). (2005). *Sacred mushroom of visions: Teonanacatl: A sourcebook on the psilocybin mushroom*. Rochester, VT: Inner Traditions/Bear & Co.

Moreno, F. A., Wiegand, C. B., Taitano, E. K., & Delgado, P. L. (2006). Safety, tolerability, and efficacy of psilocybin in 9 patients with obsessive-compulsive disorder. *Journal of Clinical Psychiatry, 67*(11), 1735–1740.

Nichols, D. E. (2004). Hallucinogens. *Pharmacology & Therapeutics, 101*(2), 131–181.

Nutt, D. J., King, L. A., & Nichols, D. E. (2013). Effects of schedule I drug laws on neuroscience research and treatment innovation. *Nature Reviews Neuroscience, 14*(8), 577–585.

Ott, J. (1996). Entheogens II: On entheology and entheobotany. *Journal of Psychoactive Drugs, 28*(2), 205–209.

Pahnke, W. N., Kurland, A. A., Unger, S., Savage, C., & Grof, S. (1970). The experimental use of psychedelic (LSD) psychotherapy. *Journal of the American Medical Association, 212*(11), 1856–1863.

Prayag, G., Mura, P., Hall, C. M., & Fontaine, J. (2016). Spirituality, drugs, and tourism: Tourists' and shamans' experiences of ayahuasca in Iquitos, Peru. *Tourism Recreation Research, 41*(3), 314–325.

Richards, T. W. (2015). *Sacred knowledge: Psychedelics and religious experiences*. New York, NY: Columbia University Press.

Rodriguez, L., & Smith, J. A. (2014). 'Finding your own place': An interpretative phenomenological analysis of young men's experience of early recovery from addiction. *International Journal of Mental Health and Addiction, 12*(4), 477–490.

Ross, S. (2012). Serotonergic hallucinogens and emerging targets for addiction pharmacotherapies. *Psychiatric Clinics of North America, 35*(2), 357–374.

Ross, S., Bossis, A., Guss, J., Agin-Liebes, G., Malone, T., Cohen, B., . . . & Su, Z. (2016). Rapid and sustained symptom reduction following psilocybin treatment for anxiety and depression in patients with life-threatening cancer: A randomized controlled trial. *Journal of Psychopharmacology, 30*(12), 1165–1180.

Schultes, R. E., Hofmann, A., & Rätsch, C. (2001). *Plants of the gods: Their sacred, healing and hallucinogenic powers*. Rochester, VT: Inner Traditions.

Sessa, B. (2005). Can psychedelics have a role in psychiatry once again? *British Journal of Psychiatry, 186*, 457–458.

Smart, R. G., Storm, T., Baker, E. F., & Solursh, L. (1966). A controlled study of lysergide in the treatment of alcoholism. *Quarterly Journal of Studies on Alcohol, 27*, 469–482.

Strassman, R. J. (1984). Adverse reactions to psychedelic drugs: A review of the literature. *The Journal of Nervous and Mental Disease, 172*(10), 577–595.

Strassman, R. J. (1995). Hallucinogenic drugs in psychiatric research and treatment perspectives and prospects. *The Journal of Nervous and Mental Disease, 183*(3), 127 138.

Taussig, M. T. (1986). *Shamanism, colonialism, and the wild man: A study in terror and healing*. Chicago, IL: University of Chicago Press.

Tupper, K. W. (2008). The globalization of ayahuasca: Harm reduction or benefit maximization? *International Journal of Drug Policy, 19*(4), 297–303.

Tupper, K. W., Wood, E., Yensen, R., & Johnson, M. W. (2015). Psychedelic medicine: A re-emerging therapeutic paradigm. *Canadian Medical Association Journal, 187*(14), 1054–1059.

Tylš, F., Páleníček, T., & Horáček, J. (2014). Psilocybin–summary of knowledge and new perspectives. *European Neuropsychopharmacology, 24*(3), 342–356.

Weil, A. (2004). *The natural mind: A revolutionary approach to the drug problem.* Boston, MA: Houghton Mifflin Harcourt.

Zamaria, J. A. (2016). A phenomenological examination of psilocybin and its positive and persisting aftereffects. *NeuroQuantology, 14*(2), 285–296.

6

Using a Group Counseling Intervention to Treat Inmates' Symptoms of Mental Illness

ROBERT M COX, RICHARD K. JAMES, REBECCA J. GRADY, *and* MICHAEL S. SKIRIUS[5]

The role of correctional systems and incarceration as behavioral modifiers and crime deterrents in the United States is not a new conversation. For over 100 years, law enforcement, correctional professionals, academics, and behavioral health clinicians have been examining the etiologies of criminal behavior and methods of intervention and treatment with incarcerated populations to glean ideas useful in crime reduction (Bromberg, 1941; Charles, 1933; Gault, 1925). Many of the issues discussed by Bromberg (1941) before World War II, such as increasing numbers imprisoned, the high cost of incarceration, and a paucity of appropriate treatments for offenders, would fit into 21st-century discussions about crime and punishment. While incarceration rates and the

5. Robert m Cox, Department of Marriage and Family Therapy, Pfeiffer University-Charlotte. Richard K. James, Memphis, Tennessee. Rebecca J. Grady, Tampa, Florida. Michael S. Skirius, Counseling, Educational Psychology, and Research, The University of Memphis. Correspondence concerning this article should be addressed to Robert m Cox, Human Relations Coordinator, Substance Abuse Track, Pfeiffer University-Charlotte, 1515 Mockingbird Lane, Suite 100, Charlotte, NC 28209. E-mail: robert.cox@pfeiffer.edu. This research was initially conducted for Robert m Cox's doctoral dissertation.

overall costs of crime have risen since 1941, much of how society deals with criminal actors has remained static. One major example of this pattern is the significant increase in the population of incarcerated offenders with mental illness (OMI). Prison mental health systems, constrained by limited budgets, small behavioral health workforces, and a long-standing lack of evidence-supported programming for mental illness, struggle to promote OMIs' adjustment to the institutional environment, prepare them for a successful transition back into the community, or even treat their symptoms of mental illness (Daniel, 2007; Morgan et al., 2012), potentially contributing to the extraordinary return-to-custody rates reported for OMI.

The U. S. prison population was 1,526,800 persons at yearend 2015 (Carson & Anderson, 2016). Using 2011–2012 data, the U. S. Bureau of Justice Statistics (BJS) reported that 37% of prisoners in state and federal correctional systems reported a mental health history, which is double the rate of mental illness in the general population (Center for Behavioral Health Statistics and Quality, 2016). Thus, there are an estimated 565,000 OMI nationwide at any time; approximately 80% of OMI have recidivated multiple times (James & Glaze, 2006).

OMI recidivate almost twice as fast as their non-mentally ill peers; the more severe the symptoms, the quicker they return to custody (Bales, Nadel, Reed, & Blomberg, 2017). The median time for those with serious mental illness to return to prison is 385 days, which is just over half the time that those without serious mental illness averaged before returning to prison (Cloyes, Wong, Latimer, & Abarca, 2010). While ultimately the desired outcome of behavioral health treatment for OMI is criminal desistence, pre-discharge treatment can increase inmate safety and reduce prisoner management costs in terms of increased institutional adjustment, reduced medical costs, and decreased length of stay (Blitz, Wolff, & Shi, 2008; Merten, Bishop, & Williams, 2012; Morgan et al., 2012).

The correctional system, legally charged to provide treatment for mental illness that is comparable with community standards (Rich, Allen, & Williams, 2015), is given the discretion to determine how individual facilities provide treatment. As there is no universal standard for correctional mental health treatment systems, behavioral health care provided by the prison system is often inadequate (Cloyes et al., 2010). In many correctional facilities, the mental health treatment system is restricted to efficiently meeting OMIs' basic, immediate needs, often focusing on symptom identification, symptom control with psychotropic medications, segregation during acute psychiatric emergencies, and perfunctory discharge planning (Brandt, 2012; Hills, Siegfried, & Ickowitz, 2004), to the neglect of rehabilitation programming designed to promote institutional adjustment and criminal desistence through the treatment of mental illness—a situation true for four decades or more (Cullen & Jonson, 2017; Morgan et al., 2012; Snyder, 2007). Despite the relationship of recidivism risk with anxiety, depression, and psychological trauma (Coid & Ullrich, 2010), an inmate with a depressive or anxiety disorder is less likely than OMI with psychotic illness to receive any treatment (Reingle Gonzalez & Connell, 2014). In fact, less than a third of OMI in state-run correctional facilities received treatment for mental health or co-occurring substance abuse, a significant predictor of recidivism for OMI (Baillargeon et al., 2010; Blank-Wilson, Draine, Barrenger, Hadley, & Evans, 2014; Hall, Miraglia, Lee, Chard-Wierschem, & Sawyer, 2012). Whether OMI receive treatment or not, approximately 95% will return to their communities at some point (Carson, 2014; Cloyes et al., 2010), often without new symptom management skills, a practical aftercare plan, or linkage to community resources (Gagliardi, Lovell, Peterson, & Jemelka, 2004). Consequently, there is an urgent need for a cost-effective evidence-supported rehabilitation treatment program specifically for OMI.

Inmates' Symptoms of Mental Illness

Crime and correctional settings can be iatrogenic and exacerbating of mental illness. Common symptoms of mental illness reported by inmates, and often associated with poor institutional adjustment and criminal recidivism, include anxiety, depression, psychological trauma, and low self-esteem. OMI reported prevalence rates for anxiety near 35%—well above those found in the general population (Allnutt, Wedgwood, Wilhelm, & Butler, 2008; Drapalski, Youman, Stuewig, & Tangney, 2009; Shinkfield & Graffam, 2010). Hypervigilance, sleep disturbance, defensiveness, and irritability are commonly reported anxiety symptoms in prisons (Reinhardt & Rogers, 1998). For OMI, anxiety may result in poorer environmental adjustment as well as increased mental health symptoms and medical problems, substance abuse, and weapons violations (Felson, Silver, & Remster, 2012).

Symptoms of depression, especially psychomotor agitation, sleep disturbances, loss of interest, persistent irritability or anger, excessive guilt or helplessness, and changes in sexual interest and appetite, were reported by 40% of OMI (James & Glaze, 2006). Incarceration, associated with a 45% increase in the odds of experiencing lifetime major depression, more than doubles the odds of developing a 12-month dysthymic disorder (Schnittker, Massoglia, & Uggen, 2012).

Trauma exposure, a nearly universal experience among OMI, can come from being a victim or a perpetrator of crime (Wolff, Huening, Shi, & Frueh, 2014); it is common for OMI to be both. Male prisoners report their top three traumas as witnessing death or serious injury, physical assault, and childhood sexual abuse (Miller & Najavits, 2012). Victims of violence often present with dissociation, substance abuse, depression, and PTSD (Ardino, 2012). Trauma sequelae include elevated suicide risk, psychosis, and sleep problems (Babson & Feldner, 2010; Blaauw, Arensman, Kraaij, Winkel, & Bout, 2002; Saavedra & Álvarez, 2013). Both trauma exposure and PTSD are strongly associated with physical aggression, hostility, substance abuse, violent crime and increased risk of involvement in the criminal justice system (Ardino, 2012; Bevilacqua et al., 2012; Donley et al., 2012; Miller & Najavits, 2012; Neller, Denney, Pietz, & Thomlinson, 2006; Swogger, Conner, Walsh, & Maisto, 2011). Increased levels of PTSD are found in offenders who felt regret or experienced guilty thoughts about their criminal actions (Crisford, Dare, & Evangeli, 2008; Gray et al., 2003).

Confusingly, both high self-esteem and low self-esteem are linked to crime. Garofalo, Holden, Zeigler-Hill, and Velotti (2015) found the level of awareness for and understanding of emotions, acceptance of emotional responses, engagement in goal-directed behavior, ability to abstain from impulsive behavior while experiencing emotional distress, and access to effective emotion regulation strategies may moderate self-esteem and aggression among prisoners. While self-esteem can predict criminal behavior (Boduszek, Hyland, Dhingra, & Mallett, 2013; Ostrowsky, 2010), the mechanisms through which self-esteem and criminal action operate is poorly understood. Consequently, effectively treating prisoners' anxiety, depression, PTSD, and low self-esteem should increase their environmental success, the odds of positive reintegration back into the community, and decrease recidivism risk.

Evidence-Supported Cognitive-Behavioral Treatments for OMI

Although the research is clear that treatment works, and despite more than 40 years of research, little or none of the manualized programming generally accepted as behavioral health treatment for inmates was designed for the complex pre-discharge needs of OMI (Bronson & Berzofsky, 2017; Hills et al., 2004; James & Glaze, 2006; Sammons & McGuinness, 2015). Moreover, all of these programs require significant on-going operational costs without corresponding inmate improvements.

While the sparse research literature on effectiveness in changing inmate behaviors over the long-term is focused primarily on those without mental illness, programs employing Risk-Need-Responsivity (R-N-R) principles (Andrews & Bonta, 2010) and cognitive-behavioral therapies (CBT) have been found to reduce recidivism and promote criminal desistence (Bauer, Morgan, & Mandracchia, 2011; Cullen & Jonson, 2017; Landenberger & Lipsey, 2005; Morgan et al., 2012). Research into the effectiveness of treatment for OMI indicates that treatment increases coping skills and compliance with facility rules while it reduces mental illness symptoms and criminal and psychiatric recidivism (Landenberger & Lipsey, 2005; Loeffler, Prelog, Unnithan, & Pogrebin, 2010; Morgan et al., 2012). The R-N-R principles support interventions that *respond* to research-identified criminal risk factors using interventions designed to reduce the *criminogenic need* for criminal actions among those at highest *risk* for re-offending (Andrews & Bonta, 2010). CBT used with offenders attempts to transfer skills to correctional program participants that will remedy either a cognitive deficit or thinking patterns that are creating barriers to prosocial functioning (Wilson, Bouffard, & Mackenzie, 2005).

Several commercial evidence-supported interventions are available to meet the general treatment needs of non-mentally ill prisoners. Two well-known, and the most researched (Wilson et al., 2005), commercial interventions are Moral Reconation Therapy (MRT) and Reasoning and Rehabilitation (R & R). A third program, The Good Lives Model (Ward & Stewart, 2003), is a strengths-based interpretation of R-N-R principles (Andrews & Bonta, 2010). A fourth program, Changing Lives and Changing Outcomes (CLCO), is one of the few programs designed on R-N-R foundations specifically for OMI.

Moral Reconation Therapy (Little & Robinson, 1990) was developed to provide behavioral, social, and moral education to the general offender population through skill building, cognitive-restructuring, and development of participants' moral reasoning (Correctional Counseling, Inc., 2015). A recent meta-analysis of 33 research evaluations found that MRT is associated with reduced ($r = 0.16$) criminal behavior by adult and juvenile offenders (Ferguson & Wormith, 2013).

The Reasoning and Rehabilitation program (R & R; Ross, Fabiano, & Ewles, 1988) was developed as an intervention for youths or adults who are evidencing antisocial behaviors or delinquent or criminal behavior. R & R employs a problem-solving approach that includes nine program components delivered in 35 manualized two-hour sessions. Effectiveness research of the R & R program determined a 14% decrease in recidivism among participants of 19 international evaluation studies (Tong & Farrington, 2008).

While both MRT and R & R are popular and well-researched evidence-supported models, there are several limitations to their implementation. First, while both MRT and R & R can be effective at reducing recidivism among the general offender population, newer research shows less effectiveness than earlier studies (Ferguson & Wormith, 2013; Tong & Farrington, 2008); neither program uses R-N-R principles. Second, research on both programs studied applications with non-OMI populations. Third, the initial and maintenance costs of using either MRT or R & R can be economically prohibitive for correctional systems, which must train program facilitators, and for inmates, who are required to purchase program materials. Both programs require upfront training for psychoeducational group leaders, participant manuals, and ongoing training for both new and veteran leaders.

Alternatively, the Good Lives Model (GLM), first proposed by Ward and Stewart (2003) for use with sexual offenders, is a strengths-based approach to offender treatment that is designed to promote criminal desistance. GLM differs from MRT and R & R in that it adds to an R-N-R foundation by switching treatment providers' focus away from risk reduction technologies and toward the development of offenders' intrinsic motivation, skills, and resources to live a self-interested ("good") life (Ward & Fortune, 2013). Early research by the GLM's developer and colleagues suggests that GLM may enhance the efficacy of programs that adhere to R-N-R principles by equipping clients with the tools to live personally meaningful and fulfilling lives (Ward & Fortune, 2013; Willis, Ward, & Levenson, 2014). One limitation of the GLM approach is that it was no more effective than a traditional relapse prevention approach in empirical studies (Barnett, Manderville-Norden, & Rakestrow, 2014; Harkins, Flak, Beech, & Woodhams, 2012). A second limitation of the GLM, which may also be its greatest strength, is the focus on participants' long-term identity change and the promotion of criminal desistence through trauma-informed and future-focused treatment. This approach may not be a good fit with contemporary criminological theory and facility management practice.

Morgan, Kroner, and Mills (2018) developed Changing Lives and Changing Outcomes (CLCO) as a manualized treatment program using R-N-R principles specifically for OMI. CLCO includes nine modules delivered over 76 sessions focused on promoting recovery from mental illness and restructuring cognitive distortions associated with criminal thinking patterns. Preliminary research into CLCO does show promise in short-term behavior change indicative of reduced substance use and increased prosocial behaviors (Morgan et al., 2018; Van Horn et al., 2018). Limitations of CLCO include the prerequisite training as a counselor or other mental health professional required for implementation of the program (Morgan et al., 2018), the intensity of the treatment, and the lack of data on program effectiveness.

As this brief review demonstrates, several decades of treatment outcome research related to the specific needs of OMI has not significantly increased the number of programs being developed and tested with scientific rigor (Rice & Harris, 1997; Snyder, 2007) or increased program quality. The lack of program development is partially attributable to two factors: the environmental restrictions of forensic settings limit rigid research structures, and the investment required to develop an evidence-based program is beyond the resources of most correctional systems (Daniel, 2007; Liebman et al., 2013; Morgan et al., 2012; Scott-Hayward, 2009). The net result is a lack of appropriate intervention and preemptive planning such that two-thirds of OMI will return to custody within three years post-release (Bales & Mears, 2008).

Regardless of the etiology of their mental illness symptoms, we believe institutional adjustment and recidivism reduction involve the treatment of mental illness while addressing OMIs' criminogenic needs. As many of the identifying characteristics of anxiety, depression, psychological trauma, and low self-esteem correlate, a counseling intervention that trains OMI to be aware of their emotional distress and to respond appropriately should yield rewards in institutional adjustment, symptom alleviation, and criminal recidivism risk reduction. The Adult Recidivism Reduction Alternative (ARRAY) group counseling program is designed to address OMIs' complex pre- and post-discharge needs as they prepare for transition out of prison and back into their home communities without burdening correctional facilities' thin resources. The purpose of this research is to determine the effects of participation in the pilot ARRAY pre-release intervention on OMIs' symptoms of mental illness commonly correlated with recidivism.

The Adult Recidivism Reduction Alternative

The pilot ARRAY program is a research-based intervention designed to reduce recidivism risk through pre-release group counseling for OMI to develop symptom management skills as well as a practical relapse prevention plan while operating within institutional boundaries and increasing security without affecting cost. The 12-session ARRAY intervention, created for OMI with a one to two-year release horizon, is delivered to a closed participant group over 12 consecutive weeks in 1½ hour group sessions. The program is designed to assist with pre-release institutional adjustment, provide treatment for symptoms of mental illness, promote desistance from antisocial and criminogenic behaviors, and prepare OMI to maintain gains at re-entry. ARRAY was delivered by masters-level counseling interns under supervision by doctoral-level licensed counselors with correctional behavioral health setting experience. Participants were adult men in a regional correctional facility assigned to a mental health unit (MHU) based on a diagnosis of mental illness made by facility physicians.

Program Delivery

As discussed elsewhere (Cox, Lenz, & James, 2015; Cox, Skirius, Lenz, James, & Packard, 2017), each weekly ARRAY session plan includes didactic introduction of a symptom management or relapse prevention skill, discussion of skill application in the environment, skill demonstration, and scaffolded skills practice, with group leaders acting as coaches. Specific sessions address substance use and adherence to medication recommendations. Key to the model is a unique ARRAY feature where participants actively map the session onto a whiteboard for discussion. This *mapping technology* utilizes the active involvement of group participants coached by program facilitators. Following skills practice, group leaders assist participants in a review of the session map by asking what distress indicators (*yellow lights*) participants noticed during the session, as well as which safe and unsafe coping skills were used in response to the yellow lights. Participants were facilitated to notice the consequences of the coping skills and whether relapse risk was high (*red lights*) or low (*green lights*).

Instrumentation

This pilot study employed the Emotional Problem Scales–Corrections (EPS-C; Daigle, Strohmer, & Loew, 2015) as a pre- and post- intervention assessment instrument to measure participants' change as a result of participation in the ARRAY program. Although the EPS-C includes eight clinical scales, only the anxiety, depression, self-esteem, and PTSD scales were employed to measure the intensity of distress for emotional problems commonly reported by OMI in this study.

The EPS-C (Daigle et al., 2015) consists of 128 items organized into clinical scales measuring anxiety, depression, low self-esteem, poor impulse control, post-traumatic stress disorder (PTSD), substance abuse, suicide potential, and thought and behavior disorder. Several validity scales are included in the instrument. The EPS-C was normed on over 1000 individuals in correctional settings in the United States, and validity is supported for each of the eight clinical scales. Test-retest data for the clinical scales range between .76 and .90. Cronbach Alpha scores for the clinical scales range between .84 and .90.

The EPS-C (Daigle et al., 2015) was directly derived from the Emotional Problems Scales-Self Report Inventory (EPS–SRI). Prout and Strohmer (2010) developed the EPS-SRI in response to the need for an appropriate clinical assessment instrument to evaluate emotional and behavioral difficulties in individuals with lower IQ's and reading levels. The EPS-SRI, normed on over 700 individuals in the United States and

Canada, consists of 146 items, and has scales that assess anxiety, depression, low self-esteem, poor impulse control, and thought and behavior disorder.

The EPS-C offers several advantages as an evaluation tool for the effect of the ARRAY program as it is designed specifically for forensic settings and exhibits both discriminative and predictive validity for risk of misconduct. The EPS-C is a brief self-report instrument administrable at a reading level appropriate for prisoners with learning disabilities and low reading levels.

Research Design

The design of this pilot study was a quantitative quasi-experimental pre- and post-intervention comparison of a group of adult male inmates with mental illness resident on the mental health unit of a regional prison located in the United States' mid-south region. The aim of this study was to determine if there are differences in the dependent variables of anxiety, depression, PTSD, and self-esteem, as measured by the EPS-C over time. This design has the efficiency, flexibility, and goodness of fit necessary for the available time-frame and setting. All participants were volunteers recruited from the same secure housing unit; randomization of the group into treatment and non-treatment samples was impractical, due to the physical limits of the facility and the selective nature of the procedure.

Study Participants

Seventy-one volunteers initiated engagement with ARRAY. Of the 71 participants, 33 completed the intervention accounting for a 53% attrition rate. Reasons for dropping out of the study included difficulty trusting other group members, difficulty with the intervention techniques, movement out of the MHU, and disruptive behaviors in session. The ARRAY experimental group is composed of those who responded to the EPS-C at the pre-intervention administration, finished the treatment program, and responded to the EPS-C at post-intervention administration. The ARRAY group ($n = 33$) is further broken down into two subgroups based upon time of measurement. The ARRAY pre-group was measured before participation in the intervention and the ARRAY post-group following completion.

Participant Demographics

All study participants were residents on the prison mental health unit (MHU) at the time of the study. Referral to the MHU occurs following a diagnosis of mental illness by a physician either at the time of intake into the facility or by referral from the general population. While individual diagnostic profiles were not available to the research team, ARRAY participants presented to the study with mood disorders, psychotic disorders, and substance use disorders.

The demographic breakdown of the ARRAY experimental group indicates a general tendency to be male (100%), heterosexual (100%), unmarried (69.7%), White (60.6%), older than 35 years old (54.6%), and to have educational achievement of a general education certificate or higher (84.9%). In contrast, the general offender population at the prison where this pilot study was conducted had the following demographic breakdown: male (74.7%), heterosexual (54.3%), unmarried (47.4%), African American (62.5%) inmates between the age of 18 and 35 years old (59.6%) with an educational attainment level of a general education certificate or higher (52.1%). The implications of these demographic differences for the OMI and the ARRAY intervention are unclear; however, these areas are ripe for continued research.

Research Questions

Previous research (Cox et al., 2015; Cox et al., 2017) determined that ARRAY is effective in reducing symptoms of depression and anxiety in a small number of individuals, and consistent with the correctional treatment literature, that effectiveness increases with treatment intensity. The current pilot study increases the variety of mental health concerns addressed through one 12-week iteration of the ARRAY intervention with a larger participant sample. The general research question answered by this pilot study is whether there are differences in the group means of the pre- and post-intervention scores on the EPS-C anxiety, depression, PTSD, and self-esteem scales for the pilot ARRAY intervention.

Procedure

After receiving Institutional Review Board approval, the research team recruited potential study participants through face-to-face methods. Interested OMI were screened for a history of criminal recidivism, ability to participate in a counseling group, and a stated desire for behavioral change that promotes a prosocial, or at least non-criminal, lifestyle. Those who presented unstable mood or psychotic symptoms, could not appropriately interact with others for a 90-minute counseling group session, or denied desire for behavioral change were excluded from participation. An invitation to sign the informed consent form and participate in the study was offered to potential participants once the research team answered all of their questions.

Statistical Analysis

Separate analyses were conducted for each dependent variable using the repeated measures dependent samples *t*-test. Although there is a Type 1 error threat with this design, analysis using multiple *t*-tests was chosen to improve distinction between the results.

Results

The general research question to be answered by this pilot study is whether there are differences in the group means of the pre- and post-intervention scores on the EPS-C anxiety, depression, PTSD, and self-esteem scales for the ARRAY intervention group.

Table 1 summarizes the pre- to post-intervention results for each variable examined in this study. Group sample sizes differ for each variable: anxiety ($n = 33$), depression ($n = 32$), PTSD ($n = 33$), low self-esteem ($n = 31$). We calculated effect sizes for the dependent samples using the test statistics t, n, and r and Lenhard and Lenhard's (2016) online effect size calculator. The ARRAY intervention had a moderate significant effect on improvement of participants' symptoms of depression, PTSD, and self-esteem, as measured using the EPS-C. The modest improvements reported in anxiety symptomology by participants were not statistically significant.

Discussion

Following the intervention, participants reported reduced anxiety, less depressive distress, reductions in PTSD-related distress, and higher self-esteem, which adds support to this pilot program as an effective pre-release intervention for treatment of inmates' mental illness. ARRAY participation did not provide statistically significant relief from anxiety symptoms.

Anxiety, a feature of the prison experience, is difficult to manage in an uncertain environment. OMI's lifetime exposure to traumatic events could also encumber symptom alleviation. The correctional rehabilitation literature on trauma exposure and mental illness (Neller et al., 2006; Saavedra & Álvarez, 2013) may offer additional clues to the psychological experiences of inmates related to the development of effective rehabilitation programming. Inmates report histories of exposure to traumatic events, with associated PTSD prevalence rates as high as 60% in some prisoner samples (Wolff et al., 2014). Prison environmental factors heighten PTSD symptoms (e.g., hypervigilance), depressive symptoms (e.g., excessive guilt, shame), and hinder effective stress management such that treatment program developers should consider trauma and shame as factors for further exploration.

Mapping Technology

A primary ARRAY intervention is a unique mapping technology that allows participants to visualize idiosyncratic affective, behavioral, and cognitive indicators, or yellow lights, of anxiety, depression, PTSD, and low self-esteem. Coping responses that mask distress (e.g., substance use, aggression, crime) are unsafe because of their tendency to increase the risk for criminal behavior (red lights). Alternatively, safe coping responses (e.g., challenging irrational thoughts, removal from risky situations, emotional regulation) reduce distress and subsequent relapse risk (green lights). Participants learn to use a simple 5-box schematic to map out the relationship between their yellow lights and the consequences of coping skills they use to manage them. During ARRAY sessions, participants took turns mapping group conversations onto a whiteboard, which the group processed as a session activity. This activity reinforced the use of the ARRAY tools through the active mapping exercise as well as through the processing of the map.

ARRAY, though it remains in development, provides an accessible adjunctive group counseling intervention option to supplement existing correctional mental health treatment systems. One of the strengths of the intervention is that it can be effectively delivered by supervised entry-level counselor-trainees, which indicates the potential for the program to be deliverable by trained and supervised correctional facility staff, thereby reducing operational costs.

Implications

Our findings lead us to believe that the ARRAY program does have promise as a treatment for mental illness experienced by OMI. Ultimately, criminal recidivism reduction is the goal of interventions like ARRAY; therefore, follow-up research with OMI who completed ARRAY and were discharged from prison to determine return-to-custody times is indicated, as is the continued development of the program for inmates' pre-release. The preliminary success found in this pilot study merits determination of ARRAY's value as a post-release intervention. Therefore, several implications for participants and program development deserve attention.

Anxiety is endemic in correctional settings, as is psychological trauma; consequently, additional research into the experience of anxiety by OMI would clarify program adjustments helpful in symptom reduction. The relationship between anxiety, psychological trauma, and functioning deserves exploration from a neurobiological perspective (Focquaert, 2018).

This pilot study examined the effects of a program for increasing OMIs' functioning while incarcerated. Several program components seemed to have more impact than others. The mapping technology employed to visualize relationships between thoughts and actions seemed well-received by participants. But there is little evidence about the independent contribution this program component adds to the overall ARRAY model. Thus, dismantling studies on the mapping and visual modeling as a behavior change technology, independent of skills coaching, is one example of an area where future research could strengthen ARRAY.

Program admission procedures included a fairly rigorous screening. However, an attrition rate above 50% is troubling. While institutional variables have an impact on attrition, it seems clear that the demand of preparing weekly assignments of a very personal and introspective nature may prove problematic for some members. Although this may be the cost of doing business, so to speak, more positive reinforcement and individual attention may limit attrition. Follow-up with individual participants seems to increase participant engagement, indicating that additional research into the efficacy of individual counseling sessions and the therapeutic alliance is warranted.

The number of OMI, and the fact that 95% will return to their communities at some point (Carson & Golinelli, 2013), means that counselors are likely to interact with former prisoners or their families. However, community mental health programming is often seen by OMI as inadequate (Lovell, Gagliardi, & Peterson, 2002). One factor for this perception may be related to counselor training. Few texts or protocols provide a comprehensive presentation of correctional mental health from the perspective of OMI, so counselors may lack training specific to the needs of OMI. Further research, training, or site placements in accredited counselor education programs to service delivery for OMI does not appear to be a high priority (Mintz, Ellmo, Ritter, Falvey, & James, 2016), which should be a cause of national concern to the profession. ARRAY offers a culturally informed program that can be used by entry-level counselors.

The findings of this pilot study have several potential implications for ARRAY participants. The program improved participants' mental health. ARRAY provides an accessible model for OMI to use in making behavioral changes. The model is flexible enough for participants to use in a variety of situations and simple enough to be remembered even when participants find themselves in high-risk relapse situations. Therefore, participation in the ARRAY program has benefits for those who engage in the program. If ARRAY is effective in raising self-esteem and reducing the effects of PTSD and depression for OMI, then it follows that ARRAY may be useful for the general inmate population as well as in community corrections.

Limitations

Data Limitations

With a 47% completion rate, a data limitation of the ARRAY program is participants' tenure in the program. Reasons for non-completion vary by individual and include institutional housing reassignment, discharge from the facility, and voluntary withdrawal from the program. Dropouts tended to occur within four weeks of enrollment. Controlling for length of stay in the program may provide insight into any differences between those who voluntarily withdrew from the program near the beginning and those administratively withdrawn after extended participation. A second research limitation of this study is the lack of a control group, such as a treatment as usual sample of those who did not participate in ARRAY or those who initiated ARRAY but dropped out before completing the intervention group. Additionally, there is a lack of correspondence in the demographic variables between the ARRAY participant sample and the prison's general population; therefore, the findings of this pilot study are not representative of the general inmate population.

Program Limitations

ARRAY was delivered by masters- and doctoral-level counselors-in-training who had no prior training in ARRAY or corrections within a 15-week academic term. While supervised by doctoral-level licensed professional counselors with correctional experience, there was a period during the early ARRAY sessions when group facilitators were learning both the ARRAY model and group counseling skills. This learning curve may have affected the outcomes of the program. Facilitators did report increased comfort delivering ARRAY with gained experience. The intensity of participation is an area of limitation, as ARRAY is delivered in 12 weekly group sessions. Increasing either the number of weekly sessions, adding individual sessions, or creating opportunity for participants to re-enroll may change the effectiveness of the intervention.

Future Research

Future ARRAY research opportunities include exploration of the differences among OMI and non-OMI comparison groups on each of the variables. Differences in the demographics of the comparison groups, especially for ethnicity, age, educational achievement, and incarceration experience, may be explored to determine interactions between demographic variables and program variables. Future research with ARRAY could also study the program's effect with women.

Continued research may be conducted to determine an effective ARRAY dosage for participants. Some research (Cox et al., 2017) has been done on this question, revealing that participants' anxiety, depression, and somatic distress continued to decline with increased participation in the ARRAY program when measured with the Patient Health Questionnaire (Lowe, Kroenke, Herzog, & Grafe, 2004).

Findings of this pilot study were that depression, low self-esteem, and PTSD were significantly relieved by participation in the ARRAY program. Anxiety was reduced somewhat, but not to a statistically significant amount, which may be related to environmental factors. Future ARRAY research may determine how ARRAY can be improved to provide greater relief of participants' anxiety-related distress within the prison environment. Consideration of trauma-informed care principles as they apply to the correctional system may improve the prison environment and decrease anxiety correspondingly.

As noted at the onset of this paper, the conversation about how to interrupt criminal recidivism by OMI dates beyond the middle of the last century. To determine the utility of ARRAY in reducing recidivism, follow-up studies with program participants are needed. Research into the effect of ARRAY participation on institutional adjustment (e.g., use of sanctions and use of medical resources) would provide insight into the effectiveness of the program on facility security. Research into return-to-custody times as well as the use of outpatient community mental health services, emergency departments, and psychiatric hospitalization would provide insight into the effectiveness of the program on criminal and psychiatric recidivism.

Conclusion

The Adult Recidivism Reduction Alternatives (ARRAY) program is one of the few research-supported protocols available for counselors to use with persons with mental illness who are involved with the criminal justice system. ARRAY may also be used in pre-sentencing and post-discharge venues to treat OMI and to support the goals of the criminal justice system.

The ARRAY integrative group counseling program holds promise as an effective model for the treatment of mental illness experienced by prisoners. The findings of this pilot study point to reduced distress from the symptoms of depression, PTSD, and low self-esteem experienced by OMI. Treatment of prisoners' mental illness decreases institutional and societal costs related to crime and punishment. Therefore, while ARRAY remains developmental, the foundations of the program are in place, which present a rare opportunity for furthering the correctional research literature on what works in the rehabilitation of OMI using a resource-efficient model.

Table 1

Results of t-tests for the experimental group at pre- and post-intervention, by EPS-C scale

		Pre-intervention		Post-intervention					
Variable	*n*	M	SD	M	SD	*t***	p	95% CI	*d**
Anxiety	33	14.36	6.42	13.24	5.99	1.406	.169	[-.50, 2.75]	.18
Depression	32	11.10	6.98	7.16	5.22	3.803	.001	[1.82, 6.05]	.62
PTSD	33	7.25	2.55	6.22	2.56	2.375	.024	[.15, 1.92]	.40
Low Self-Esteem	31	9.48	6.79	6.42	5.72	3.191	.003	[1.10, 5.03]	.48

Note. *d computed for dependent samples using *t, n, and r* using the online effect size calculator found at http://www.psychometrica.de/effect_size.html#dep **n for each group differs.

References

Allnutt, S., Wedgwood, L., Wilhelm, K., & Butler, T. (2008). Temperament, substance use and psychopathology in a prisoner population: Implications for treatment. *Australian and New Zealand Journal of Psychiatry, 42*(11), 969–975. doi:10.1080/00048670802415350

Andrews, D. A., & Bonta, J. (2010). *The psychology of criminal conduct* (5th ed.). New Providence, NJ: Anderson Publishing.

Ardino, V. (2012). Offending behaviour: The role of trauma and PTSD. *European Journal of Psychotraumatology, 3*. doi:10.3402/ejpt.v3i0.18968

Babson, K. A., & Feldner, M. T. (2010). Temporal relations between sleep problems and both traumatic event exposure and PTSD: A critical review of the empirical literature. *Journal of Anxiety Disorders, 24*(1), 1–15. doi:10.1016/j.janxdis.2009.08.002

Baillargeon, J., Penn, J. V., Knight, K., Harzke, A. J., Baillargeon, G., & Becker, E. A. (2010). Risk of reincarceration among prisoners with co-occurring severe mental illness and substance use disorders. *Administration and Policy in Mental Health and Mental Health Services Research, 37*(4), 367–374. doi:10.1007/s10488-009-0252-9

Bales, W. D., & Mears, D. P. (2008). Inmate social ties and the transition to society: Does visitation reduce recidivism? *Journal of Research in Crime and Delinquency, 45*(3), 287–321. doi:10.1177/0022427808317574

Bales, W. D., Nadel, M., Reed, C., & Blomberg, T. G. (2017). Recidivism and inmate mental illness. *International Journal of Criminology and Sociology, 6*, 40–51. doi:10.6000/1929-4409.2017.06.05

Barnett, G. D., Manderville-Norden, R., & Rakestrow, J. (2014). The good lives model or relapse prevention: What works better in facilitating change? *Sexual Abuse: A Journal of Research and Treatment, 26*(1), 3–33. doi:10.1177/1079063212474473

Bauer, R. L., Morgan, R. D., & Mandracchia, J. T. (2011). Offenders with severe and persistent mental illness. In T. J. Fagan & R. K. Ax (Eds.), *Correctional Mental Health: From Theory to Best Practice* (pp. 189–212). Thousand Oaks, CA: Sage Publications.

Bevilacqua, L., Carli, V., Sarchiapone, M., George, D. K., Goldman, D., Roy, A., & Enoch, M. A. (2012). Interaction between FKBP5 and childhood trauma and risk of aggressive behavior. *Archives of General Psychiatry, 69*(1), 62–70. doi:10.1001/archgenpsychiatry.2011.152

Blaauw, E., Arensman, E., Kraaij, V., Winkel, F. W., & Bout, R. (2002). Traumatic life events and suicide risk among jail inmates: The influence of types of events, time period and significant others. *J Trauma Stress, 15*(1), 9–16. doi:10.1023/a:1014323009493

Blank Wilson, A., Draine, J., Barrenger, S., Hadley, T., & Evans, A., Jr. (2014). Examining the impact of mental illness and substance use on time till re-incarceration in a county jail. *Administration and Policy in Mental Health and Mental Health Services Research, 41*(3), 293–301. doi:10.1007/s10488-013-0467-7

Blitz, C. L., Wolff, N., & Shi, J. (2008). Physical victimization in prison: the role of mental illness. *Int J Law Psychiatry, 31*(5), 385–393. doi:10.1016/j.ijlp.2008.08.005

Boduszek, D., Hyland, P., Dhingra, K., & Mallett, J. (2013). The factor structure and composite reliability of the Rosenberg Self-Esteem Scale among ex-prisoners. *Personality and Individual Differences, 55*(8), 877–881. doi:10.1016/j.paid.2013.07.014

Brandt, A. L. S. (2012). Treatment of Persons With Mental Illness in the Criminal Justice System: A Literature Review. *Journal of Offender Rehabilitation, 51*(8), 541–558. doi: 10.1080/10509674.2012.693902

Bromberg, W. (1941). Psychotherapy in a court clinic. *American Journal of Orthopsychiatry, 11*(4), 770–774. doi:10.1111/j.1939-0025.1941.tb05867.x

Bronson, J., & Berzofsky, M. (2017). *Indicators of mental health problems reported by prisoners and jail inmates,* 2011–12 *(NCJ 250612).* Washington, DC: U.S. Department of Justice.

Carson, E. A. (2014). *Prisoners in 2013*. Bureau of Justice Statistics. Retrieved from http://www.bjs.gov/content/pub/pdf/p13.pdf.

Carson, E. A., & Anderson, E. (2016). *Prisoners in 2015*. (NCJ 250229). Washington DC: U.S. Department of Justice. Retrieved from http://www.bjs.gov/index.cfm?ty=pbdetail&iid=5869.

Carson, E. A., & Golinelli, D. (2013). *Prisoners in 2012: Trends in admissions and releases,* 1991–2012 (Revised). *Prisoners Series.* Retrieved from http://www.bjs.gov/index.cfm?ty=pbdetail&iid=4842

Center for Behavioral Health Statistics and Quality. (2016). *Key substance use and mental health indicators in the United States: Results from the 2015 National Survey on Drug Use and Health (HHS Publication No. SMA* 16-4984, *NSDUH Series H-51).* Retrieved from http://www.samhsa.gov/data/

Charles, C. M. (1933). A comparison of the intelligence quotient of three different mental tests applied to a group of incarcerated delinquent boys. *Journal of Applied Psychology, 17*(5), 581–584. doi:10.1037/h0075331

Cloyes, K. G., Wong, B., Latimer, S., & Abarca, J. (2010). Time to prison return for offenders with serious mental illness released from prison: A survival analysis. *Criminal Justice and Behavior, 37*(2), 175–187. doi:10.1177/0093854809354370

Coid, J., & Ullrich, S. (2010). Antisocial personality disorder and anxiety disorder: a diagnostic variant? *Journal of Anxiety Disorders, 24*(5), 452–460. doi:10.1016/j.janxdis.2010.03.001

Correctional Counseling, Inc. (2015). *About criminal thinking treatment*. Retrieved from https://www.ccimrt.com/mrt_programs/criminal-justice/

Cox, R. m, Lenz, A. S., & James, R. K. (2015). A Pilot Evaluation of the ARRAY Program With Offenders With Mental Illness. *Journal of Counseling & Development, 93*(4), 471–480. doi:10.1002/jcad.12045

Cox, R. m, Skirius, M. S., Lenz, A. S., James, R. K., & Packard, C. (2017). The Effects of Repeated Exposure to the ARRAY Program With Offenders With Mental Illness. *Journal of Addictions & Offender Counseling, 38*(2), 98–114. doi:10.1002/jaoc.12033

Crisford, H., Dare, H., & Evangeli, M. (2008). Offence-related posttraumatic stress disorder (PTSD) symptomatology and guilt in mentally disordered violent and sexual offenders. *The Journal of Forensic Psychiatry & Psychology, 19*(1), 86–107. doi:10.1080/14789940701596673

Cullen, F. T., & Jonson, C. L. (2017). *Correctional Theory: Context and Consequences* (2nd ed.). Thousand Oaks, CA: Sage.

Daigle, R. P., Strohmer, D. C., & Loew, M. M. (2015). *Emotional Problem Scales – Self Report Inventory (Corrections).* In. Cordova, TN.: Integrated Assessment (LLC).

Daniel, A. E. (2007). Care of the mentally ill in prisons: Challenges and solutions. *Journal of the American Academy of Psychiatry and the Law Online, 35*(4), 406–410.

Donley, S., Habib, L., Jovanovic, T., Kamkwalala, A., Evces, M., Egan, G., . . . Ressler, K. J. (2012). Civilian PTSD symptoms and risk for involvement in the criminal justice system. *Journal of the American Academy of Psychiatry and the Law Online, 40*(4), 522–529.

Drapalski, A. L., Youman, K., Stuewig, J., & Tangney, J. (2009). Gender differences in jail inmates' symptoms of mental illness, treatment history and treatment seeking. *Criminal Behaviour and Mental Health, 19*(3), 193–206. doi:10.1002/cbm.733

Felson, R. B., Silver, E., & Remster, B. (2012). Mental disorder and offending in prison. *Criminal Justice and Behavior, 39*(2), 125–143. doi:10.1177/0093854811428565

Ferguson, L. M., & Wormith, J. S. (2013). A meta-analysis of moral reconation therapy. *Int J Offender Ther Comp Criminol, 57*(9), 1076–1106. doi:10.1177/0306624x12447771

Focquaert, F. (2018). Neurobiology and crime: A neuro-ethical perspective. *Journal of Criminal Justice.* doi:https://doi.org/10.1016/j.jcrimjus.2018.01.001

Gagliardi, G. J., Lovell, D., Peterson, P. D., & Jemelka, R. (2004). Forecasting recidivism in mentally ill offenders released from prison. *Law and Human Behavior, 28*(2), 133–155. doi:10.2307/4141742

Garofalo, C., Holden, C. J., Zeigler-Hill, V., & Velotti, P. (2015). Understanding the connection between self-esteem and aggression: The mediating role of emotion dysregulation. *Aggressive Behavior.* doi:10.1002/ab.21601

Gault, R. H. (1925). Criminology. *Psychological Bulletin, 22*(10), 575–591. doi:10.1037/h0064947

Gray, N. S., Carman, N. G., Rogers, P., MacCulloch, M. J., Hayward, P., & Snowden, R. J. (2003). Post-traumatic stress disorder caused in mentally disordered offenders by the committing of a serious violent or sexual offence. *The Journal of Forensic Psychiatry & Psychology, 14*(1), 27–43. doi:10.1080/1478994031000074289

Hall, D. L., Miraglia, R. P., Lee, L. G., Chard-Wierschem, D., & Sawyer, D. (2012). Predictors of general and violent recidivism among SMI prisoners returning to communities in New York state. *Journal of the American Academy of Psychiatry and the Law Online, 40*(2), 221–231.

Harkins, L., Flak, V. E., Beech, A. R., & Woodhams, J. (2012). Evaluation of a community-based sex offender treatment program using a good lives model approach. *Sex Abuse, 24*(6), 519–543. doi:10.1177/1079063211429469

Hills, H., Siegfried, C., & Ickowitz, A. (2004). *Effective prison mental health services: Guidelines to expand and improve treatment.* Washinton, D. C.: U. S. Department of Justice, National Institute of Corrections.

James, D. J., & Glaze, L. E. (2006). *Mental health problems of prison and jail inmates NCJ 213600.* Retrieved from http://www.bjs.gov/index.cfm?ty=pbdetail&iid=789

Landenberger, N. A., & Lipsey, M. W. (2005). The positive effects of cognitive–behavioral programs for offenders: A meta-analysis of factors associated with effective treatment. *Journal of Experimental Criminology, 1*(4), 451–476. doi:10.1007/s11292-005-3541-7

Lenhard, W. & Lenhard, A. (2016). *Calculation of effect sizes.* Retrieved from: http://www.psychometrica.de/effect_size.html. Bibergau (Germany): Psychometrica.

Liebman, R. E., Burnette, M. L., Raimondi, C., Nichols-Hadeed, C., Merle, P., & Cerulli, C. (2013). Piloting a psycho-social intervention for incarcerated women with trauma histories: Lessons learned and future recommendations. *Int J Offender Ther Comp Criminol, 58*(8), 894–913. doi:10.1177/0306624x13491073

Little, G. L., & Robinson, K. D. (1990). Reducing recidivism by changing how inmates think: The systematic approach of moral reconation therapy. *American Jails, 4*(3), 12–16.

Loeffler, C. H., Prelog, A. J., Unnithan, N. P., & Pogrebin, M. R. (2010). Evaluating shame transformation in group treatment of domestic violence offenders. *Int J Offender Ther Comp Criminol, 54*(4), 517–536. doi:10.1177/0306624X09337592

Lovell, D., Gagliardi, G. J., & Peterson, P. D. (2002). Recidivism and use of services among persons with mental illness after release from prison. *Psychiatric Services, 53*(10), 1290–1296. doi:10.1176/appi.ps.53.10.1290

Lowe, B., Kroenke, K., Herzog, W., & Grafe, K. (2004). Measuring depression outcome with a brief self-report instrument: sensitivity to change of the Patient Health Questionnaire (PHQ-9). *Journal of Affective Disorders, 81*(1), 61–66. doi:10.1016/S0165-0327(03)00198-8

Merten, M. J., Bishop, A. J., & Williams, A. L. (2012). Prisoner health and valuation of life, loneliness, and depressed mood. *American Journal of Health Behavior, 36*(2), 275–288. doi:10.5993/AJHB.36.2.12

Miller, N. A., & Najavits, L. M. (2012). Creating trauma-informed correctional care: a balance of goals and environment. *European Journal of Psychotraumatology, 3*. doi:10.3402/ejpt.v3i0.17246

Mintz, L. B., Ellmo, F., Ritter, L. M., Falvey, V. F., & James, R. K. (2016). *Where's the social justice for offenders with mental illness? A call to the counseling profession.* Paper presented at the 35th Annual F. E. Woodall Conference for the Helping Professions, Delta State University, Cleveland, MS.

Morgan, R. D., Flora, D. B., Kroner, D. G., Mills, J. F., Varghese, F., & Steffan, J. S. (2012). Treating offenders with mental illness: A research synthesis. *Law and Human Behavior, 36*(1), 37–50. doi:10.1037/h0093964

Morgan, R. D., Kroner, D. G., & Mills, J. F. (2018). *A treatment manual for justice involved persons with mental illness: Changing lives and changing outcomes.* New York: Routledge.

Neller, D. J., Denney, R. L., Pietz, C. A., & Thomlinson, R. P. (2006). The relationship between trauma and violence in a jail inmate sample. *Journal of Interpersonal Violence, 21*(9), 1234–1241. doi:10.1177/0886260506290663

Ostrowsky, M. K. (2010). Are violent people more likely to have low self-esteem or high self-esteem? *Aggression and Violent Behavior, 15*(1), 69–75. doi:http://dx.doi.org/10.1016/j.avb.2009.08.004

Prout, H. T., & Strohmer, D. C. (2010). *Emotional Problem Scales: The Self-Report Inventory.* Cordova, TN: Integrated Assessment, LLC.

Reingle Gonzalez, J. M., & Connell, N. M. (2014). Mental health of prisoners: Identifying barriers to mental health treatment and medication continuity. *American Journal of Public Health, 104*(12), 2328–2333. doi:10.2105/ajph.2014.302043

Reinhardt, V., & Rogers, R. (1998). Differences in anxiety between first-time and multiple-time inmates: a multicultural perspective. *Journal of the American Academy of Psychiatry and the Law Online, 26*(3), 375–382.

Rice, M. E., & Harris, G. T. (1997). The treatment of mentally disordered offenders. *Psychology, Public Policy, and Law, 3*(1), 126–183. doi:http://dx.doi.org/10.1037/1076-8971.3.1.126

Rich, J. D., Allen, S. A., & Williams, B. A. (2015). The need for higher standards in correctional healthcare to improve public health. *J Gen Intern Med, 30*(4), 503–507. doi:10.1007/s11606-014-3142-0

Ross, R. R., Fabiano, E. A., & Ewles, C. D. (1988). Reasoning and rehabilitation. *Int J Offender Ther Comp Criminol, 32*(1), 29–35. doi:10.1177/0306624x8803200104

Saavedra, J., & Álvarez, M. L. (2013). Association between traumatic experiences and psychosis among incarcerated men. *J Nerv Ment Dis, 201*(9), 773–779. doi:10.1097/NMD.0b013e3182a21488

Sammons, M. T., & McGuinness, K. M. (2015). Combining psychotropic medications and psychotherapy generally leads to improved outcomes and therefore reduces the overall cost of care. *The Tablet,* (April). Retrieved from http://www.apadivisions.org/division-55/publications/tablet/2015/04/combininations.aspx

Schnittker, J., Massoglia, M., & Uggen, C. (2012). Out and down: Incarceration and psychiatric disorders. *Journal of Health and Social Behavior, 53*(4), 448–464. doi:10.1177/0022146512453928

Scott-Hayward, C. S. (2009). *The fiscal crisis in corrections: Rethinking policies and practices.* Retrieved from New York, NY: www.vera.org/files/The-fiscal-crisis-in-corrections_July-2009.pdf

Shinkfield, A. J., & Graffam, J. (2010). The relationship between emotional state and success in community reintegration for ex-prisoners. *Int J Offender Ther Comp Criminol, 54*(3), 346–360. doi:10.1177/0306624X09331443

Snyder, H. N. (2007). Nothing works, something works—But still few proven programs. *Corrections Today, 69*(6), 6–28.

Swogger, M. T., Conner, K. R., Walsh, Z., & Maisto, S. A. (2011). Childhood abuse and harmful substance use among criminal offenders. *Addictive Behaviors, 36*(12), 1205–1212. doi:10.1016/j.addbeh.2011.07.025

Tong, L. S. J., & Farrington, D. P. (2008). Effectiveness of "reasoning and rehabilitation" in reducing reoffending. *Piscothema, 20*(1), 20–28.

Van Horn, S. A., Morgan, R. D., Brusman-Lovins, L. B., Littlefield, A. K., Hunter, J. T., Gigax, G., & Ridley, K. (2018). Changing lives and changing outcomes: "What works" in an intervention for justice-involved persons wiht mental illness. *Psychological Services*(June 14), 1–8. doi:10.1037/ser0000248

Ward, T., & Fortune, C.-A. (2013). The Good Lives Model: Aligning risk reduction with promoting offenders' personal goals. *European Journal of Probation, 5*(2), 29–46. doi:10.1177/206622031300500203

Ward, T., & Stewart, C. A. (2003). The treatment of sex offenders: Risk management and good lives. *Professional Psychology: Research and Practice, 34*(4), 353–360. doi:http://dx.doi.org/10.1037/0735-7028.34.4.353

Willis, G. M., Ward, T., & Levenson, J. S. (2014). The Good Lives Model (GLM): An evaluation of GLM operationalization in North American treatment programs. *Sexual Abuse: A Journal of Research and Treatment, 26*(1), 58–81. doi:10.1177/1079063213478202

Wilson, D. B., Bouffard, L. A., & Mackenzie, D. L. (2005). A quantitative review of structured, group-oriented, cognitive-behavioral programs for offenders. *Criminal Justice and Behavior, 32*(2), 172–204. doi:10.1177/0093854804272889

Wolff, N., Huening, J., Shi, J., & Frueh, B. C. (2014). Trauma exposure and posttraumatic stress disorder among incarcerated men. *Journal of Urban Health: Bulletin of the New York Academy of Medicine, 91*(4), 707–719. doi:10.1007/s11524-014-9871-x

7

Person Centered Therapy with Adult Male Prisoners Diagnosed with Gender Dysphoria

Amanda Hinds *and* Melinda M. Gibbons[6]

Gender Dysphoria is significantly different in *The Diagnostic and Statistical Manual of Mental Disorders* (5th edition; *DSM–5*; American Psychiatric Association [APA], 2013) from Gender Identity Disorder in the *Diagnostic and Statistical Manual of Mental Disorders-IV-Text Revision* (*DSM-IV-TR*; APA, 2000). For the purpose of this discussion, one of the most striking and relevant differences is the recognition of nonbinary gender identity as a norm experienced by many, as opposed to being a form of pathological thinking (Dailey, Gill, Karl, & Barrio Minton, 2014). The shift in focus is clearly evidenced by the change in nomenclature from disorder to dysphoria in the *DSM*-5 and the removal of Gender Dysphoria from the sexual dysfunctions and paraphilias categories (APA, 2013). Gender identity issues do not necessarily result from sexuality or associated matters but rather from feelings of confusion or degradation related to environmental context (DeFeo, 2015). By separating Gender Dysphoria from sexual dysfunctions and paraphilias, the

6. Amanda Hinds and Melinda M. Gibbons, Department of Educational Psychology and Counseling, University of Tennessee, Knoxville. Correspondence concerning this article should be addressed to Amanda Hinds, 441 Claxton Complex, 1122 Volunteer Boulevard, Knoxville, TN 37996–3542. E-mail: ahinds@vols.utk.edu

message is clear that gender identity is no longer the focus of diagnosis but rather the distress resulting from the incongruence (Dailey et al., 2014). Adult male inmates with Gender Dysphoria experience unique and difficult issues, both individually and systemically, related to their gender identity (APA, 2013; Dailey et al., 2014; DeFeo 2015; Edney, 2004). The prison environment is segregated by biological gender, and conformity is strictly enforced through institutional policy, complicating issues for inmates whose gender identity is not male (Edney, 2004). The purpose of this manuscript is to identify general criteria of Gender Dysphoria and the challenges experienced by incarcerated, adult, biological males. Based on the challenges faced by this unique population, we suggest a shift to person-centered therapy. A hypothetical case illustration utilizing person-centered therapy is provided, and implications for future research are discussed.

Gender Dysphoria

Gender is no longer considered a simple two-option biological assignment. According to the American Psychiatric Association, assigned or natal-gender refers to a person's physical sex at time of birth (Parekh, 2016). Gender identity, on the other hand, is one's internal identification as being male or female, or somewhere on the male-to-female spectrum. A person can have an assigned gender of male but a gender identity of female. Relatedly, gender expression denotes how someone demonstrates their gender to others (Parekh, 2016). Expression may include dress, appearance, or other behaviors, and may or may not be congruent with their gender identity. Transgender refers to people whose gender identity differs from their assigned gender and is not a mental health disorder. Lastly, Gender Dysphoria is not equivalent to transgender, but arises when negative emotions occur from incongruence between one's biological gender and perceived gender identity.

Given its own chapter in the *DSM-5*, Gender Dysphoria refers to "the distress that may accompany the incongruence between one's experienced or expressed gender and one's assigned gender" (APA, 2013, p. 451). Many nuances exist related to this diagnosis, but in general terms, clients must have a significant incongruence with their assigned gender and the gender with which they identify (APA, 2013). The incongruence is felt in many ways, but many of the defining features concern the desire to be the opposite gender, to be treated as the opposite gender, and to have the physical characteristics of the other gender (APA, 2013). As mentioned above, significant impairment and distress must result from this incongruence for the diagnosis (APA, 2013). To merit this diagnosis, clients must experience this distress for at least six months, and the distress can be demonstrated in a variety of ways, from outward expression to internal discomfort. For more specifics related to this diagnosis, readers should consult the *DSM-5* (APA, 2013).

According to Dziengel (2015), a person might choose to hide their gender identity to avoid losing social support or being ostracized from their social group. Depending on the accepted standards in the unique setting, the individual may choose to stay indefinitely hidden (Dziengel, 2015). Often, environments that force conformity foster a culture of discrimination against any that do not conform (Brower, 2013). Clients with Gender Dysphoria may be more open with some people and perhaps not open at all with others, thereby choosing not to express their identity anywhere other than the counseling session due to fear of retaliation or discrimination (Brower, 2013; Dziengel, 2015). Prisons are one environment where gender expression is tightly regulated, and inmates are forced to conform to their assigned gender. The prohibition of gender nonconforming behaviors in the institution can increase risk of both physical and mental victimization (APA, 2013; Dailey et al., 2014; DeFeo, 2015; Edney, 2004). In such an environment, it is likely the individual would experience significant psychological distress, such as depression, self-hatred, loneliness, and shame, possibly leading to a diagnosis of Gender Dysphoria if their gender identity is not affirmed or supported (Chaney, Filmore & Goodrich, 2011; Levitt & Ippolito, 2014; Sanchez & Vilain, 2009).

Natal-Male Inmates with Gender Dysphoria

It is difficult to estimate the number of natal-male inmates diagnosed with Gender Dysphoria for a number of reasons. Reasons include privacy concerns, failure of the client to report symptoms, refusal to participate in research, and lack of diagnosis by providers (Brown & McDuffie, 2009; Jenness, 2010). According to a report from Flores, Herman, Gates, and

Brown (2016), there are approximately 1.4 million individuals in the United States that identify as transgender, with some experiencing Gender Dysphoria. In addition, others struggling with gender identity but who do not identify as transgender may also experience Gender Dysphoria. The *DSM*-5 gives the estimated prevalence of Gender Dysphoria for adult natal males at .005 to .014 percent of the general population, but it does not include statistics for the prevalence in penal institutions (APA, 2013). According to Brown and McDuffie (2009), there are approximately 750 inmates total in the United States in prison facilities managed at the state level, with potentially 100 more in federally managed facilities, who identify as transgender and, given the considerations described previously, may meet criteria for Gender Dysphoria. More recently, Osborne and Lawrence (2016) suggested the prevalence of transgender inmates in the U.S. was closer to 1 in 500, with 3,000—4,000 struggling with Gender Dysphoria. Although this number is minuscule when compared to the 1.53 million incarcerated individuals in the United States (Bureau of Justice, 2015), these figures are likely under-representative due to the continued stigma attached to sexual identity and gender identification (Brown & McDuffie, 2009; Jenness, 2010).

Despite the number being small, the issues surrounding inmates with Gender Dysphoria are significant as, according to Brown and McDuffie (2009), only 20% of facilities have formal policies to address issues experienced by this population, and many more institutions resolve matters in ways not clearly outlined in a formal manner. These policies explored topics such as continued hormone therapy, new prescribing of hormones, requirements concerning psychiatric evaluations, expert consultation options, housing, and gender-affirming surgery (Brown & McDuffie, 2009). Given the lack of direction at the institutional level and the newness of the diagnosis, mental health counselors working in correctional facilities would benefit from additional information.

Problems Experienced at the Institutional Level

Several institutional-level problems exist for prisoners with Gender Dysphoria. A primary challenge for those in prison with Gender Dysphoria relates to how inmates are separated into these institutions. Prisons operate on the segregation of inmates based on their biological gender and not gender identity (Edney, 2004). Therefore, a natal-male inmate, who is living as a female when not incarcerated, would still be placed in a male prison. Therefore, prisoners with Gender Dysphoria often are subjected to discrimination and increased risk of attacks from other inmates, and prisons face increased legal liability when charged with keeping the individuals safe (Jenness, 2010; Jenness & Fenstermaker, 2013, 2015). As Stohr (2015) stated:

> The incarceration of transgender inmates, particularly transgender women in men's prisons, has been fraught with difficulties, missteps, ignorance, and abuse. . . .Transgender women and men have existed in what must at times seem like a war zone in which they are the perpetual target of scorn, harassment, and assault (p. 127).

The placement of inmates by natal gender is done intentionally and often in spite of protests from individuals with nonconforming gender identities.

Another problem is the mission of the organization itself. Penal institutions are charged with security first and foremost. Therefore, a significant power differential exists between staff and inmates as well as among inmates themselves (Jenness & Fenstermaker, 2015). Stohr (2015) highlighted that power in prisons resides first with the staff and then filters down. For example, Ferdik and Smith (2016) explored the types of power demonstrated by correctional officers and found they most often utilized power related to respect, or power related to authority rights. In other words, staff believed they had the right to power over prisoners, but also tried to engender respect between prisoners and officers. However, the most powerful inmates are often those readily accepted by other inmates, and inmates with Gender Dysphoria or those who identify as transgender are likely unaccepted due to their lack of conformity to traditional views of what natal male inmates are supposed to do, be, and look like (Stohr, 2015).

As mentioned earlier, due to this rejection of their identity and prohibition of openly representing their gender identity, inmates who comfortably identified as transgender outside of prison may come to meet criteria for Gender Dysphoria (APA, 2013; Dailey et al., 2014; DeFeo 2014; Edney, 2004). Jenness and Fenstermaker (2015) explained that while placed in these institutions, gender dysphoric inmates may participate in unsafe practices such as pairing up or engaging in sexual acts with other inmates, despite not desiring to do so, because of the benefit of being protected by other inmates. Practices such as these showcase the vulnerability of inmates diagnosed with Gender Dysphoria and the daily struggles they face in an institution segregated by biological sex. Although institutions may not force inmates into these practices overtly, the degradation and dehumanization of inmates with nonconforming gender identities through forced conformity directly impact the decisions made (Jenness & Fenstermaker, 2015). Security precautions make it impossible for inmates with Gender Dysphoria to live as they feel they should be able to and as whom they perceive they truly are, as demonstrated in the next section.

Problems at the Individual Level

Prisons run in an overtly strict manner due to the focus on safety and security, and successful operation is dependent on conformity. All prisoners must dress and appear similar, creating an environment which does not affirm nonconforming gender identities and potentially leads to a diagnosis of Gender Dysphoria (Arkles, 2012; Levitt & Hiestand, 2004; Levitt & Ippolito, 2014). Arkles (2012) noted that these regulations force prisoners to "adhere to dominant social norms through dress. . .using dress that does not match dominant norms as a form of punishment and humiliation" (p. 866). Arkles (2012) further suggested that dress directly relates to personal dignity, identity, and communication, so for inmates who identify as transgender, dress regulations may actually further their emotional distress, possibly contributing to a diagnosis of Gender Dysphoria. In effect, inmates with nonconforming gender identities are punished for their differences.

Prisoners whose gender is nonconforming often face emotional and mental health struggles in prison. Marlow, Winder, and Elliott (2015) interviewed prison staff about their experiences with transgender prisoners to learn more about their perspectives on working with this group. They noted the staff believed many prisoners experienced negative psychological issues and most experienced harassment, whether they were formally diagnosed with Gender Dysphoria or not. Relatedly, Brown (2014) reviewed written correspondence from 129 transgender inmates and identified feelings of Gender Dysphoria from 22% and reports of mistreatment or abuse from 42% of the inmates. Prisoners with nonconforming gender identities appear to face significant mental health issues associated with gender identity, which can result in Gender Dysphoria.

Brown and McDuffie (2009) noted only 20% of institutions had policies regarding the treatment or placement of inmates with a nonconforming gender identity. The identified policies indicated that 71% of housing assignments were based on biological sex, psychiatric evaluations were required, treatment issues (such as hormone therapy) were referred to a committee, and gender-affirming surgery was prohibited or discouraged (Brown & McDuffie, 2009). However, Stohr (2015) found that new regulations at the federal level are recommending decisions based on the individual inmate, considering individual needs and medical appropriateness. The medical treatment of Gender Dysphoria is outside the scope of this manuscript, but it is important to note that hormone replacement therapy, gender-affirming surgery and the risk of auto-castration or autopenectomy are topics of much discussion in the literature (Brown, 2010; Mann, 2006; Oparah, 2012; Tarzwell, 2006). Health care policies often prevent inmates from obtaining particular medical interventions, discontinue medical treatments upon admission to prison, and have the potential to impact the inmates' mental status (Brown & McDuffie, 2009). This denial of health care, to which the person may have had access in the free world, is yet another example of this population being prevented from living as they desire.

Some professionals would also argue that assigning a Gender Dysphoria diagnosis is still pathologizing to nonbinary and gender nonconforming individuals. Moleiro and Pinto (2015) noted that by including any diagnosis related to gender variance in the DSM, it still may suggest that it is a disorder to be fixed or addressed. In addition, they mention that inclusion as a mental disorder may exacerbate prejudice and discrimination against this group. Overall, this is a complicated issue with systemic implications. For now, however, the diagnosis does offer a way to provide aid, both medical and psychological, to clients struggling with aspects of their gender identity.

Typical Treatments Utilized in Prison

All of the problems mentioned above will no doubt have an effect on an inmate's mental health status (Chaney et al., 2011; Levitt & Ippolito, 2014; Sanchez & Vilain, 2009). As one inmate recalled, "every day, I struggle with trying to stay alive and not wanting to die. Sometimes I think being a martyr would be better than having to live with all this" (Jenness & Fenstermaker, 2015, p. 15). The problems discussed above demonstrate how this population loses the very right to live out one of their most basic identifications as a human, if that identification is not connected to natal-gender. A focus on treatment for those with Gender Dysphoria is likely to help alleviate some of the distress experienced by these clients.

Typical mental health treatments for prisoners center on theories such as cognitive behavioral therapy (CBT), which essentially challenges offenders' thoughts to target problematic behaviors (Dahlen & Johnson, 2010; Wilson, Bouffard, & MacKenzie, 2005). Wilson et al. (2005) noted that the cognitive approach typically views mental health issues as a result of a dysfunctional thought process. When working with clients diagnosed with Gender Dysphoria, CBT can be used to help clients replace internalized negative thoughts, usually heard repeatedly from society, with positive ones (Chaney et al., 2011). However, feelings of isolation and loneliness due to the inability to express their gender identity present a unique issue (Chaney et al., 2011). This issue may require treatment which provides a safe space for discussion, is gender affirming, does not label the client, and promotes self-empowerment (Chaney et al., 2011). As a result, incorporating a person-centered approach into treatment for incarcerated natal males with Gender Dysphoria may be an important way to address their unique needs.

Person-Centered Therapy

Person-centered therapy was founded by Carl Rogers in the 1950's and consists of a set of necessary conditions for the therapeutic relationships. The necessary conditions as laid out by Rogers (1957) emphasized the therapeutic behaviors of unconditional positive regard, empathy, and congruence to convey acceptance of clients. Person-centered therapy directly targets incongruent feelings related to distress by promoting unconditional acceptance of clients (Brice, 2011; Murphy, Cramer, & Joseph, 2012; Rogers, 1957). While these conditions do not necessarily tell a counselor how to proceed in therapy, they do set forth a set of conditions which will allow for growth on the client's part and, if these conditions are met over a period of time, change on the part of the client will naturally follow (Rogers, 1957). The relationship between the counselor and the client is the core of this approach.

Kirk and Belovics (2008) asserted that clients with Gender Dysphoria have many of the same needs as others, such as the need for respect and to be accurately and adequately represented in everyday life. These needs may be denied in a prison setting (Arkles, 2012; Levitt & Hiestand, 2004; Levitt & Ippolito, 2014; Stohr, 2015). It is here that person-centered therapy becomes relevant. As Livingstone (2008) stated:

> In a person-centered approach to therapy, the confused, tentative, and almost incoherent thinking of an individual who knows he has been evaluated as abnormal is really respected by being deemed well worth understanding. It feels well past time that the trans-identified population was deemed well worth understanding and met with genuineness, empathy, and unconditional positive regard of a facilitative phenomenological approach. (p. 138)

Clients struggling with Gender Dysphoria in the correctional system may feel devalued as humans and, as a result, their mental health can decline (Chaney et al., 2011; Levitt & Ippolito, 2014; Sanchez & Vilain, 2009). Person-centered therapy, with its direct focus on valuing the client as a person, becomes particularly relevant with this population. Prisoners with Gender Dysphoria live a daily existence in which they are not accepted for who they are, not only by their peers but also by those with direct power over them (Jenness & Fenstermaker, 2015; Stohr, 2015).

Person-Centered Therapy and Inmates with Gender Dysphoria

People struggling with Gender Dysphoria experience incongruence between their biological gender and identified gender resulting in significant distress and impairment in their daily lives (APA, 2013). Utilizing a person-centered approach with incarcerated inmates diagnosed with Gender Dysphoria creates what may be the only safe space they experience where they can feel fully accepted (Brice, 2011; Murphy et al., 2012;

Rogers, 1957). Not only do these clients experience internal incongruence, but they also feel incongruence with an environment over which they have no control (Jenness, 2010; Jenness & Fenstermaker 2013, 2015). However, the client can experience control in person-centered therapy, which provides a safe environment to discuss distress (Brice, 2011; Livingstone, 2008; Murphy et al., 2012; Rogers, 1957).

Counselors communicate unconditional positive regard and empathic understanding throughout the counseling process (Rogers, 1957). Those diagnosed with Gender Dysphoria in a penal institution can benefit from this unconditional positive regard and empathy, as they likely experienced many critical or disinterested reactions from others in their lives (Brice, 2011). This safe space and positive interaction with the counselor provide a stark contrast to the daily environment of the prison which is based on punishment and order. The condition of acceptance also is critical with this particular population, as they may experience daily degradation and dehumanization (Stohr, 2015). By providing acceptance, the counselor empowers the client to better navigate systemic hurdles as well as other personal difficulties (Howard & Schustack, 2009). For example, rather than acting out behaviorally due to being denied access to services, an inmate might be empowered to seek out alternative solutions when faced with systemic barriers (Brown & McDuffie, 2009).

Because the diagnosis of Gender Dysphoria is so new, few empirical studies exist on counseling interventions for this group. One study that interviewed clients who identify as transgender does lend some support for the use of person-centered counseling with gender-nonconforming clients. Participants in the Mizock and Lundquist (2016) study were asked about counselor interactions that were unhelpful or uncomfortable for them. Participants highlighted generalizing, pathologizing, and trying to repair a problem as major issues with therapists; as a result, the authors noted the need for counselors to be open, accepting, and nonjudgmental, all core characteristics of person-centered counseling. It can be assumed that these characteristics would be important for counselors working with clients with Gender Dysphoria, as well.

The prison system as discussed above relies on conformity and does not encourage individuality. Natal male inmates with Gender Dysphoria feel unaccepted due to their gender identity, which is seen as an individual and nonconforming choice (Stohr, 2015). Also noteworthy is the very recommendation by the *DSM-5* (APA, 2013) that the distress felt by clients diagnosed with Gender Dysphoria might well be reduced or eliminated by providing treatments which focus on being supportive and accepting. The following hypothetical case illustration demonstrates how person-centered therapy might work with this population.

Case Illustration

State Maximum Penal Institution (SMPI) is a fictional maximum custody state prison which houses 2,500 male inmates. Maximum custody implies that this institution holds all custody levels of inmates up to and including those considered maximum security who are segregated from general population. However, even though maximum-security inmates can be held here, not all inmates are considered maximum security and some may be treated/segregated as maximum-security inmates based on other factors. Inmates in maximum security are confined to a cell by themselves and only permitted to have one hour of recreational time per day, which is spent in a large caged-in area where they have no physical proximity to other inmates. Due to the high level of security risk, therapy sessions in this setting are conducted through the crack in the inmate's door, and only during crisis situations are the inmates permitted to be removed from their cell. When removed from their cells these inmates are required to be handcuffed, waist chain applied, legs shackled with a tether which attaches to the waist chain or leg shackles, and overseen by two correctional officers. Inmates in maximum security are required to wear all white scrubs, including white socks and white boxer shorts under their state issued pants. Despite not being maximum security, our client has been segregated due to the recent diagnosis of Gender Dysphoria and the safety issues associated with this diagnosis, as perceived by security staff.

Samantha is a 30-year-old natal-gender male incarcerated at SMPI and has served 1 year of a 10-year sentence for aggravated assault. This inmate was introduced to the counselor as Scott due to policy requiring all inmates be referred to as the name on their birth certificate. Samantha has been diagnosed with Gender Dysphoria and reports she is currently living in high security due to her openness as identifying with the female gender. Samantha was openly living as a transgender female prior to incarceration. However, since being incarcerated, Samantha has experienced significant distress related to her being forced to conform to her assigned gender (rather than following her conviction) and her feelings and reactions of another gender. Due to these factors, the facility psychiatrist assigned the diagnosis of Gender Dysphoria and referred Samantha for individual counseling.

Samantha reports she prefers to be called Samantha, but this has not been allowed as security staff members are required to call inmates by their legal name. Samantha reports she has a minimum-security level but, due to multiple threats from other inmates and previous assaults, she has been segregated for her protection. She feels this is not fair as she has earned the privileges afforded to those with a lower security level. She feels distressed that she has been forced to wear all men's clothing, including undergarments, and reports she openly lived as a female outside of prison. She also reports ridicule, harassment, and degrading statements and gestures from not only other inmates but also security staff. Samantha states she does not feel that therapy will do her any good as she does not need to be "fixed" and mental health staff will only judge her like all the rest of the staff.

During the very first session with Samantha, the counselor made it a point to address her as Samantha and acknowledged that she did indeed identify with another gender. The therapist also tried to communicate unconditional acceptance and positive regard. Samantha seemed somewhat taken aback by this approach and expressed to the therapist a feeling of "being set up to get knocked down again." Using the person-centered approach, the counselor validated this concern and expressed understanding that previous situations and systemic factors may have led to this form of thinking. The counselor reassured Samantha that the therapy session was a safe and confidential place to discuss concerns. The counselor did make a point to discuss the limits of confidentiality in a prison setting to build trust further. With this information, Samantha was placed in the position of power or control by being able to choose what she wanted to discuss within those boundaries. While hesitant, Samantha seemed to be considering what the counselor was saying in session.

The next few sessions focused on continuing to build a therapeutic relationship with Samantha. She often expressed frustration at having to meet with the counselor at the door and feeling this was not very confidential. The counselor communicated empathy by expressing how difficult it must be to be incarcerated and also experience limited choices when seeking help. The counselor also used this as an opportunity to work out a plan with security to have Samantha placed in a noncontact visitation gallery for sessions. Placement in a more private setting allowed Samantha to discuss her issues in confidence while still maintaining proper security procedures. This change seemed to put Samantha at ease and reaffirm that the counselor was there to help and cared about her issues. Samantha began discussing conflicts with security and a feeling of being under constant scrutiny because of the desire to live as a woman. Due to this feeling, Samantha revealed that she often lashed out at security for perceived slights or insults related to gender identity. At this point, the counselor validated Samantha's concerns to some degree by expressing how frustrating that must be. However, the counselor did make a mistake by stating, "You have to remember Samantha, they have to worry about murderers every day so worrying about your desire to be called a different name might not be that important to them." Samantha became distant at this point and stated, "You just don't understand. You're just like all the rest."

The counselor sought supervision and at the next session was able to communicate to Samantha that she was sorry for making it seem as though her problems were not significant. By addressing the issue directly and validating that these issues were indeed important to Samantha, she again felt the caring of the therapist and was able to move forward. Samantha was once again comforted by being acknowledged as an integral part of the counseling relationship and being afforded the dignity of an apology, something not typically received in a prison setting.

As the weeks continued and Samantha began to feel more accepted in the therapeutic relationship, she began opening up more problems she was experiencing in her day-to-day life. Examples of these issues included communication issues with other inmates, communication with staff, inability to regulate her moods, and a fear of reaching out to medical staff for evaluation. Due to the strong therapeutic relationship formed by the counselor, Samantha and the counselor were able to address several of these issues together. Samantha began demonstrating an ability to communicate with other inmates in a positive manner and, when subjected to insults and taunts, she discovered that writing alleviated much of the distress. The counselor also submitted a referral to psychiatry for a medication evaluation. During the evaluation, Samantha was able to communicate openly with the psychiatrist concerning her mood swings. Samantha also found that, if she submitted requests through the proper channels with security, the response was sometimes obtained in a timely fashion. Samantha felt encouraged by her acceptance from the counselor and began the process of seeking medical treatment, as well.

As Samantha became more comfortable in the therapeutic relationship, she also became more comfortable with herself. She began showing more self-accepting behaviors such as making more important decisions on her own and reflecting on the outcome with the counselor. Samantha was also able to reflect that discrimination in her current setting was likely not going to disappear overnight. Instead of instinctively lashing out at each person who made an insulting remark, Samantha reflected on her situation and considered how she wanted to address each interaction. By the end of counseling, Samantha felt a stronger sense of self-worth and autonomy and increased her self-acceptance. The distress associated with her diagnosis of Gender Dysphoria appeared to lessen, with reductions in her sadness and anxiety related to gender identity. In addition, Samantha was able to make progress due to the private and accepting nature of the counseling space, which allowed her to assuage some of the incongruities between her forced gender expression and her gender identity.

Discussion and Implications

In this case illustration, the counselor used core conditions from person-centered counseling to establish a safe and accepting therapeutic relationship. The counselor was able to have Samantha pulled out to a more private setting and, therefore, was able to demonstrate acceptance, unconditional positive regard, and validation of the importance of the client's problems. By demonstrating these qualities and communicating both directly and indirectly that the client was worthy of respect and caring, the counselor was able to foster more independence and address several issues. Samantha was able to open up to the therapist, became more open with others in her daily life, and was able to engage in more appropriate behaviors to achieve her goals.

One of the challenges for incarcerated clients with Gender Dysphoria is the gender-specific requirements attached to this setting. Enacted for safety and control purposes, these restrictions make it necessary for inmates with nonconforming gender identities to lose many of their personal expression opportunities, potentially creating a sense of Gender

Dysphoria. Counselors using a person-centered approach can offer a space for these clients to feel a small sense of control in an institution known for demanding conformity (Stohr, 2015). This allows the client to express their gender identity in a safe environment, thereby relieving distress due to incongruity between gender expression and gender identity. This approach provides a way to work with inmates with Gender Dysphoria while acknowledging their uniqueness and demonstrating unconditional positive regard (Cooper & McLeod, 2011; Rogers, 1957).

It is important to note there will be limitations inherent in any therapeutic intervention in a correctional setting but particularly in a maximum-security setting. As mentioned above, prisons are charged with security first and foremost and, to maintain a safe environment, conformity is enforced by those with the power (Stohr, 2015). Many institutions would not permit the ability to conduct private sessions, particularly with a maximum-security inmate, likely due to lack of space that would fit the needs of security and the mental health staff. Additionally, the decision to call an inmate by a different name or afford them what could be perceived as special privileges is likely to be frowned upon by many institutions (Arkles, 2012; Stohr, 2015). However, these limitations could be challenged by counselors who provide ongoing education to institutional staff and advocate for better policies and treatment options. Such advocacy and multicultural competence are expectations for counselors, as delineated by the *ACA Code of Ethics* (American Counseling Association, 2014).

Future researchers may explore environmental challenges unique to prisons, which contribute to the distress of individuals with Gender Dysphoria. In an environment (such as prison) where a person's nonconforming identity is unsupported, it is likely the individual would experience significant psychological distress, such as depression, self-hatred, loneliness, and shame (Chaney et al., 2011; Levitt & Ippolito, 2014; Sanchez & Vilain, 2009). However, it might be said that inmates' distress is caused by interactions in a transphobic, cis-normative environment, which is not gender affirming, accepting, or safe and promotes unsafe practices for transgender inmates (Jenness, 2010; Jenness & Fenstermaker, 2013, 2015; Stohr, 2015). While outside the scope of this manuscript, the experiences of transgender prisoners prior to, during, and after incarceration might provide more insight as to how transgender prisoners do or do not meet criteria for Gender Dysphoria.

This paper proposes the use of person-centered therapy for incarcerated natal males diagnosed with Gender Dysphoria. There are problems experienced by this population both at the institutional and individual level. These clients are subjected to more challenges than many inmates because of the structural requirements of prison systems. By providing one area of safe space for these clients to feel congruent with their gender choice, person-centered therapy fosters growth and more independence. Achieving growth and independence allows the client to navigate systemic barriers more effectively and achieve a higher degree of wellness on an individual level.

References

American Counseling Association. (2014). *ACA Code of Ethics.* Alexandria, VA: Author.

American Psychiatric Association. (2000). *Diagnostic and statistical manual of mental disorders: DSM-IV-TR.* Washington, DC: Author.

American Psychiatric Association. (2013). *Diagnostic and statistical manual of mental disorders* (5th ed.). Washington, DC: Author.

Arkles, G. (2012). Correcting race and gender: Prison regulation of social hierarchy through dress. *New York University Law Review, 87*, 859–949.

Brice, A. (2011). "If I go back, they'll kill me. . ." Person-centered therapy with lesbian and gay clients. *Person-Centered & Experiential Psychotherapies, 10*, 248–259. doi:10.1080/14779757.2011.626624.

Brower, T. (2013). What's in the closet: Dress and appearance codes and lessons from sexual orientation. *Equality, Diversity, and Inclusion: An International Journal, 32*, 491–502. doi: 10.1108/EDI-02-2013-0006

Brown, G. R. (2010). Autocastration and autopenectomy as surgical self-treatment in incarcerated persons with gender identity disorder. *International Journal of Transgenderism 12*, 31–39. doi:10.1080/15532731003688970.

Brown, G. R. (2014). Qualitative analysis of transgender inmates' correspondence: Implications for departments of correction. *Journal of Correctional Health Care, 20*, 334–342. doi: 10.1177/1078345814541533

Brown, G. R. & McDuffie, E. (2009). Health care policies addressing transgender inmates in prison systems in the united states. *Journal of Correctional Health Care 15*, 280–291. doi: 10.1177/1078345809340423

Chaney, M. P., Filmore, J. M., & Goodrich, K. M. (2011). No more sitting on the sidelines. *Counseling Today, 53*(11), 34–37.

Cooper, M. & McLeod, J. (2011). Person-centered therapy: A pluralistic perspective. *Person-Centered & Experiential Psychotherapies 10*, 210–223. doi: 10.1080/14779757.2011.599517.

Corey, G. (n.d.). Article 29: Designing an integrative approach to counseling practice. *Vistas*, 271–291.

Dahlen, K. & Johnson, R. (2010). The humanism is in the details: An insider's account of humanistic modifications to a cognitive behavioral treatment program in a maximum-security prison. *The Prison Journal, 90*, 115–135.

Dailey, S., Gill, C., Karl, S., & Barrio Minton, C. *DSM-5 learning companion for counselors.* Alexandria, VA: American Counseling Association

Defeo, J. (2015). Understanding sexual, paraphilic, and gender dysphoria disorders in dsm-5. *Journal of Child Sexual Abuse, 24*, 210–215. doi: 10.1080/10538712.2015.1004293

Dziengel, L. (2015). A be/coming out model: Assessing factors of resilience and ambiguity. *Journal of Gay & Lesbian Social Services 27*, 302–325. doi: 10.1080/10538720.2015.1053656

Edney, D. R. (2004). Mass media and mental illness: A literature review. *Canadian Mental Health Association*, 1–27.

Ferdik, F. V. & Smith, H. P. (2016). Maximum security correctional officers: An exploratory investigation into their social bases of power. *American Journal of Criminal Justice, 41*, 498–521. doi: 10.1007/s12103–015-9307–5

Flores, A. R., Herman, J. L., Gates, G. J., & Brown, T. N. T. (2016). *How many adults identify as transgender in the United States?* Los Angeles, CA: The Williams Institute.

Jenness, V. (2010). From policy to prisoners to people: A "soft mixed methods" approach to studying transgender prisoners. *Journal of Contemporary Ethnography 39*, 517–553. doi: 10.1177/0891241610375823

Jenness, V. & Fenstermaker, S. (2013). Agnes goes to prison: Gender authenticity, transgender inmates in prisons for men, and pursuit of "the real deal." *Gender & Society, 28*, 5–31. doi: 10.1177/0891243213499446

Jenness, V. & Fenstermaker, S. (2015). Forty years after brownmiller: Prisons for men, transgender inmates, and the rape of the feminine. *Gender & Society, 30*, 14–29. doi: 10.1177/0891243215611856

Kirk, J. & Belovics, R. (2008). Understanding and counseling transgender clients. *Journal of Employment Counseling 45*, 29–45.

Levitt, H., & Hiestand, K. (2004). A quest for authenticity: Contemporary butch gender. *Sex Roles: A Journal of Research, 50*, 605–621. doi:10.1023/B:SERS.0000027565.59109.80

Levitt, H. M., & Ippolito, M. R. (2014) Being transgender: The experience of transgender identity development, *Journal of Homosexuality, 61*(12), 1727–1758, doi: 10.1080/00918369.2014.951262

Livingstone, T. (2008). The relevance of a person-centered approach to therapy with transgendered or transsexual clients. *Person-Centered & Experiential Psychotherapies, 7*, 135–144. doi:10.1080/14779757.2008/9688459

Mann, R. (2006). The treatment of transgender prisoners, not just an American problem – a comparative analysis of American, Australian, and Canadian prison policies concerning the treatment of transgender prisoners and a "universal" recommendation to improve treatment. *Law and Sexuality 15*, 91–133.

Marlow, K., Winder, B., & Elliott, H. J. (2015). Working with transgendered sex offenders: prison staff experiences. *Journal of Forensic Practice, 17*, 241–254. doi: 10.1108/JFP-02–2015-0013

Mizock, L, & Lundquist, C. (2016). Missteps in psychotherapy with transgender clients: promoting gender sensitivity in counseling and psychological practice. *Psychology of Sexual Orientation and Gender Diversity, 3*, 148–155. doi: 10.1037/sgd0000177

Moleiro, C., & Pinto, N. (2015). Sexual orientation and gender identity: Review of concepts, controversies and their relation to psychopathology classification systems. *Frontiers in Psychology, 6.* doi: 10.3389/fpsyg.2015.01511

Murphy, D., Cramer, D. & Joseph, S. (2012). Mutuality in person-centered therapy: A new agenda for research and practice. *Person-Centered & Experiential Psychotherapies, 11*, 109–123. doi: 10.1080/14779757.2012.668496.

Oparah, J. C. (2012). Feminism and the (trans)gender entrapment of gender nonconforming prisoners. *UCLA Women's Law Journal 18*, 239–271.

Osborne, C. S., & Lawrence, A. A. (2016). Male prison inmates with gender dysphoria: When is sex reassignment surgery appropriate? *Archives of Sexual Behavior, 45*, 1649–1663. doi: 10.1007/s10508-016-0700-z

Parekh, R. (2016). *What is gender dysphoria?* Retrieved from: https://www.psychiatry.org/patients-families/gender-dysphoria/what-is-gender-dysphoria

Rogers, C. R. (1957). The necessary and sufficient conditions of therapeutic personality change. *The Journal of Consulting and Clinical Psychology* 60, 827–832. doi:10.1037/0022-006X.60.6.827

Sanchez, F. J., & Vilain, E. (2009). Collective self-esteem as a coping resource for male-to-female transsexuals. *Journal of Counseling Psychology*, 56, 202–209. doi:10.1037/a0014573

Stohr, M. K. (2015). The hundred years' war: The etiology and status of assaults on transgender women in men's prisons. *Women & Criminal Justice*, 25(1–2), 120–29. doi: 10.1080/08974454.2015.1026154.

Tarzwell, S. (2006). The gender lines are marked with razor wire: Addressing state prison policies and practices for the management of transgender inmates. *Columbia Human Rights Law Review, 38*, 167–219.

U.S. Census Bureau (2011). *Age and sex composition: 2010.* Washington, DC: U.S. Government Printing Office.

U.S. Department of Justice (2016). *Prisoners in 2015.* Washington, DC: U.S. Government Printing Office.

Whaley, K. (n.d.) (In)validating transgender identities: Progress and trouble in the DSM-5. Retrieved January 21, 2018 from http://www.thetaskforce.org/invalidating-transgender-identities-progress-and-trouble-in-the-dsm-5/.

Wilson, D. B, Bouffard, L. A., & Mackenzie, D. L. (2005). A quantitative review of structured, group-oriented cognitive-behavioral programs for offenders. *Criminal Justice and Behavior* 32(2), 172–204. doi: 10.1177/0093854804272889

8

Professional Counselors' and Students' Current Knowledge, Training, and Experience with Process Addictions

Angie D. Cartwright, Leigh Falls Holman, Judith A. Nelson, Kristy Carlisle, Christine Baker, Regina Moro, Sarah Monakes Whitmire, Stephanie Carroll, *and* LaTasha Y. Hicks Becton[7]

With the publication of *The Diagnostic and Statistical Manual of Mental Disorders* (5th edition; *DSM–5*; American Psychiatric Association [APA], 2013a), behavioral addictions have been acknowledged for the first time by the APA. The only behavioral addiction currently listed in the chapter on Substance-Related and Addictive Disorders

7. Angie D. Cartwright, Counseling and Higher Education, University of North Texas; Leigh Falls Holman, Department of Counseling, Educational Psychology, and Research, University of Memphis; Judith A. Nelson, Department of Counselor Education, Sam Houston State University; Kristy Carlisle, Department of Counseling and Human Services, Old Dominion University; Christine Baker, School of Psychology and Counseling, Regent University; Regina Moro, Department of Counselor Education, Boise State University; Sarah Monakes Whitmire, Marriage and Family Therapy Graduate Program, Pfeiffer University; Stephanie Carroll, Department of Special Education, Rehabilitation, and Counseling, Auburn University; LaTasha Y. Hicks Becton, Department of Counseling and Educational Development, University of North Carolina at Greensboro. Correspondence concerning this article should be addressed to Angie D. Cartwright, University of North Texas, 1155 Union Circle #310829, Denton, TX 76203–5017. E-mail: angie.wilson@unt.edu.

is gambling disorder. However, other disorders commonly thought to be behavioral addictions were included in Section III as needing further study, including nonsuicidal self-injury and Internet gaming disorders. Additionally, the chapters on eating disorders and obsessive-compulsive disorders acknowledge neurobiological similarities between some of these diagnoses and those of addictive behaviors. The American Society of Addiction Medicine's (ASAM) definition of addiction identifies several potential addictive behaviors including sex, spending, gambling, and eating (ASAM, 2016). However, only after years of work and reviews of scientific evidence did ASAM (2011) decide to define addiction not by its source, but by its process. Thus, the term "process addiction" (PA) came into use.

PAs are defined as any compulsive-like behaviors that interfere with normal living and result in a significant negative impact on functioning in personal or professional activities. Gambling, Internet, sex, exercise, and eating addictions are among those identified as PAs (Sussman, Lisha, & Griffiths, 2011). Since the late 1980s, PAs have been described as a set of behaviors that can alter an individual's mood in a way that is pleasurable and that can lead to dependency (Schaef, 1987).

The Council for Accreditation of Counseling and Related Programs (CACREP) required that accredited programs include PAs in their curriculum beginning in 2009 by infusing the language of process addictions and addictive behaviors throughout the standards' revisions. At that time, the International Association of Addiction and Offender Counselors (IAAOC) Process Addictions Committee (PAC) conducted a thorough review to determine if, and to what degree, process or behavioral addictions were included in the textbooks being used to train counselors. We found that there were no textbooks that discussed the addictive process as encompassing both substances and behaviors as potential targets for the addiction. Some texts referenced behavioral or process addictions, but with very few details.

As a result, we decided to conduct a series of studies using a mixed-methods design to examine the state of self-perceived knowledge and training directed toward the assessment, diagnosis, and treatment of PAs. We wondered first about whether counselor educators who were teaching addiction classes at the time perceived themselves to be prepared to teach their students about process addictions (Crozier & Agius, 2012). Our pilot study of counselor educators in two southern states revealed that the majority of those who were teaching addiction counseling classes did not feel adequately knowledgeable about process addictions in general or specific process addictions, such as pathological gambling and eating disorders, among others.

Next, we examined whether counselors in the field felt prepared to assess, diagnose, and refer or treat PAs as this was not a standard part of their training (Crozier & Agius, 2012). Wanting to have some methodological similarity between the counselor educators and other counselors, we limited the participants to the same states where our study of counselor educators was conducted. We found that a significant number of counselors surveyed were treating people with process addictions while reporting that they had received little or no training in doing so. Those who had received training reported that it was primarily related to eating disorders, sexual addiction, and relationship addictions.

Finally, we surveyed counseling students (Nelson, Wilson, & Holman, 2015) to determine their perceptions of training experiences and self-efficacy in screening, assessment, diagnosis, and treatment of process addictions. Among these students, 68% were pursuing a Master's degree in Counseling and the remaining participants were pursuing a second counseling degree (Educational Specialist or Doctorate). Additionally, 68% of the participants reported being between their fourth semester and their practicum or internship at the time they completed the survey. Both quantitative and qualitative analyses indicated that, although participants were generally aware of PAs, they did not identify focused training in screening or assessing for PAs. Although they did acknowledge being exposed to diagnostic criteria for some of these disorders, such as eating disorders and gambling, they reported they did not have access to training regarding the treatment of these disorders beyond being encouraged to pursue independent reading.

All three studies were small pilot studies of a participant pool limited to two states. We determined that in order to understand whether our findings were generalizable beyond this small group, we needed to conduct a larger national study. During the process of designing and completing these three studies, the PAC developed instruments to measure perceived level of knowledge and training, as well as sense of self-efficacy, for assessing, diagnosing, and treating PAs. Part of this process included seeking feedback from an expert panel and "beta-testing" the instruments with a group of volunteers who met the targeted participant populations. These instruments provided the foundation for the instrument used in the current study.

Process Addictions

Clinical literature on PAs, also conceptualized as behavioral addictions and obsessive-compulsive or impulse control disorders, indicates some people demonstrate addictive-type behavior to food, exercise, Internet use and gaming, sex, work, spending, and other behaviors (Sussman et al., 2011). According to Smith (2012), behaviors that are addictive have a similar neurobiological influence on the brain's reward system that negatively impacts functioning as those individuals who present with substance use disorders. However, although clinicians are reporting a significant increase in people presenting with these issues, several of these behaviors do not meet the evidence threshold necessary for publication in the DSM. This is due to the fact that sufficient epidemiological and neurobiological studies have not been conducted at this time to support the clinical findings that PAs are significantly presenting in clinical settings. Our study surveyed participants on several PAs supported by the literature, including gambling disorder, Internet gaming disorder, Internet addiction, eating disorders, exercise addiction, sex addiction, compulsive spending, and work addiction. Therefore, we describe the literature on each process addiction to provide a foundation regarding counselors' training needs. However, the responses to our questions, which covered all of the disorders, yielded responses which endorsed only a few of the disorders in large enough numbers for us to analyze and include in the results. Hence, the results and discussion will focus on PAs in general and the two disorders of sex addiction and eating disorders specifically. The PAs included in the review of relevant literature are the most common and relevant to the current study.

Gambling Disorder

The only PA identified in the *DSM-5* as an addictive behavior is gambling disorder (APA, 2013b). Pathological gambling was first recognized in the *DSM-III* (APA, 1980) as an impulse control disorder based on criteria identified in clinical settings (Reilly & Smith, 2013). The *DSM-IV*

(APA, 1994) later revised the criteria to resemble substance dependence disorder. However, both sets of criteria, which were primarily based on clinical data, were criticized as being insufficiently tested by research. Additionally, there was concern expressed among academicians and clinicians that the behavior exists on a continuum that was not reflected in the diagnostic criteria of the time (Hasin, O'Brien, Auriacombe, Borges, Bucholz, et al., 2014; Petry, Blanco, Auriacombe, Borge, & Buscholtz, et al., 2014; Slecza, Braun, Piontek, Buhringer, & Kraus, 2015). The *DSM-5* changed pathological gambling to gambling disorder to show how the behavior occurs along a continuum of severity consistent with other addictive disorders. Additionally, and perhaps more significantly, the disorder is no longer classified as an impulse control disorder. It was added to a new chapter, Substance-Related and Addictive Disorders, as the first recognized behavioral or process addiction. "This new term and its location in the new manual reflect research findings that a gambling disorder is similar to substance-related disorders in clinical expression, brain origin, comorbidity, physiology, and treatment" (APA, 2013c, p. 1).

Estimates vary widely as to the true prevalence of gambling disorders in the United States. The APA (2013a) suggests past-year prevalence rates range from 0.2% to 0.3%, whereas others suggest 0.5% (Substance Abuse and Mental Health Services Administration [SAMHSA], 2014) to 1% (Petry & Blanco, 2012) of the general population. With the current United States population at over 343.3 million individuals (United States Census Bureau, 2017), these rates suggest upwards of approximately 3.4 million Americans struggled with gambling disorder in the past year. When looking at distinct subgroups, this percentage grows (Petry & Blanco, 2012). For example, it is estimated that approximately 3.2% of active duty military members meet criteria for the disorder (National Council on Problem Gambling, 2015), and anywhere from 0.01% to 10.6% of adults aged 60 years and older (Subramaniam et al., 2015).

A diagnosis of gambling disorder can be given when four of the nine diagnostic criteria are present within an individual (APA, 2013a). The criteria strongly represent those for substance use disorders, such as the concepts of tolerance (i.e., increasing monetary amounts over time), preoccupation with the activity, using the activity as a distraction from unsettling emotional experiences, and experiencing significant stressors due to participation in the activity (APA, 2013a). In addition, a significant change in the newer release was the removal of participation in illegal activities from the criteria list due to the limited use of the criterion and the lack of benefit for an accurate diagnosis (Petry, 2010). Although the prevalence rates suggest there is a significant portion of Americans struggling with this disorder, help seeking behavior is limited to only 10% of individuals with the disorder (SAMHSA, 2014).

Given the incidence and prevalence of the disorder, all counselors need to be qualified to assess and diagnose it, even if they intend to refer out for treatment. A concern noted in previous studies revealed that not only were practicing counselors and counseling students reporting little to no training, counselor educators were also reporting that they did not understand the disorder (Crozier & Agius, 2012; Nelson et al., 2015; Wilson & Johnson, 2013).

Internet Gaming Disorder

The APA (2013c) produced a fact sheet on substance-related and addictive disorders and indicated that Internet gaming disorder (IGD) is being considered for future inclusion in the addictive behaviors section of the DSM, because research similarly supports this behavior as an addictive process. Currently, IGD is found in Section III (Conditions Warranting Further Research) of the *DSM*-5 and is still being researched due to the lack of evidence to support the inclusion of the disorder in the manual (APA, 2013b).

Excessive Internet gaming is linked to psychosocial and psychiatric distress similar to other addictive disorders. Psychosocial problems include the absence of real-world relationships (Allison, von Wahlde, Shockley, & Gabbard, 2006), inhibited social relationships (Carlisle & Carrington, 2015), aggression and hostility (Chan & Rabinowitz, 2006), inattention and maladaptive coping (Batthyány, Müller, Benker, & Wölfling, 2009), social inadequacy (Carlisle & Carrington, 2015), decreased academic achievement (Jeong & Kim, 2010; Rehbein, Psych, Kleimann, Mediasci, & Mossle, 2010), and sacrificing real-world activities in order to partake in virtual activities (Griffiths, Davies, & Chappell, 2004; Rehbein et al., 2010). Other studies point to the relationship between IGD and psychiatric issues, such as depression (Carlisle & Carrington, 2015; Peng & Liu, 2010, van Rooij et al., 2011; Yen, Ko, Yen, Chang, & Cheng, 2009), loneliness (Lemmens, Valkenburg, & Peter, 2010), and suicidal ideations (Rehbein et al., 2010). Some researchers consider IGD to be a sub-category of Internet addiction (IA), but since being online is not a requirement for IGD and much of the significant literature provides evidence that it is a separate disorder (Peng & Liu, 2010, van Rooij et al., 2011), we separate the two.

While examining the prevalence of IGD, significant consequences of excessive play were discovered (Jeong & Kim, 2010). However, these studies do not reflect consistent assessment instruments or criteria for diagnosis. In an effort to standardize criteria so that future research can determine the probability of this disorder being included in the *DSM*-5, nine common factors found consistently in the literature were chosen as criteria: preoccupation, withdrawal, tolerance, loss of control, continued use irrespective of problem awareness, neglect of other activities, escapism/mood modification, deception, and jeopardizing relationships and work (APA, 2013a).

Eating Disorders

The APA (2013a) discusses in the *DSM*-5 introductory material on the chapter on *Feeding and Eating Disorders* that preliminary neurobiological research on disorders, such as anorexia nervosa, bulimia nervosa, and the new diagnosis of binge eating disorder, demonstrate similar brain structures and processes to those affected with addictive disorders. This is the first indication that the APA may be considering the possibility that eating disorders would be best categorized within the addictive disorders section, as are process addictions.

The prevalence of anorexia nervosa and bulimia nervosa among young females is 0.4% and 1.0%-1.5%, respectively (APA, 2013a). Individuals diagnosed with anorexia nervosa experience a pathological fear of weight gain, severely restrict their dietary intake, have significantly low body weight, and severely poor body image. Similar to anorexia nervosa, individuals exhibiting symptoms of bulimia nervosa experience poor body image and engage in behaviors to minimize weight gain and exacerbate weight loss. Additional symptoms of bulimia nervosa are persistent episodes of binge eating and engaging in compensatory behaviors, such as self-induced vomiting or extreme exercise (APA, 2013a).

While individuals diagnosed with anorexia nervosa or bulimia nervosa are motivated by intense fear of weight gain, individuals experiencing the binge-eating disorder do not engage in compensatory behaviors to reduce body weight. Some common features of binge eating disorder are recurrent episodes of binge eating, eating rapidly and to the point of discomfort, eating excessive amounts of food when not hungry, and experiencing shame or depression after a binge episode. The prevalence of binge-eating disorder is more commonly diagnosed in women than men, roughly a 1.6%-0.8% ratio, respectively (APA, 2013a).

Sex Addiction

Although omitted from publication in the *DSM-5*, hypersexual disorder, commonly referred to as sex addiction (SA), was seriously considered for inclusion. Controversy among clinicians and researchers regarding the definition, diagnosis, and treatment of SA resulted in difficulties for clinicians who increasingly report these clients presenting for treatment in community counseling settings. Experts in sexuality disagree on the exact nature of SA (Bancroft & Vukadinovic, 2004; Kafka, 2010; Reay, Attwood, & Gooder, 2013). Riemersma and Sytsma (2013) identify two forms of sexual addiction: classic as described by Carnes (1991) related to abuse and poor attachment in childhood; and contemporary, a rapid-onset type of sexual addiction, which has emerged due to the explosive growth of online sexual images (Delmonico & Griffin, 2008). There is no formal diagnosis for SA, and Hagedorn (2009) believed this was a clear reason why there is little motivation "to create empirically founded training protocols for clinicians" (p. 190). And yet the literature clearly supports the legitimacy of SA as a diagnosable and treatable disorder (American Society of Addiction Medicine, 2011; Carnes, 2001; Hagedorn, 2009; Samenow, 2013).

Methodology

For the current study, an online survey was constructed and disseminated by members of the PAC. A mixed-methods approach was utilized in order to obtain both quantitative and qualitative data about PAs from counselor educators, counseling students, and professional counselors.

We utilized a mixed-methods concurrent triangulation design as well as a phenomenological approach in our study. Mixed-methods research combines qualitative and quantitative techniques in collecting and analyzing data that strengthens a research design (Creswell, 2014) and draws on the strengths of both the quantitative and qualitative to minimize weaknesses inherent in each (Johnson & Onwuegbuzie, 2004). We used Zip SurveyTM to collect data in a secure platform that allowed us to encourage participation from various geographic locations across the country.

This research study was guided by four research questions: (a) What are the participants' perceptions of their current general knowledge, understanding, and comfort levels on screening, assessment, diagnosis, and treatment of PAs, generally (quantitative research question)? (b) For eating disorders and sexual addiction, in particular, what are participants' perceptions of training, experience, and comfort level with assessing and providing counseling services for this condition (quantitative research question)? (c) What are the educational and training experiences participants have had in assessment, diagnosis, and treatment of PAs (qualitative research question)? (d) To what extent do the participants' reported experiences of being trained on the assessment, diagnosis, and treatment of PAs support the participants' survey responses regarding their general knowledge, understanding, and comfort levels on the assessment, diagnosis, and treatment of PAs (mixed research question)?

The purpose of the study was to collect information regarding the current state of the counseling profession regarding general knowledge, understanding, and comfort levels with assessment, diagnosis, and treatment of PAs. Both description and exploration of the data were important to the project, which is conducive to utilizing a mixed-methods approach (Collins, Onwegbuzie, & Sutton, 2006). The mixed-methods design utilized in this study was the convergent parallel mixed-methods design in which the quantitative and qualitative data are collected simultaneously, analyzed separately, and then compared to see if the results of one confirm or weaken the results of the other (Creswell, 2014).

Participants

The study was conducted nationally and was approved by the Institutional Review Board of a university in the southwestern United States before contacting potential participants. Participants in the current study consisted of 407 counseling practitioners, counselor educators, and students in counseling Master's and Ph.D. programs. Participants were asked to identify their current work or educational situation by choosing "all that apply." Overall, there were 407 participants in this study. Of those 407, 37% (n = 177) were counseling practitioners, 17% (n = 82) were counselor educators, 26% (n = 122) were Master's degree students, and 14% (n = 65) were doctoral students in counseling. Participants choosing "other" included 7% (n = 32) and chose descriptions, such as social worker, clinical supervisor, counseling psychologist, substance abuse counselor, clinical psychologist, and correctional health care manager. Among the participants, 42% (n = 170) identified as being a member of a professional addictions association and 58% (n = 237) did not. Males constituted 26% (n = 108) of the participants and females, 74% (n = 299). Participants included the following racial/ethnic groups: 11% (n = 46) African American; 0.5% (n = 2) American Indian; 1.5% (n = 6) Asian; 80% (n = 324) Caucasian; 3% (n = 12) Hispanic; and 4% (n = 17) other selections, including choices such as both Hispanic and Caucasian, multiracial, and Latina. Four participants elected not to identify their racial/ethnic group.

Instrument

A survey instrument was developed by members of the PAC for the purpose of conducting a national study of students in counselor education programs, counselor-educators, and counseling practitioners on their opinions and experiences with PA. The survey questions were based on the literature relevant to PAs and our pilot study instrument (Crozier & Agius, 2012; Nelson et al., 2015; Wilson & Johnson, 2013). Following completion of the pilot study, the questions were revised to accomplish several goals: to delete questions that appeared to be redundant, to revise questions that were not clear to participants, and to include questions that would focus on counselor training regarding PAs. Questions were germane to the participants' knowledge of PA, their experiences with clients, and their experiences in counselor education training programs. Grounded in current survey methods research guidelines (Dillman, Smyth, & Christian, 2009), the surveys were sent to all members of the

PAC to assess for content validity, and they were revised based on the feedback obtained. The 23-item survey included both closed-ended and open-ended questions and was designed for completion in 20 minutes or less. In addition to the descriptive survey questions, open-ended text boxes were provided for participants to elaborate on their responses in order to give a rich description of their experiences, and respondents were asked about their comfort level related to PAs. One item was used to assess comfort level with PAs in general, and participants had five response options (very comfortable, comfortable, ambivalent, not comfortable, and not applicable). However, three questions assessed the respondents training related to screening, diagnosing, and assessing specific process addictions, and they were provided 10 response options (eating disorders, exercise, Internet, gaming, gambling, relationships, sex, work, spending, and other). Additionally, respondents were asked about the importance of PAs and were provided four response options (very important, important, neutral, and not important).

Data Collection

Zip SurveyTM was used to post the surveys and collect responses as well as to analyze the demographic and quantitative data. Prospective participants received an email with a link to the survey requesting their participation. Surveys were distributed via counseling listservs throughout counselor education programs and by researchers utilizing professional networking. In addition, during national conferences, individuals were encouraged to participate in the study by snowball correspondence. The actual response rate for this study is not able to be calculated due to the fact that the call for participants was placed on professional listservs. Furthermore, this study was conducted to provide demographic information regarding knowledge of PAs among the three groups. Upon opening the survey link, the participants were prompted to read the informed consent and agree that they understood the nature of the study before continuing to the survey questions. The participants were assured that their responses were anonymous. The survey company collected the responses and aggregated the data into charts and Excel files. The qualitative responses obtained from participants, who shared their ideas and experiences through textboxes in the survey, were also utilized as data in this study.

Data Analysis

Quantitative data analysis. In addition to Zip SurveyTM, the researchers utilized the Statistical Package for Social Sciences (SPSS, IBM Corp., 2013) to analyze and organize quantitative data. With SPSS, researchers were able to explore the descriptive characteristics of the participants and their responses.

Qualitative data analysis. The participants provided their qualitative responses in textboxes (i.e., written form), and we chose to use one item to analyze for this study because it most accurately addressed the research question regarding the participants' training experiences. According to Moustakas (1994), qualitative data must be in a written form in order to adequately organize and formulate themes. We utilized Creswell's (2014) protocol for qualitative data analysis to answer the primary research question: what are participants' experiences of being trained on the assessment, diagnosis, and treatment of PAs? One member of the research team first organized and prepared the data for analysis. The researchers then read the open text submissions to gain a general idea of the large domains that stood out in the data. Next, we began coding the data by writing notes in the margins of the textual responses and color coding words and phrases that were related. We then began to identify relationships among the larger domains and to refine the initial codes into themes. Next, the research team worked to interconnect themes and, lastly, we discussed and reached consensus on how the themes would be represented in the findings section. Trustworthiness and credibility included peer debriefing, clarifying researcher bias, triangulation, checking transcripts for accuracy, and asking all research team members to reach a consensus on the final themes and interpretation.

Merged data analysis. As was the case in the pilot studies (Crozier & Agius, 2012; Nelson et al., 2015; Wilson & Johnson, 2013), Onwuegbuzie and Johnson's (2006) recommendations for legitimation (validity) in mixed-methods research were followed. More specifically, participants of the study, members of the research team, and an outside consultant provided feedback regarding interpretation of the data to achieve inside-outside legitimation. Once both sets (qualitative and quantitative) of data were analyzed, a consultant was utilized to assess the qualitative codes, and other members of the research team were utilized to provide a second review of the qualitative data. The second review occurred in order to verify the findings of the qualitative data analysis. After both sets of data were analyzed separately, all results were merged. The results were visually compared by members of the research team as an informal method to determine convergence, divergence, or a combination of the two. The rationale for this approach is to triangulate the findings to provide a better understanding of the research purpose (Creswell & Plano Clark, 2011), as well as increase the validity of the results of the study (Gall, Gall, & Borg, 2003).

Since our study was a concurrent triangulation design, mixing occurred at the interpretation stage (Creswell & Plano Clark, 2011). We used the side-by-side comparison for merged data analysis by "presenting the quantitative results and the qualitative findings together. . .so that they can be easily compared" (Creswell & Plano Clark, 2011, p. 223). All data pertaining to quantitative and qualitative quotations were reported to "specify how the qualitative quotes either confirm or disconfirm the quantitative results" (Creswell & Plano Clark, 2011, p. 223). Our primary interest in the qualitative portion of the study was to corroborate findings from the quantitative portion of the study and to ensure a wider exploration of the multiple experiences of the participants relating to PAs. This approach is utilized to "confirm, cross-validate or corroborate findings within a single study" (Creswell, 2003, p. 217).

Results

The results section has been organized into three categories: quantitative results, qualitative results, and merged results.

Quantitative Results

Table 1 provides a summary of the descriptive quantitative results. Specifically, participants provided responses to answer the quantitative research question: "What are the participants' perceptions of their current general knowledge, understanding, and comfort levels on screening, assessment, diagnosis, and treatment of PAs, generally?" The cumulative responses of all participants are described in the following section. With regards to screening for process addictions, 45% (n = 184) reported that they were not screening for process addictions, 53% (n = 214) reported screening for process addictions, and 2% (n = 9) did not respond to the question. Similarly, approximately 48% (n = 196) reported that they were treating counseling clients with process addictions at the time of the study, 50% (n = 203) reported that they were not treating clients with process addictions, and 2% (n = 9) did not respond to the question. Furthermore, the participants revealed that many of them, 43% (n =174), were very comfortable or comfortable providing counseling services related to process addictions.

Additionally, we sought to answer the following research question: for eating disorders and sexual addiction, what are participants' perceptions of training, experience, and comfort level with assessing and providing counseling services for this condition? Eating disorders and sexual addiction appeared to be the most recognizable PAs, thus participants' responses related to eating disorders and sexual addictions were explored in detail. A little over half (53%; n = 215) stated that they were very comfortable or comfortable assessing for eating disorders. However, of those 215 respondents, only 53% (n = 114) reported receiving training to assess eating disorders. When respondents provided information on diagnosing eating disorders, a little less than half (48%; n = 196) reported that they were providing counseling services related to eating disorders at the time they took the survey.

Responding to questions about assessing, diagnosing, and treating sexual addiction, a little over half (53%; n = 215) stated that they were very comfortable or comfortable assessing for sexual addiction. Thirty-one percent (n = 66) of the 215 stated they were very comfortable or comfortable assessing for sexual addiction and have never been trained. When respondents provided information on diagnosing sexual addiction, a little less than half (48%; n = 196) reported that they were providing sexual addiction-related counseling services at the time they took the survey. Of that 48%, about half (32%; n = 63) reported that they were diagnosing sexual addiction and had not been trained.

Qualitative Results

Given the lack of research and new category of behavioral addictions reflected in the *DSM-5*, qualitative exploration allowed us to gain a deeper understanding of participants' experiences related to PAs. The qualitative data collection and analysis answered the following research question: what are the educational and training experiences participants have had in assessment, diagnosis, and treatment of PAs? The themes that most accurately defined the experiences of the participants related to their training on PAs were as follows: *lack of training, self-training, informal training, and formal training.*

Lack of training. The theme of lack of training included statements that directly indicated that the participants had no training or very minimal training, such as a short discussion in a graduate program in one class. Of the 380 statements made by participants related to training, 36% participants *(n* = 136) indicated that their experiences were none to minimal. One participant responded, "I'm a bit disappointed that I didn't hear the term 'process addiction' until after I graduated and joined some professional organizations. I'm not even very clear on what a process addiction is, and plan to research it now." Another participant shared a brief statement regarding lack of training:

> I feel I haven't had any real training in process addictions, besides being explained what process addictions are, thus I do not feel adequately trained to diagnose or treat them as I don't know many of the warning signs/symptoms to look for in a process addict.

While some participants had never heard of process addictions, some other participants stated they had little or minimal training related to process addictions. One participant stated, "I have received no formal training in process addictions, although a great deal of time was spent discussing it in classes and in the field" and another stated, "very minimal [training on process addictions], the focus tends to be on substance abuse addictions."

Self-training. The theme of self-training included participants' statements indicating that they had read information about PAs, had searched the Internet for information, or had talked to other counselors to become informed. Of the 380 statements made by participants related to training,

9% (n = 33) of participants indicated that their training and learning experiences related to process addictions were through self-training. When speaking about process addictions and training one participant stated, "It [training] has been based on working with specific populations and then using what research is out there to come up with a means to work with individual having a process addiction." Another participant stated, "primarily self-training was through the professional literature."

Informal training. Informal training included participants' statements indicating that they had attended workshops, had taken an addiction course in their pre-service training that included PAs, had attended sessions at professional conferences, or had gained supervision by someone knowledgeable on PAs. Of the 380 statements made by participants related to training, 33% (n = 125) indicated that their training and learning experiences related to process addictions were through informal training methods. One participant shared, "I took a 3-hour academic course as part of my Master's degree and have been attending trainings and workshops on the topic for over 15 years," when asked about process addictions and their training in the area. Another participant noted that their training took place in several ways, "on the job observation and discussion with a knowledgeable expert, online courses, and literature review."

Formal training. Lastly, formal training included those participants' statements indicating that they had received training to become an addiction specialist, such as a Certified Sex Addiction Therapist. Of the 380 statements made by participants related to training, 23% (n = 86) of participants indicated that their training and learning experiences related to process addictions were through formal trainings. When asked about their training with assessing, diagnosing, and treating process addictions, one participant stated:

> I am a Certified Sex Addiction Therapist and Supervisor; I am a Certified Compulsive Gambling Counselor; I have taken workshops and three day trainings on compulsive shop-lifting and compulsive disorders as well as on workaholism and eating disorders task focused, and complete life change.

Another participant stated, "I trained with IITAP [International Institute for Trauma and Addiction] as a Certified Sex Addiction Therapist, which gave me specialist knowledge of sex addiction."

Merged Results

As is typical in the convergent parallel mixed-methods research (Creswell, 2014), the quantitative and qualitative data were analyzed separately, and then both sets were compiled into a side-by-side comparison chart to answer the mixed research question: to what extent do the participants' reported experiences of being trained on the assessment, diagnosis, and treatment of PAs support the participants' survey responses regarding their general knowledge, understanding, and comfort levels on the assessment, diagnosis, and treatment of PAs? The chart was utilized to determine convergence or divergence of quantitative results and qualitative themes. Convergence is important for enhancing findings, and divergence is essential in identifying emergent findings (Creswell & Plano Clark, 2011).

Utilizing the side-by-side comparison chart, we merged the data to provide interpretation about the overall results of this study. Results from the survey identified specific raw data and percentages to be important when interpreting the ability of counseling professionals to assess, diagnosis, and treat PAs. An analysis of one open-ended question included in the survey enhanced findings by providing a more in-depth analysis of the survey regarding the training of counseling professionals in PAs. Four major themes were identified in the open-ended question: *lack of training*, *self-training*, *informal training*, and *formal training*. Three mixed-methods themes emerged from the combined data sets: lack of training; types of training; and comfort levels in assessment, diagnosis, and treatment of PAs. Table 2 displays the results of combining the data sets.

The purpose of jointly displaying the two data sets is to compare the two sources of information and determine whether there is convergence or divergence between the two sources. As we analyzed the two merged databases in the side-by-side format, we determined that the responses to two of the qualitative questions provided convergent results. For example, in both the survey responses and the open-ended question responses, low incidences of being trained on PAs was found. Also, in the survey responses, participants indicated that they "would like" to have training in PAs, suggesting that they have not had adequate training. The open-ended question responses verified that only small percentages of the participants had any formal training on PAs, which substantiates the findings on the survey responses. Lastly, the theme regarding comfort levels with assessing, diagnosing, and treating PAs resulted in divergence. For example, relatively high percentages on the survey responses indicated that many participants (78% of practitioners, 58% of counselor-educators, and 34% of students) felt comfortable working with PAs. On the other hand, the open-ended question responses suggested that only those with formal training felt comfortable with PAs, and many who had training still did not feel comfortable.

Discussion

Almost 30 years of professional literature indicates that gambling, sex addiction, eating disorders, and Internet gaming disorder exist at clinically significant levels in the general population. Additionally, the American Society of Addictive Medicine's (ASAM, 2011) definition of addiction discusses addiction as a process rather than focusing on the target of the addiction (e.g., gambling, cocaine, sex, alcohol, etc.). Perhaps most significantly, the *DSM-5* now has a chapter that identifies addictive disorders beyond substance-use disorders, including gambling disorder as an addictive disorder and acknowledging similarities between eating disorders and certain forms of hoarding (with excessive spending), as having similar underlying behavioral and neurobiological processes as substance-use disorders. Additionally, two disorders commonly described as process or behavioral addictions, Internet gaming disorder and nonsuicidal self-injury, were added for further study.

These facts indicate that all counselors need to be prepared to at least identify, screen, and give a preliminary diagnostic label to these process addictions, whether in a general counseling setting or an addiction treatment setting. The initial findings in our pilot studies indicated that most counselor educators teaching addiction courses did not feel adequately trained in process addictions (Crozier & Agius, 2012), and the majority of practicing counselors who were diagnosing and treating PA reported having little or no training (Wilson & Johnson, 2013). However, our national survey indicates the majority of counselors, counselor educators, and students are interested and are actively pursuing training in assessment, diagnosis, and treatment of PAs, which is a positive sign. Additionally, as indicated in Table 1, the ongoing interest in training continues to be very high among all three groups. Therefore, the need for more workshops and training opportunities at professional conferences for continuing education in the area of process addictions is evident.

The fact that the only process addictions which were endorsed in significant numbers by participants were gambling disorder, sexual addiction, and eating disorders highlights the need for specific workshops on individual PAs. Although overview workshops are helpful, it is also recommended that more targeted training is made available. This may include special training on screening for process addictions in general practice settings and assessment and special diagnostic issues unique to individual process addictions, particularly those that do not have clear diagnostic guidelines in the *DSM-5* in spite of significant literature on these disorders (e.g., hypersexual arousal disorder/sex addiction). Finally, specific training and opportunities for supervised practice in working with specific PAs is important to cultivate and support within the profession. We would encourage professional organizations to seek out proposals for professional conferences and webinars that focus on these topics, including supporting a "day of learning" or special institute associated with the professional conference in order to fill a need for this training in the profession.

Many of the respondents indicated they had used Internet searches and reviewed the professional literature to gain knowledge. This indicates that organizations such as the American Counseling Association (ACA) and the International Association of Addiction and Offender Counselors (IAAOC) need to develop a repository of vetted resources of quality information that may be referenced by students, counselors, and counselor educators wanting to learn more about these topics. Additionally, ACA divisions such as the Association for Assessment and Research in Counseling (AARC) are encouraged to review instruments used for screening and assessment of various process addictions. Finally, it is a call to journal editors to consider special editions devoted to the topic of process addictions in general or specific process addictions such as gambling disorder.

Concerns regarding competency were one of the most important issues highlighted by our pilot studies. Many counselor educators indicated teaching PA material without having a knowledge base themselves. Similarly, many counselors practicing in the field at the time indicated assessing and treating these disorders without feeling they were properly trained. The *ACA Code of Ethics* (ACA, 2014) discusses the need for counselors "to practice only within the boundaries of their competence, based on their education, training, supervised experience, state and national professional credentials, and appropriate professional experience" (C.2.a., p. 8).

In spite of this, our national study seems to support the results from our pilot studies that a significant number of counselors are assessing, diagnosing, and/or treating process addictions without proper training in assessment, diagnosis, and treatment of these disorders. Specifically, only 53% of those stating they were assessing eating disorders reported receiving training to assess eating disorders. Similarly, 49% of the participants of our current study reported diagnosing eating disorders without training, and over half (55%) reported treating eating disorders without training. Clearly, if these counselors were following the guidelines in the *ACA Code of Ethics* (ACA, 2014), they would be referring out to professionals qualified to treat these specific issues.

Given these findings, we conclude there needs to be more oversight from counseling supervisors, agencies, and state licensing boards regarding counselors practicing within their areas of competence. This may also illuminate a need for increased availability for opportunities to get training and supervised experience across the country. Additionally, there may be a need for more trained professionals who can act as professional consultants on cases involving process addictions when there are no available trained professionals in the area for client referrals.

To highlight a related ethical concern, for counselors who treat substance-use disorders, it is common professional knowledge that cross-addictions are typical among addicted populations. So, if a professional specializes as a chemical dependency counselor, it is crucial that they understand how to assess and treat potentially co-morbid process addictions; otherwise they may risk clients simply substituting one addiction for another. According to the *ACA Code of Ethics* (ACA, 2014), "counselors practice in specialty areas new to them only after appropriate education, training, and supervised experience. While developing skills in new specialty areas, counselors take steps to ensure the competence of their work and protect others from possible harm" (p. 8). Therefore, practicing outside one's training, including ignoring data supporting the existence of PAs, produces client welfare issues that require professional advocacy. The data from this and our previous studies indicate that many clinicians are not fully aware of the research related to PA assessment, diagnosis, and treatment measures (Crozier & Agius, 2012; Wilson & Johnson, 2013; Nelson et al., 2015).

As reported in this study, some of these professionals are seeking informal training at professional conferences or through accessing literature either online or through professional journals. Some are even pursuing specialized certification in one or more PAs. However, training in PAs that could be a potential cross-addiction may need to be an expectation for current substance abuse counselors, with inclusion in state certification or licensing expectations. Currently, there are several extensive post-graduate training programs and certifications that clinicians can obtain in specific PAs including Certified Sex Addiction Therapist (CSAT; International Institute for Trauma & Addiction Professionals, 2011); National Certified Gambling Counselor (NCGC; National Council on Problem Gambling,2015); and Certified Eating Disorders Specialist (CEDS) in Mental Health (The International Association of Eating Disorders Professional Foundation, 2015). As some of our participants reported, they have pursued post-graduate certification programs for some process addictions.

However, these programs generally are produced by for-profit businesses and have little if any external oversight regarding curriculum or program outcomes. This potentially raises several concerns for individuals seeking training and for clinical populations who may need intervention. Is there adequate quality training at a reasonable cost to develop a knowledgeable, ethical, professional pool to serve those in need? The counseling profession must realize that these certification programs also cost significant amounts of money (up to $10,000 or more) and are not eligible for student loan assistance. This indicates a need for development of specialized addiction certification programs housed within graduate schools of counseling that include training in process addictions, in order to provide realistic training options for current students and practicing counselors. CACREP now provides standards for accrediting such programs, so there is some guidance for universities to develop them. Given that the training probably needs to be dispersed throughout the country to maximize the availability of trained professionals, we recommend ACA, IAAOC, or CACREP develop consultation services or grants for developing accredited addiction programs that include training in PAs.

Finally, CACREP training standards have required accredited graduate programs in all counseling tracks to teach PAs since 2009. In our pilot study, many counselor educators who taught addiction classes indicated that they did not feel comfortable teaching PAs (Crozier & Agius, 2012; Nelson et al., 2015; Wilson & Johnson, 2013). This may explain why counselors currently report having little training in this area; however, it is notable that almost half the counselor educators surveyed in this study indicated they were comfortable or very comfortable with teaching PA material, which is a significant improvement. This indicates a positive trend which may result in improved outcomes regarding counselor preparedness to assess, diagnose, and treat PAs in the near future. We recommend integration of these *new* disorders be infused throughout the curriculum for students to begin to understand the complexity of the issues related to PAs. Ethical case studies involving individuals treating process addictions outside their scope of practice should be included in ethics classes. A review of screening and basic assessments used for process addictions should be taught in assessment classes. The history and development of the new diagnostic category for addictive disorders, the *DSM-5* recognition in chapters on eating disorders and obsessive-compulsive disorders regarding the similarities of these disorders and addictive processes, and discussing case studies of the diagnostic dilemmas related to clients presenting with hypersexual behaviors or Internet gaming disorder should be part of coursework on diagnosis and treatment planning. These are just a few of the recommendations we have for improving the knowledge base for counselors, counselor-educators, and their students moving forward.

Limitations

Limitations are inherent in any research project, and several limitations to the current study are noted here. One limitation of our study is that our participants included three distinct groups (practitioners, students, and counselor-educators) with a wide variety of experiences, length of time in the profession, and varying job roles. While we were aware of this limitation at the time of our data collection, we chose to include all three groups to demonstrate a large continuum of training and comfort in working with PAs. Further study should include examining these groups separately in greater depth. Another limitation was that the data from the qualitative survey question were written responses in textboxes rather than interview style. This limitation resulted in limited breadth and depth of qualitative data; however, due to the participants living in various locations all over the United States, we decided to include the qualitative question in the Internet survey. For future research, a qualitative study of PA training and knowledge would inform the profession further on the results of the current study.

Strengths

Previous literature (Crozier & Agius, 2012; Nelson et al., 2015; Wilson & Johnson, 2013) called for a national study of counseling professionals' knowledge of PAs in efforts to increase awareness and promote training initiatives regarding PAs. A national sample of counseling professionals was surveyed for their perceptions and professional experiences, and the information they provided highlights the importance of training and general knowledge of PAs in the current study. Results from the current study can be implemented to highlight the importance of trainings and education related to PAs, and this manuscript strengthens the relevant literature on PAs while incorporating a mixed methods approach. The mixed methods approach is a strength of the current study because both quantitative and qualitative data are provided. Providing samples of participant's experiences may assist the reader in understanding the big picture and reduces the weaknesses in each standalone method of data collection. Future researchers are encouraged to explore PAs from a mixed methods approach in order to highlight the unique aspects of the method.

Table 1

Results of the Quantitative Data Analysis

	Practitioners	Counselor-Educators	Students
Total Number in Study	37% (n = 177)	17% (n = 82)	40% (n = 187)
Males	30% (n = 54)	45% (n = 37)	20% (n = 37)
Females	70% (n = 123)	55% (n = 45)	80% (n = 150)
African American	6% (n = 10)	11% (n = 8)	14% (n = 26)
American Indian	—	1% (n = 1)	1% (n = 1)

Asian	2% (*n* = 4)	1% (*n* = 1)	1% (*n* = 1)
Caucasian	90% (*n* = 150)	84% (*n* = 64)	80% (*n* = 142)
Hispanic	2% (*n* = 3)	3% (*n* = 3)	4% (*n* = 8)
Addictions Association	61% (*n* = 108)	46% (*n* = 38)	22% (*n* = 41)
1 to 5 Years of Experience	37% (*n* = 63)	11% (*n* = 9)	20% (*n* = 37)
6 to 10 Years of Experience	18% (*n* = 31)	26% (*n* = 21)	11% (*n* = 21)
11 to 15 Years of Experience	17% (*n* = 30)	16% (*n* =13)	3% (*n* = 6)
16 to 20 Years of Experience	12% (*n* = 21)	15% (*n* =12)	2% (*n* = 4)
21+ Years of Experience	16% (*n* = 29)	32% (*n* = 26)	1% (*n* = 1)
Training Is Very Important	78% (*n* = 136)	68% (*n* = 54)	77% (*n* = 142)
Training Is Important	19% (*n* = 33)	25% (*n* = 20)	21% (*n* = 39)
Training Not Important	3% (*n* = 5)	3% (*n* = 2)	2% (*n* = 3)
Training/Neutral	3% (*n* = 5)	5% (*n* = 4)	2% (*n* = 3)
Want to Be Trained	90% (*n* = 158)	85% (*n* = 69)	96% (*n* = 176)

Table 2

Comparison of Information from Survey Data and Text Box Responses

Mixed-method theme	Survey responses	Open-ended Survey Questions
Types of Training	90% of practitioners would like a course in PAs 85% of counselor educators would like a course in PAs 96% of students in counselor education programs would like a course in PAs	9% of participants noted self-training (reading, supervision) 33% of participants noted informal training (CEUs, workshops, conferences, graduate course) 23% of participants noted formal training (CSAT, ITTAP, addiction specialist)

Comfort levels in assessing, diagnosing and treating PAs	78% of practitioners were very comfortable or comfortable in assessing, diagnosing, and treating PAs 58% of counselor educators were very comfortable or comfortable in assessing, diagnosing, and treating PAs 34% of students were very comfortable or comfortable in assessing, diagnosing, and treating PAs	Participants with formal training were more comfortable assessing, treating, and diagnosing PAs. A wide variety of screening tools were being utilized (e.g., CAGE, SAST, verbal screenings, and CAMH Gambling Screen). While some were trained in assessing and treating they were not comfortable providing counseling services specifically related to PAs.

References

Allison, S. E., von Wahlde, L., Shockley, T., & Gabbard, G. O. (2006). The development of the self in the era of the Internet and role-playing fantasy games. *The American Journal of Psychiatry, 163*(3), 381–385. doi:10.1176/appi.ajp.163.3.381

American Counseling Association. (2014). *Code of ethics.* Alexandria, VA: Author.

American Psychiatric Association. (2013a). *Diagnostic and statistical manual of mental disorders* (5th ed.). Washington, DC: Author.

American Psychiatric Association. (2013b). *Highlights of changes from DSM-IV-TR to DSM-5.* Retrieved from http://www.dsm5.org/Documents/changes%20from%20 dsm-iv-tr%20to%20dsm-5.pdf

American Psychiatric Association. (2013c). *Substance-related and addictive disorders.* Retrieved from http://www.dsm5.org/documents/ substance%20use%20 disorder%20fact%20sheet.pdf

American Psychiatric Association. (1994). *Diagnostic and statistical manual of mental disorders* (4th ed.). Washington, DC: Author.

American Psychiatric Association. (1980). *Diagnostic and statistical manual of mental disorders* (3rd ed.). Washington, D.C.: Author.

American Society of Addiction Medicine. (2011). *Public policy statement: Definition of addiction.* Chevy Chase, MD: Author.

Bancroft, J. & Vukadinovic, Z. (2004). Sexual addiction, sexual compulsivity, sexual impulsivity, or what? Toward a theoretical model. *Journal of Sex Research, 41*(3), 225–234. doi:10.1080/00224490409552230

Batthyány, D., Müller, K. W., Benker, F., & Wölfling, K. (2009). Computer game playing: Clinical characteristics of dependence and abuse among adolescents. *Wiener Klinsche Wochenschrift, 121*(15–16), 502–509. doi:10.1007/s00508–009-1198–3

Carlisle, K. L. & Carrington, C. (2015). The social experience of Internet gamers: A pilot study. *VISTAS 2015*. Retrieved from http://www.counseling.org/knowledge-center/ vistas

Chan, P. A., & Rabinowitz, T. (2006). A cross-sectional analysis of video games and attention deficit hyperactivity disorder symptoms in adolescents. *Annals of General Psychiatry, 5*(1), 16–26. doi:10.1186/1744–859X-5–16

Carnes, P. (1991). *Don't call it love.* New York, NY: Bantam.

Carnes, P. J. (2001). *Out of the shadows: Understanding sexual addiction* (3rd ed.). Center City, MN: Hazelden.

Collins, K. M. T., Onwuegbuzie, A. J., & Sutton, I. L. (2006). A model incorporating the rationale and purpose for conducting mixed methods research in special education and beyond. *Learning Disabilities: A Contemporary Journal, 4*, 67–100.

Council for Accreditation of Counseling and Related Educational Programs [CACREP] (2009). 2009 standards for accreditation. Alexandria, VA: Author.

Creswell, J. W. (2003). *Research design: Qualitative, quantitative, and mixed methods approaches* (2nd ed.). Thousand Oaks, CA: Sage

Creswell, J. W. (2014). *Research design: Qualitative, quantitative, and mixed methods approaches* (4th ed.). Thousand Oaks, CA: Sage.

Creswell, J. W., & Plano Clark, V. L. (2011). *Designing and conducting mixed methods research* (2nd ed.). Thousand Oaks, CA: Sage.

Crozier, M., & Agius, M. (2012). Counselor educators & process addictions: How we know what we know. *NC Perspectives, 7*, 32–40.

Delmonico, D. L., & Griffin, E. J. (2008). Cybersex and the E-teen: What marriage and family therapists should know. *Journal of Marital and Family Therapy, 34*(4), 431–444. doi:10.1111/j.1752–0606.2008.00086.x

Dillman, D., Smyth, J., & Christian, L. (2009). *Internet, mail, and mixed-mode surveys: The Tailored Design Method.* New York: Wiley.

Gall, M. D., Gall, J. P., & Borg, W. R. (2003). *Educational research: An introduction* (7th ed.). Boston, MA: Allyn & Bacon.

Griffiths, M. D., Davies, M. N. O., & Chappell, D. (2004). Demographic factors and playing variables in online computer gaming. *Cyberpsychology & Behavior, 7*(4), 479–487. doi:10.1089/cpb.2004.7.479

Hagedorn, B. (2009). Sexual addiction counseling competencies: Empirically based tools for preparing clinicians to recognize, assess, and treat sexual addiction. *Sexual Addiction & Compulsivity, 16*(3), 190–209. doi:10.1080/10720160903202604

Hasin, D. S., O'Brien, C. P., Auriacombe, M., Borges, G. Bucholz, K., et al. (2014). DSM-5 criteria for substance use disorders: Recommendations and rationale. *American Journal of Psychiatry, 170*(8), 834–851.

IBM Corp. (Released 2013). *IBM SPSS Statistics for Windows*, Version 22.0. Armonk, NY: IBM, Corp.

International Institute for Trauma & Addiction Professionals. (2011). *About CSAT certification & training.* Retrieved from http://www.iitap.com/certification/csat-certification-and-training.

Jeong, E. J., & Kim, D. W. (2010). Social activities, self-efficacy, game attitudes, and game addiction. *Cyberpsychology, Behavior & Social Networking, 14*(4), 213–221. doi:10.1089/cyber.2009.0289

Johnson, R. B., & Onwuegbuzie, A. J. (2004). Mixed methods research: A research paradigm whose time has come. *Educational Researcher, 33*, 14–26. doi:10.1177/155889806298224

Kafka, M. P. (2010). Hypersexual disorder: A proposed diagnosis for *DSM-5* [Review]. *Archives of Sexual Behavior. 39*(2), 377–400. doi:10.1007/s10508–009-9574–7

Lemmens, J. S., Valkenburg, P. M., & Peter, J. (2010). Psychosocial causes and consequences of pathological gaming. *Computers in Human Behavior, 27*(1), 144–152. doi:10.1016/j.chb.2010.07.015

Moustakas, C. (1994). *Phenomenological research methods.* Thousand Oaks, CA: Sage.

National Council on Problem Gambling. (2015). *Gambling in the military.* Retrieved from http://www.ncpgambling.org/wp-content/uploads/2014/04/Military-Gambling-Fact-Sheet-Mar-2015.pdf

Nelson, J., Wilson, A., & Holman, L. (2015). Training students in counselor education programs in process addictions: A pilot study. In S. Southern & K. Hilton (Eds), *Annual Review of Addictions and Offender Counselors II* (pp. 65- 81). Eugene, OR: Recourse Publishing.

Onwuegbuzie, A. J., & Johnson, B. (2006). The validity issues in mixed research. *Research in Schools, 13*(1), 48–63.

Peng, W., & Liu, M. (2010). Online gaming dependency: A preliminary study in China. *Cyberpsychology, Behavior and Social Networking, 13*(3), 329–333. doi:10.1089/cyber.2009.0082

Petry, N.M. (2010). Pathological gambling and the DSM-V. *International Gambling Studies, 10*(2), 113–115. doi: 10.1080/1445979502010.501086

Petry, N. M., Blanco, C., Auriacombe, M., Borge, G., Buscholtz, K., et al., (2014). An overview of and rationale for changes proposed for pathological gambling in DSM-5. *Journal of Gambling Studies, 30*(2), 493–502.

Petry, N.M, & Blanco, C. (2012). National gambling experiences in the United States: Will history repeat itself? *Addiction, 108,* 1032–1037. doi: 10.1111/j.1360–0443.2012.03894.x

Reay, B., Attwood, N., & Gooder, C. (2013). Inventing sex: The short history of sex addiction. *Sexuality & Culture, 17*(1), 1–19. doi:10.1007/s12119-012-9136-3

Rehbein, F., Psych, G., Kleimann, M., Mediasci, G., & Mossle, T. (2010). Prevalence and risk factors of video game dependency in adolescence: Results of a German nationwide survey. *Cyberpsychology, Behavior and Social Networking, 13*(3), 269–277. doi:10.1089/cyber.2009.0227

Reilly, C., & Smith, N. (2013). *The evolution of pathological gambling in the DSM-5.* National Center for Responsible Gambling. Retrieved from http://www.ncrg.org/sites/ default/files/uploads/docs/white_papers/ncrg_wpdsm5_may2013.pdf.

Riemersma, J., & Sytsma, M. (2013). A new generation of sexual addiction. *Sexual Addiction & Compulsivity, 20*(4), 306–322. doi:10.1080/10720162.2013.843067

Samenow, C. P. (2013). SASH policy statement (revised): The future of problematic sexual behaviors/sexual addiction. *Sexual Addiction & Compulsivity, 20*(4), 255–258. doi:10.1080/10720162.2013.847752

Schaef, A. W. (1987). *When society becomes an addict.* New York, NY: Harper Collins.

Selzer, M. (1971). The Michigan Alcoholism Screening Test: The quest for a new diagnostic instrument. *American Journal of Psychiatry, 127*, 1653–1658. doi:10.1176/ajp.127.12.1653

Slecza, P., Braun, B., Piontek, D., Buhringer, G., & Kraus, L. (2015). DSM-5 criteria for gambling disorder: Underlying structure and applicability to specific groups of gamblers. *Journal of Behavioral Addictions, 4*(4), 226–235.

Smith, D. E. (2012). The process addictions and the new ASAM definition of addiction. *Journal of Psychoactive Drugs, 44*(1), 1–4. doi:10.1080/02791072.2012.662105

Subramaniam, M., Wang, P., Soh, P., Vaingankar, J.A., Chong, S.A., Browning, C.J., & Thomas, S.A. (2015). Prevalence and determinants of gambling disorder among older adults: A systematic review. *Addictive Behaviors, 41,* 199–209. doi:10.1016/j.addbeh.2014.10.007

Substance Abuse and Mental Health Services Administration. (2014). *Gambling problems: An introduction for behavioral health services providers.* HHS Publication No. SMA-14-4851. Retrieved from http://www.ncpgambling.org/samhsa-releases-gambling-addiction-an-introduction-for-behavioral-health-providers/

Sussman, S., Lisha, N., & Griffiths, M. (2011). Prevalence of the addictions: A problem of the majority or the minority. *Evaluations and the Health Professions, 34*(1), 3–56. doi:10.1177/0163278710380124 The International Association of Eating Disorders Professional Foundation. (2015). *Certification.* Retrieved from http://www.iaedp.com/certification/certification.htm.

United States Census Bureau. (2017). *Population clock.* Retrieved from http://www.census.gov/en.html

van Rooij, A. J., Schoenmakers, T. M., Vermulst, A. A., van den Eijnden, R. M., & Van De Mheen, D. (2011). Online video game addiction: Identification of addicted adolescent gamers. *Addiction, 106*(1), 205–212. doi:10.1111/j.1360-0443.2010.03104.x

Wilson, A., & Johnson, P. (2013). Counselors and process addiction: The blind spot in our field. *The Professional Counselor, 2*(1), 16–22.

Yen, C., Ko, C., Yen, J., Chang, Y., & Cheng, C. (2009). Multi-dimensional discriminative factors for Internet addiction among adolescents regarding gender and age. *Psychiatry & Clinical Neurosciences, 63*(3), 357–364. doi:10.1111/j.1440-1819.2009.01969.x

9

The Systematic Influence of Past and Current Traumas

Understanding Substance Use in Native American Adolescent Populations

KATHLEEN BROWN-RICE *and* ANDREW GERODIAS[8]

Introduction

Native American (NA) youth have continually been found to be at greater risk for anxiety, substance abuse, and depression than other racial groups (Dickerson & Johnson, 2012; Roberts, Spillane, Colby, & Jackson, 2017; Olson & Wahab, 2006). Suicide rates for NA adults and youth are higher than the national average, with suicide being the leading cause of death for NAs for all ages (CDC, 2015). For NA adolescents, suicides are more frequently alcohol-related than suicides in other adolescents (Olson & Wahab, 2006). Substantial disparity related to substance

8. Kathleen Brown-Rice, Department of Counselor Education, Sam Houston State University; Andrew Gerodias, Division of Counseling and Psychology in Education, University of South Dakota. Correspondence concerning this article should be addressed to Kathleen Brown-Rice, Department of Counselor Education, College of Education, Sam Houston State University, CEC130, 1932 Bobby K. Marks Drive, Huntsville, TX 77340. E-mail: kar084@shsu.edu.

abuse has been found between NAs and other ethnic groups when examining binge drinking and hard drug use (Akins, Lanfear, Cline, & Mosher, 2013). A recent extensive study of Midwestern and Canadian NA youth found that by age 13, approximately 35% had used marijuana, 47% had drunk alcohol, and 64% had smoked cigarettes in the past year (Sittner, 2016). Regrettably, no structured interventions have been developed to address the specific and diverse needs of NA adolescents in a culturally appropriate manner (Novins et al., 2012).

The theory of historical trauma has been established to explain the problems that persist in many NA communities (Brave Heart & Debruyn, 1998; Brown-Rice, 2013; Gone, 2009; Myhra, 2011). This theory postulates that historical events have resulted in historical losses (i.e., loss of culture, loss of people, loss of land, loss of family structure) that in turn created loss-associated symptoms (e.g., substance abuse, depression, anxiety, suicide, internalized oppression, loss of ethnic identity; Brown-Rice, 2013; Whitbeck, Adams, Hoyt, & Chen, 2004). Further, recent authors have suggested that persistent suffering by NA people may be related to ongoing traumas and stressors occurring in many NA communities—in addition to historical losses (Kirmayer, Gone, & Moses, 2014). Thus, examining current and past experiences of trauma is crucial to gaining a better understanding of the problems faced by NA youth and to developing or refining prevention and treatment strategies. The purpose of this article is to organize and examine the relevant literature on the prevalence of alcohol and other drug use in this population and analyze the influence of past and current traumas. Additionally, specific strategies to assist professional counselors in their clinical practice are identified. A case study is provided to demonstrate how to use this theory with an adolescent client.

Prevalence of Use

The NA adolescent population is highly heterogeneous. There are over 560 federally recognized tribal governments in the US (Bureau of Indian Affairs, 2015) and 617 First Nations communities in Canada (Indigenous and Northern Affairs Canada, 2015). Therefore, it is important not to make generalizations about this population (Gone, 2009). Acknowledging that within group differences exist, the impact of alcohol and other drug use has been identified as a critical issue for NA youth (SAMHSA 2010).

Commonly Abused Substances

The most commonly abused substances by individuals who identify as NA are tobacco and alcohol (Kropp et al., 2013; SAMHSA, 2010). A qualitative study found the use of tobacco is related to the community's tolerant attitudes toward smoking, generational use of cigarettes, and cigarettes being easily accessed through friends and family (Dennis & Momper, 2012). NA adolescents have also been found to use marijuana and OxyContin at significantly higher rates and engage in more binge drinking, relative to other racial/ethnic groups (Stanley, Harness, Swaim, & Beauvais, 2014).

Walls, Sittner, Hartshorn, and Whitbeck (2013) found that rates of problem drinking and monthly marijuana use increased across adolescence in NA youth, with the steadiest growth happening before age 15. In a study of marijuana use among 717 NA adolescents, Cheadle and Hartshorn (2012) found that users beginning from ages 11 to 13 were 6.5 times more likely to have a substance use problem than abstainers, with girls being found to be more at risk for early use. Similarly, O'Connell, Novins, Beals, Whitesell, and the AI-SUPERPFP Team (2011) found individuals who used alcohol before age 14 were more than twice as likely as those who initiated use at older ages to meet criteria for alcohol or marijuana use disorders. The odds of meeting diagnostic criteria of abuse were two to five times higher for participants who used both alcohol and marijuana than those who used only one substance. Further, marijuana use at an early age has been found to be a gateway drug to later alcohol abuse in NA youth (Whitesell et al., 2012).

Within Group Differences

There has been limited research regarding within group differences in this population. When looking at gender differences, a national study examined NA adolescent alcohol and other drug use to assess lifetime and 30-day use of alcohol, marijuana, inhalants, and methamphetamine; researchers found female use was equal to or greater than use by their male counterparts for all four substances (Miller, Stanley, & Beauvais, 2012). Variations have also been found related to sexual orientation. Balsam, Huang, Fieland, Simoni, and Walters (2004) compared substance use of heterosexual NAs and gay, lesbian, bisexual, or transgender (collectively referred to as two-spirit in NA culture) counterparts. It was found that the two-spirit NAs reported that a) they began drinking alcohol two years earlier (12.6 years), b) were more inclined to drink to manage mood and tension, and c) were more likely to use illicit drugs other than marijuana.

While the stereotype might be that NAs live on reservations, the fact is that 71% of NAs live in urban settings (US Census, 2011). De Ravello, Jones, Tulloch, Taylor, and Doshi (2014) performed a study across the US with students in 9th through 12th grades. Their analyses of two national surveys found that NA students were at a much higher risk than urban peers of other ethnicities for substance use and sexually risky behaviors. Dickerson et al. (2012) also identified that members of the NA population have been consistently at an elevated risk of possible substance abuse and addiction, and found that NA youth were consistently younger at age of first use —at an average of two years —compared to other ethnicities surveyed. The results of their analyses also found that NA individuals had more than twice the occurrences of injecting their drug over the last 30 days.

Past and Current Traumas

The literature on NA adolescent substance use is vast. However, little attention by researchers has been given to why these issues persist generation to generation. As Whitesell et al., (2007) so pointedly stated, "We know more about what disparities exist [in NA communities] than we do why they exist, and thus we are not well poised to design programs that will significantly reduce these disparities" (p. 279).

Historical Trauma

To explain this inequality, Brave Heart and Debruyn (1998) developed the concept of historical trauma. This theory argues that the current issues facing many NA communities are the result of "a legacy of chronic trauma and unresolved grief across generations" perpetrated on them by the European dominant culture (Brave Heart & DeBruyn, 1998, p. 60). At the core of this theory is the assertion that past trauma is conveyed to subsequent generations, resulting in an intergenerational cycle of trauma (Sotero, 2006). Specifically, NAs were subjected to traumas defined by specific historical losses that have resulted in ongoing historical loss-associated symptoms (Whitbeck et al., 2004). Historical losses are related to loss of people (e.g., to disease or genocide), loss of land (e.g., to treaties or confiscation), loss of family (e.g., to boarding schools, forced relocation, reservations), and loss of culture (i.e., through forced assimilation and laws forbidding practice of Native customs; Brave Heart & Debruyn, 1998).

Symptoms associated with historical trauma are categorized as psychological, social/environmental, and physiological distress (Brown-Rice, 2013). Psychological concerns relate to substance abuse, depression, anxiety, suicide, internalized oppression, and loss of ethnic identity (CDC, 2015; Chandler, Lalonde, Sokol, & Hallett, 2003). Societal/environmental concerns relate to child sexual abuse, domestic violence, geographic isolation, unemployment, and poverty (Denny, Holtzman, Goins, & Croft, 2005; US Census Bureau, 2012). Physiological concerns include heart disease, obesity, chronic liver disease, tuberculosis, and diabetes (CDC, 2015; IHS, 2009). To measure NA historical trauma, Whitbeck et al. (2004) developed the Historical Loss Scale and the Historical Loss Associated Symptoms Scale. These scales found adolescents reported continual thoughts related to historical loss (e.g., distrust of the intentions of the White culture, thoughts about the loss of culture and traditional language, thoughts about the impact of alcoholism on their community; Whitbeck, Walls, Johnson, Morrisseau, & McDougall, 2009).

Researchers have begun to investigate the relationship between historical trauma and substance use. Pokhrel and Herzog (2014) surveyed Native Hawaiian college students and found historical trauma was positively correlated with perceived discrimination. Moreover, perceived discrimination was positively correlated with participants' use of cigarettes. It has also been found that historical trauma symptoms are significantly correlated with NA adults past month alcohol use and lifetime use of non-marijuana illicit drugs (Wiechelt, Gryczynski, Johnson, & Caldwell, 2012). When looking specifically at NA adolescents and substance use, only one study was located. However, the findings were significant: NA youths self-reported historical trauma was found to be a risk factor for cigarette smoking (Soto, Baezconde-Garbanati, Schwartz, & Unger, 2015).

Cycle of Trauma

A history of systematic and forced colonization and discrimination has resulted in substantial, repeated traumas inflicted on multiple generations of NA people (Brave Heart, Chase, Elkins, & Altschul, 2011; Brown-Rice, 2013) and created a cycle of trauma in many NA communities (Evans-Campbell, 2008). This susceptibility to trauma is directly related to the marginalization of NA people and the internalized discrimination resulting from dominant White culture's racist policies toward this population (Brave Heart et al., 2011). Historical losses resulted in historical loss symptoms that created a systematic vulnerability to develop "layers of [interpersonal and intrapersonal] violence" in many NA communities (Willmon-Haque & Big Foot, 2008). In fact, one study found that 94% of NA youth reported having experienced a trauma (e.g., unexpected death, injury or assault, crime, witnessing trauma, natural disaster with loss, and sexual abuse; Ehlers, Gizer, Gilder, Ellingson, & Yehuda, 2013). Further, NA adolescents in substance abuse treatment were surveyed and it was found that these youth averaged 4.1-lifetime traumas, with threat of injury and witnessing injury being most common, and molestation and rape being least common (Deters, Novins, Fickenscher, & Beals, 2006). It was found that a diagnosis of stimulant abuse was significantly associated with meeting the criteria for posttraumatic stress disorder.

Unfortunately, for many NA communities, the historical traumas impact the functioning of families today. Adults who have been abused and neglected may in turn unintentionally enter into a cycle of violence with their own children (Walker, 1999). For many years, NA children were forcibly removed from their tribal communities to government and church-run boarding schools, where many were physically and sexually abused (Brave Heart & Debruyn, 1998). This practice resulted in the traditional NA family structure being severed (Cole, 2006), unhealthy parenting styles being formed (Brave Heart et al, 2011), and an unintentional generational cycle of violence and abuse being perpetrated on the current NA youth (Brown-Rice, 2013).

As noted above, the reasons why NA adolescent use and abuse substances are complex. The multifaceted "relationship between substance abuse and traumatic stress is often explained solely by the limited self-medicating hypothesis"; however, this "focuses on personality pathology" and negates the "sociopolitical and historical factors" (Myhra, 2011, p.

19). Thus, counselors and researchers need to develop and implement prevention and intervention strategies that address the unique needs of this population. In that, the high levels of substance use "is predicted by pervasive and enduring disadvantage rather than intrinsic ethnic characteristics" (Akins et al., 2013, p. 510).

Implications for Counselors

Compared to the overall population, NAs tend to underutilize mental health services, have higher no show and drop-out rates, and are less likely to respond to treatment (NAMI, 2003). Although substance abuse interventions have been implemented with this population, they are generally unsuccessful due to professional counselors not understanding the cultural uniqueness of NA people (Gone & Alcántara, 2007), lack of collaboration with local tribal members (Lane & Simmons, 2011), and lack of validation of past and current traumas inflicted on NA people by counselors who are members of the dominant European-American culture (Brown-Rice, 2013).

Social Suffering

Medical and behavior health clinicians cannot adequately address the substance use problems in many NA communities "without understanding not only social suffering but also how narratives about trauma and social suffering are constructed" (Goodkind et al., 2012). In this vein, counselors need to consider the effects of European American colonialism and its long-term impact on NA culture, identity, and spirituality (Gone & Alcántara, 2007), which has led to systematic discrimination and disparity. Strategies should integrate psychoeducation on historical trauma which include NA indigenous practices and the validation that discrimination and racism exist (Brown-Rice, 2013).

Evidence-based counseling interventions (i.e., cognitive-behavioral therapy, dialectical behavior therapy) that incorporated NA specific cultural and spiritual practices have been found to be effective (Beckstead, Lambert, DuBose, & Linehan, 2015; Novins et al., 2012; Patchell, Robbins, Lowe, & Hoke, 2015). Patchell et al. (2015), for example, found a Native Talking Circle Intervention based on tribal-specific beliefs and values was significantly effective in treating substance use among at-risk NA Plains tribal adolescents. The researchers compared the treatment condition of NA adolescents receiving culturally-specific prevention activities (10 weekly sessions conducted by a counselor and cultural expert) with the condition of NA adolescents obtaining standard prevention interventions (D.A.R.E. program conducted by a police officer for 10 weeks). It was found that substance use among youth in the cultural-based group significantly declined from baseline level, whereas substance use among adolescents in the standard group continued to increase post-intervention after 12 months (Lowe, Liang, Henson, & Riggs, 2016). Therefore, counselors should consider contacting local cultural experts to utilize clients' unique tribal practices while designing substance use treatment options.

Protective Factors

Another important consideration is for counselors to identify protective factors within this population. Scholars have hypothesized that NA cultural identity is a protective factor in preventing or treating substance abuse (Barlow et al., 2010; Dickerson & Johnson, 2012). However, Kropp et al. (2013) found that engaging in cultural practices was not correlated with substance use patterns or age of onset of use. The reasons for this discrepancy may be due to the researchers' lack of attention to participant cultural identity level. Counselors "must not make assumptions about a client's cultural identification" and should "assess which cultural contexts are relevant for the client" (Weaver & Brave Heart, 1999, p. 29). Another rationale for these unexpected results concerns internalized discrimination. Due to forced colonization processes on NAs, there can be a self-perception of shame attached to their cultural identity (Dell & Hopkins, 2011). Such shame can result in the client's belief that he/she is inferior and can potentially trigger initial or continual substance use. Thus, "[d]ecolonization must then play a significant role in the planned intervention so that the client can connect to their cultural identity in a positive manner and see their identity as a source of strength" (Dell & Hopkins, 2011, p. 111).

Social supports have also been found to be protective factors with NA adolescents. When peer, parent, and grandparent norms were investigated as protective factors for NA youth intentions to use substances, findings suggested that peer and grandparent norms were the strongest predictors of intentions to use substances (Martinez, Ayers, Kulis, & Brown, 2015). When NA adolescents' drug use after inpatient treatment was monitored, it was found that reductions in substance use post-treatment were associated with parental use of family management practices (in lieu of coercive tactics in response to problematic behavior) and engagement with NA traditional cultural practices in families (Boyd-Ball, Dishion, Myers, & Light, 2011).

Case Illustration

Naveh (pseudonym) identified as a 16-year-old NA female who is currently in the 10th grade. She shared that she is single but sexually active. She currently lives with her grandmother, Judy, along with two siblings (Lilly, 10; Ruby, 6). Naveh has lived with her grandmother for the past two years. She was taken from her mother's home due to her mother's substance use and criminal charges for distribution. Information from collateral sources indicated that the father's parental rights were taken away due to a child abuse charge seven years ago. Judy and Naveh are both enrolled members of a local tribe; however, they reside in a small rural town outside of the tribal reservation.

Naveh was referred for counseling services from the school due to slipping grades and reports of suicidal ideation. The only service available in this rural area is an outpatient counseling clinic. By the client report, she is experiencing anxiety associated with school experiences and depression due to missing her mother. She also reported using alcohol and marijuana. She uses almost every day and shared that, when she is smoking marijuana, she feels normal. She noted that she occasionally drinks alcohol. When asked about her suicidal ideations, she reported that she sees no future for herself and sometimes she thinks life would be easier if she just wouldn't wake up some days. Based on the intake, Naveh was assigned to the substance use counselor, Tracey. Tracey is a White, 30-year-old female.

Since this is the first NA client Tracey has been assigned, she chose to familiarize herself with the history of losses that have occurred to NA people. She sought to understand not just the past historical traumas but the discriminatory and oppressive environment that may be Naveh's current reality. Tracey decided in the first session to utilize the Whitbeck et al. (2004) Historical Loss Scale and the Historical Loss Associated Symptoms Scale to determine Naveh's level of historical trauma. Tracey also reviewed research indicating that higher NA identity clients may be unlikely to discuss the experience of emotional distress and substance use with counselors (Bird & Parslow, 2002; Fiske, Wetherell, & Gatz, 2009). Such decisions may be due to the belief that illness must be tolerated (Moss, 2005) or the belief that their substance use would negatively affect the family/community (Gallant, Spitze, & Grove, 2010). Tracey's additional research found that NA adolescents are most resilient when they are culturally and spiritually supported (Gray & Nye, 2001; Yoder et al., 2006) and more successful in recovery when involved in NA cultural-specific practices (Boyd-Ball et al., 2011). Further, traditional NA adolescents view themselves as holistic; in that, they do not separate the physical, emotional, spiritual, or mental self (Gone & Alcántara, 2007).

In view of this research, Tracey assessed Naveh's level of acculturation by utilizing the Native America Acculturation Scale (Garrett & Pichette, 2000). This 20-item self-report inventory can be used to differentiate those who identify themselves as NA and individuals who do not culturally identify as NA. Below is an excerpt from the first session that would be symbolic of introducing the above to the client:

Tracey: It can be difficult to talk to someone you don't know. In particular, to be able to trust me to share your story.

Naveh continues to look down.

Tracey: I can imagine it is more difficult because of me being White.

Naveh: I don't like White people.

Tracey: It seems that people that look like me have been unkind to you.

Naveh shakes her head in agreement.

Tracey: I am sorry for that.

Naveh: (looks up) You are the first White person to ever say sorry to me.

Tracey: Your people have had a tortured history in our community, which has led to a lot of pain and mistrust.

Naveh shakes her head in agreement.

Tracey: Have you ever heard of historical trauma?

Naveh shakes her head in the negative.

Tracey: Historical trauma is a theory that explains that past traumas are forced on Native American people by the dominant culture. For example, forced relocation to reservations, or boarding schools, have resulted in a legacy of pain for many Native people. Unfortunately, to deal with this pain many people will use alcohol, weed, or engage in other unhealthy behavior.

Naveh (speaking softly): So, people use weed to escape the pain.

Tracey: Do you use to escape the pain?

Naveh shakes her head in the affirmative.

Tracey: I would like us to work together to find a healthier path for you to soften your pain. Would you like that?

Naveh shakes her head in the affirmative.

Tracey: We can start by understanding more about where your pain is coming from. Would you be willing to answer a few questions?

Naveh shakes her head in the affirmative.

Tracey then introduced the Whitbeck et al. (2004) Historical Loss Scale and the Historical Loss Associated Symptoms Scale and utilized the Native America Acculturation Scale (Garrett & Pichette, 2000). Based upon the results of the Historical Loss Scale and the Historical Loss Associated Symptoms Scale, Naveh is having daily thoughts about the loss of her language, traditional spiritual ways, and how alcohol is negatively impacting her community. Tracey would utilize the literature on how traumas are transmitted across generations (see Brown-Rice, 2013) and explain this to Naveh. An understanding of how past traumas may impact present day can help the client recognize her own specific cultural triggers. A pattern of marginalizing Native people has resulted in many Native adolescents with feelings of being less than, not having a place in the "Whiteman's world," and loss of cultural identity. The results also suggest Naveh often feels sad, anxious, and uncomfortable around White people, shame about losses suffered by her people, and feelings of isolation. Given that Tracey is part of the White, dominant population, she would continue to validate Naveh's worldview in session and facilitate conversations with Naveh regarding the cross-cultural differences. It would be important for Tracey to be patient with Naveh and not assume her client is being resistant to treatment strategies. It takes time for a wounded soul to heal and for a client who has been historically marginalized to trust and open up to a clinician of the dominant culture.

The results of the Native America Acculturation Scale suggested Naveh has a strong NA cultural identity and lets Tracey know that her client may minimize her symptoms. Based on information gained from the intake session and results of the assessment, Tracey believed the most culturally competent way to approach working with Naveh involved integrating tribal-specific indigenous practices in her treatment plan. Tracey asked to meet with Naveh's grandmother to obtain her consent to bring in collaborative supports for Naveh. Specifically, Tracey asked Naveh and her grandmother where to reach out within the tribal organization to find a tribal healer. Working collaboratively with the family, Tracey contacted a tribal healer who agreed to be part of the treatment team. Tracey will also work collaboratively with Naveh's grandmother to assist the grandmother in developing family management techniques to aid Naveh's recovery. This will include parental monitoring to limit Naveh's unsupervised time and behavioral limit setting (Boyd-Ball et al., 2011).

Tracey will also work in session to assist Naveh in developing pride within herself and her cultural background. This will be accomplished through utilizing a holistic approach based upon The Medicine Wheel Model of Wellness, Balance, and Healing (The Medicine Wheel; Gray & Rose, 2012). The Medicine Wheel has been found to be an effective tool in working with NA adolescents and to assist in increasing the effectiveness of mainstream therapeutic interventions with this population (Big Foot & Schmidt, 2010). Figure 1 represents a Medicine Wheel that the first author created specific to NA adolescents. Assisting the client in understanding how historical trauma has impacted her people and her own self-efficacy, integrating her familial and community support systems, and the addition of cultural-specific strategies with mainstream substance use counseling will assist Naveh in her recovery.

Need for Future Research

Statistics indicate that a relatively high level of NA youth have mood disorders and substance use concerns (CDC, 2015; Dickerson & Johnson,

2012; Olson & Wahab, 2006). Given that NAs are underrepresented in research (Echo-Hawk, 2011), there is limited empirical examination of the correlation between the past and current experiences of trauma and substance use. While previous researchers have found that high levels of historical loss are significantly associated with NAs' use of alcohol and illicit drugs (Wiechelt et al., 2012), as well as anxiety/affective disorders and substance dependence (Ehlers et al., 2013), there is a lack of research specific to adolescents to determine effective treatment outcomes. Future researchers may investigate how interventions that incorporate indigenous practices, addressing past and current traumas to NA people, and mainstream substance use counseling are effective with NA adolescents. Given the cycle of trauma and high rates of co-morbid disorders in this population, it might also be beneficial to investigate incorporating traditional cultural practices with evidenced-based trauma treatments.

In general, however, future research needs to be conducted in ways in which NA people and communities are not marginalized (Goodkind et al., 2012). Thus, collaboration with NA communities is essential. This collaborative effort should include commitment to a long-term relationship with the community, cultural understanding, mutual respect and trust, and alignment in goals (Rajaram, Grimm, Giroux, Peck, & Ramos, 2014). We suggest that researchers reach out to tribal communities, practitioners, and clinics to ask their guidance regarding the areas where future research is needed. As there are so many within group differences in this population, the issues related to substance use and the types of substances being abused could vary greatly. Further, it is important that researchers not just focus on pathology but also protective and resiliency factors.

Conclusion

Youth and adolescents make up a large portion of the NA population, with one-third of this population being under age 18 compared to less than one-quarter of the White population (U.S. Census Bureau, 2012). These youths embody the hopes and dreams for the future of NA people (Goodkind et al., 2010). Past and current traumas have contributed to the substance use and abuse in NA adolescents. Thus, these factors must be acknowledged so that internalized beliefs and triggers can be moved to externalized, systematic factors. In particular, there is a need to recognize and heal past and current traumas (Weaver & Brave Heart, 1999). Once these traumas are validated, the focus can be on developing healthier behaviors and skills. NA youth can begin to embrace their heritage and see it as a source of strength. Specifically, professional counselors can foster the resiliency and strength that is inherent in these young people.

Figure 1. *The Medicine Wheel*

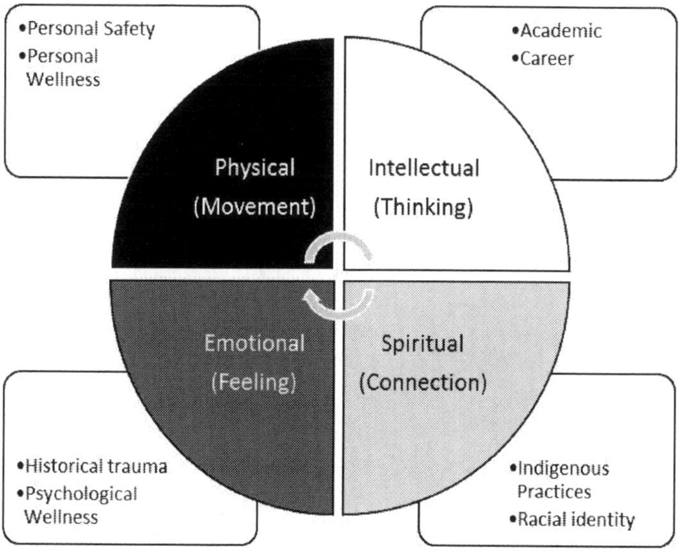

•Personal Safety
•Personal Wellness

•Academic
•Career

Physical (Movement)

Intellectual (Thinking)

Emotional (Feeling)

Spiritual (Connection)

•Historical trauma
•Psychological Wellness

•Indigenous Practices
•Racial identity

References

Akins, S., Lanfear, C., Cline, S., & Mosher, C. (2013). Patterns and correlates of adult American Indian substance use. *Journal of Drug Issues, 43*(4), 497–516.

Balsam, K. F., Huang, B., Fieland, K. C., Simoni, J. M., & Walters, K. L. (2004). Culture, trauma, and wellness: A comparison of heterosexual and lesbian, gay, bisexual, and two-spirit Native Americans. *Cultural Diversity and Ethnic Minority Psychology, 10*(3), 287–301. doi:10.1037/1099-9809.10.3.287

Barlow, A., Mullany, B. C., Neault, N., Davis, Y., Billy, T., Hastings, R., et al. (2010). Examining correlates of methamphetamine and other drug use in pregnant American Indian adolescents. *American Indian and Alaska Native Mental Health Research: The Journal of The National Center, 17*(1), 1–24.

Beckstead, D. J., Lambert, M. J., DuBose, A. P., & Linehan, M. (2015). Dialectical behavior therapy with American Indian/Alaska Native adolescents diagnosed with substance use disorders: Combining an evidence-based treatment with cultural, traditional, and spiritual beliefs. *Addictive Behaviors, 51*, 84–87. doi:10.1016/j.addbeh.2015.07.018

Big Foot, D. S., & Schmidt, S. R. (2010). Honoring children, mending the circle: cultural adaptation of trauma-focused cognitive-behavioral therapy for American Indian and Alaska Native children. *Journal of Clinical Psychology, 66*(8), 847–856.

Bird, M., & Parslow, R. (2002). Potential for community programs to prevent depression in older people. *The Medical Journal of Australia, 177*, S107-S110.

Boyd-Ball, A. J., Dishion, T. J., Myers, M. W., & Light, J. (2011). Predicting American Indian adolescent substance use trajectories following inpatient treatment. *Journal of Ethnicity in Substance Abuse, 10*(3), 181–201 21p. doi:10.1080/15332640.2011.600189

Brave Heart, M. Y. H., & DeBruyn, L. M. (1998). The American Indian holocaust: Healing historical unresolved grief. *American Indian and Alaska Native Mental Health Research, 8*(2), 60–82.

Brave Heart, M., Chase, J., Elkins, J., & Altschul, D. B. (2011). Historical trauma among indigenous peoples of the Americas: Concepts, research, and clinical considerations. *Journal of Psychoactive Drugs, 43*(4), 282–290. doi:10.1080/02791072.2011.628913

Brown-Rice, K. (2013). Examining the theoretical underpinnings of historical traumas among Native American. *The Professional Counselor: Research and Practice, 3*(3), 117–130, doi:10.15241/kbr.3.3.117

Bureau of Indian Affairs. (2015). *Who We Are.* Retrieved from http://www.bia.gov/WhoWeAre/index.htm

Centers for Disease Control and Prevention (CDC), Office of Minority Health & Health Equity. (2015). *American Indian & Alaska Native populations.* Retrieved from http://www.cdc.gov/nchs/fastats/american-indian-health.htm

Chandler, M. J., Lalonde, C. E., Sokol, B. W., & Hallett, D. (2003). Personal persistence, identity development, and suicide: Study of Native and non-Native North American adolescents. *Monographs of the Society for Research in Child Development, 68*(2), 1–130.

Cheadle, J. E., & Sittner Hartshorn, K. J. (2012). Marijuana use development over the course of adolescence among North American Indigenous youth. *Social Science Research, 41*(5), 1227–1240. doi:10.1016/j.ssresearch.2012.03.015

Cole, N. (2006). Trauma and the American Indian. In T. Witko (Ed.), *Mental health care for urban Indians: Clinical insights from Native practitioners* (pp. 115–130). Washington, DC: American Psychological Association.

Dell, D., & Hopkins, C. (2011). Residential volatile substance misuse treatment for Indigenous youth in Canada. *Substance Use & Misuse, 46*, 107–113.

Dennis, M. K., & Momper, S. L. (2012). "It's bad around here now": Tobacco, alcohol and other drug use among American Indians living on a rural reservation. *Journal of Ethnicity in Substance Abuse, 11*(2), 130–148. doi:10.1080/15332640.2012.675244

Denny, C. H., Holtzman, D., Goins, T., & Croft, J. B. (2005). Disparities in chronic disease risk factors and health status between American Indian/Alaska Native and White elders: Findings from a telephone survey, 2001 and 2002. *American Journal of Public Health, 95*, 825–827, doi:10.2105/AJPH.2004.043489

De Ravello, L., Jones, E. S., Tulloch, S., Taylor, M., & Doshi, S. (2014). Substance use and sexual risk behaviors among American Indian and Alaska Native high school students. *Journal of School Health, 84*(1), 25–32.

Deters, P. B., Novins, D. K., Fickenscher, A., & Beals, J. (2006). Trauma and posttraumatic stress disorder symptomatology: Patterns among American Indian adolescents in substance abuse treatment. *American Journal of Orthopsychiatry, 76*(3), 335–345. doi:10.1037/0002–9432.76.3.335

Dickerson, D. L., Fisher, D. G., Reynolds, G. L., Baig, S., Napper, L. E., & Anlin, M. D. (2012). Substance use patterns among high-risk American Indians/Alaska Natives in Los Angeles County. *The American Journal on Addiction, 21*(1), 445–452. doi:10.1111/j.1521–0391.2012.00258.x

Dickerson, D. L., & Johnson, C. L. (2012). Mental health and substance abuse characteristics among a clinical sample of urban American Indian/Alaska Native youths in a large California Metropolitan area: A descriptive study. *Community Mental Health Journal, 48*(1), 56–62. doi: 10.1007/s10597–010-9368–3

Echo-Hawk, H. (2011). Indigenous communities and evidence building. *Journal of Psychoactive Drugs, 43*(4), 269–275. doi:10.1080/02791072.2011.628920

Ehlers, C. L., Gizer, I. R., Gilder, D. A., Ellingson, J. M., & Yehuda, R. (2013). Measuring historical trauma in an American Indian community sample: Contributions of substance dependence, affective disorder, conduct disorder and PTSD. *Drug & Alcohol Dependence, 133*(1), 180–187. doi:10.1016/j.drugalcdep.2013.05.011

Evans-Campbell, T. (2008). Historical trauma in American Indian/Native Alaska communities: A multilevel framework for exploring impacts on individuals, families, and communities. *Journal of Interpersonal Violence, 23*(3), 316–338. doi: 10.1177/0886260507312290

Fiske, A., Wetherell, J., & Gatz, M. (2009). Depression in older adults. *Annual Review of Clinical Psychology, 5*, 363–389.

Gallant, M.P., Spitze, G., & Grove, J.G. (2010). Chronic illness self-care and the family lives of older adults: A synthetic review across four ethnic groups. *Journal of Cross-Cultural Gerontology, 25*(1), 21–43.

Garrett, M. T., & Pichette, E. F. (2000). Red as an apple: Native American acculturation and counseling with or without reservation. *Journal of Counseling & Development, 78*(1), 3–13. doi: 10.1002/j.1556–6676.2000.tb02554x

Gone, J. P. (2009). A community-based treatment for Native American historical trauma: Prospects for evidence-based practice. *Journal of Consulting & Clinical Psychology, 77*(4), 751–762. doi: 10.1037/a0015390

Gone, J. P., & Alcántara, C. (2007). Identifying effective mental health interventions for American Indians and Alaska Natives: A review of the literature. *Cultural Diversity and Ethnic Minority Psychology, 13*(4), 356–363, doi:10.1037/1099–9809.13.4.356

Goodkind, J., LaNoue, M., Lee, C., Freeland, L., & Freund, R. (2012). Feasibility, acceptability, and initial findings from a community-based cultural mental health intervention for American Indian youth and their families. *Journal of Community Psychology, 40*(4), 381–405.

Goodkind, J. R., Ross-Toledo, K., John, S., Hall, J. L., Ross, L., Freeland, L., & . . . Lee, C. (2010). Promoting healing and restoring trust: Policy recommendations for improving behavioral health care for American Indian/Alaska Native adolescents. *American Journal of Community Psychology, 46*(3/4), 386–394. doi: 10.1007/s10464–010-9347–4

Gray, N., & Nye, P. S. (2001). American Indian and Alaska Native substance abuse: Co-morbidity and cultural issues. *American Indian and Alaska Native Mental Health Research, 10*(2), 67–84.

Gray, J. S., & Rose, W. J. (2012). Cultural adaptation for therapy with American Indians and Alaska Natives. *Journal of Multicultural Counseling and Development, 40*(2), 82–92. doi:10.1002/j.2161-1912.2012.00008.x

Indian Health Services (IHS). (2009). *IHS fact sheets: Indian health disparities.* Retrieved from http://info.ihs.gov/Disparities.asp

Indigenous and Northern Affairs Canada. (2015). *First Nations.* Retrieved from https://www.aadnc-aandc.gc.ca/eng/1100100013791/1100100013795

Kirmayer, L. J., Gone, J. P., & Moses, J. (2014). Rethinking historical trauma. *Transcultural Psychiatry, 51*(3), 299–319. doi: 10.1177/1363461514536358

Kropp, F., Somoza, E., Lilleskov, M., Moccasin, M. G., Moore, M., Lewis, D., & ... Winhusen, T. (2013). Characteristics of Northern Plains American Indians seeking substance abuse treatment in an urban, non-tribal clinic: A descriptive study. *Community Mental Health Journal, 49*(6), 714–721. doi: 10.1007/s10597-012-9537-7

Lane, D. C., & Simmons, J. (2011). American Indian youth substance abuse: Community-driven interventions. *Mount Sinai Journal of Medicine, 78*(3), 362–372. doi:10.1002/msj.20262

Lowe, J., Liang, H., Henson, J., & Riggs, C. (2016). Preventing substance use among Native American early adolescents. *Journal of Community Psychology, 44*(8), 997–1010. doi:10.1002/jcop.21823

Martinez, M. J., Ayers, S. L., Kulis, S., & Brown, E. (2015). The relationship between peer, parent, and grandparent norms and intentions to use substances for urban American Indian youths. *Journal of Child & Adolescent Substance Abuse, 24*(4), 220–227. doi:10.1080/1067828X.2013.812529

Miller, K. A., Stanley, L. R., & Beauvais, F. (2012). Regional differences in drug use rates among American Indian youth. *Drug & Alcohol Dependence, 126*(1/2), 35–41. doi:10.1016/j.drugalcdep.2012.04.010

Moss, M. (2005). Tolerated illness concept and theory for chronically ill and elderly patients as exemplified in American Indians. *Journal of Cancer Education, 20*(1), 17–22.

Myhra, L. L. (2011). "It runs in the family": Intergenerational transmission of historical trauma among urban American Indians and Alaska Natives in culturally specific sobriety maintenance programs. *American Indian and Alaska Native Mental Health Research: The Journal of The National Center, 18*(2), 17–40.

National Alliance for the Mentally Ill. (2003). *American Indian and Alaskan Native Resource Manual.* Retrieved from http://www2.nami.org/Content/ContentGroups/Multicultural_Support1/CDResourceManual.pdf

Novins, D. K., Boyd, M. L., Brotherton, D. T., Fickenscher, A., Moore, L., & Spicer, P. (2012). Walking on: Celebrating the journeys of Native American adolescents with substance use problems on the winding road to healing. *Journal of Psychoactive Drugs, 44*(2), 153–159. doi:10.1080/02791072.2012.684628

O'Connell, J. M., Novins, D. K., Beals, J., Whitesell, N. R., Spicer, P., & The AI-SUPERPFP, T. (2011). The association between substance use disorders and early and combined use of alcohol and marijuana in two American Indian populations. *Journal of Substance Use, 16*(3), 213–229. doi:10.3109/14659891.2010.545857

Olson, L., & Wahab, S. (2006). American Indians and suicide: a neglected area of research. Trauma, *Violence & Abuse, 7*(1), 19–33 15p.

Patchell, B. A., Robbins, L. K., Lowe, J. A., & Hoke, M. M. (2015). The effect of a culturally tailored substance abuse prevention intervention with Plains Indian adolescents. *Journal of Cultural Diversity, 22*(1), 3–8.

Pokhrel, P., & Herzog, T. A. (2014). Historical trauma and substance use among Native Hawaiian college students. *American Journal of Health Behavior, 38*(3), 420–429 10p. doi:10.5993/AJHB.38.3.11

Rajaram, S. S., Grimm, B., Giroux, J., Peck, M., & Ramos, A. (2014). Partnering with American Indian communities in health using methods of strategic collaboration. *Progress in Community Health Partnerships: Research, Education, and Action, 8*(3), 387–395. doi:10.1353/cpr.2014.0036

Roberts, M. E., Spillane, N. S., Colby, S. M., & Jackson, K. M. (2017). Forecasting disparities with early substance-use milestones. *Journal of Child & Adolescent Substance Abuse, 26*(1), 56–59. doi:10.1080/1067828X.2016.1184601

Sittner, K. J. (2016). Trajectories of substance use: Onset and adverse outcomes among North American indigenous adolescents. *Journal of Research on Adolescence (Wiley-Blackwell), 26*(4), 830–844. doi:10.1111/jora.12233

Sotero, M. M. (2006). A conceptual model of historical trauma: implications for public health practice and research. *Journal of Health Disparities Research and Practice, 1*(1), 93–108.

Soto, C., Baezconde-Garbanati, L., Schwartz, S. J., & Unger, J. B. (2015). Stressful life events, ethnic identity, historical trauma, and participation in cultural activities: Associations with smoking behaviors among American Indian adolescents in California. *Addictive Behaviors, 50*, 64–69. doi:10.1016/j.addbeh.2015.06.005

Stanley, L. R., Harness, S. D., Swaim, R. C., & Beauvais, F. (2014). Rates of substance use of American Indian students in 8th, 10th, and 12th grades living on or near reservations: Update, 2009–2012. *Public Health Reports, 129*(2), 156–163.

Substance Abuse and Mental Health Services Administration. (SAMHSA; 2010). *Results from the 2009 National Survey on Drug Use and Health: Volume I. Summary of National Findings* (Office of Applied Studies, NSDUH Series H-38A, HHS Publication No. SMA 10–4586 Findings). Rockville, MD.

United States Census Bureau. (2011). *American Indian and Alaska Natives.* Retrieved from: http://www.census.gov/aian/census_2010/

Walker, M. (1999). The inter-generational transmission of trauma: The effects of abuse on their survivor's relationship with their children and on the children themselves. *European Journal of Psychotherapy, Counselling and Health, 2*(3), 281–296.

Walls, M., Sittner Hartshorn, K. J., & Whitbeck, L. B. (2013). North American indigenous adolescent substance use. *Addictive Behaviors, 38*(5), 2103–2109. doi:10.1016/j.addbeh.2013.01.004

Weaver, H. N., & Brave Heart, Y. H. (1999). Examining two facets of American Indian identity exposure to other cultures and the influences of historical trauma. *Journal of Human Behavior in the Social Environment, 2*, 19–33.

Whitbeck, L. B., Adams, G. W., Hoyt, D. R., & Chen, X. (2004). Conceptualizing and measuring historical trauma among American Indian people. *American Journal of Community Psychology, 33*(3–4), 119–130. doi:10.1023/B:AJCP.0000027000.77357.31

Whitbeck, L. B., Walls, M. L., Johnson, K. D., Morrisseau, A. D., & McDougall, C. M. (2009). Depressed affect and historical loss among North American Indigenous adolescents. *American Indian and Alaska Native Mental Health Research: The Journal of The National Center, 16*(3), 16–41.

Whitesell, N. R., Beals, J., Mitchell, C. M., Keane, E. M., Spicer, P., & Turner, R. J. (2007). The relationship of cumulative and proximal adversity to onset of substance dependence symptoms in two American Indian communities. *Drug and Alcohol Dependence, 91*(2–3), 279–288. doi:10.1016/j.drugalcdep.2007.06.008

Whitesell, N. R., Kaufman, C. E., Keane, E. M., Crow, C. B., Shangreau, C., & Mitchell, C. M. (2012). Patterns of substance use initiation among young adolescents in a northern plains American Indian tribe. *The American Journal of Drug and Alcohol Abuse, 38*(5), 383–388. doi:10.3109/00952990.2012.694525

Wiechelt, S. A., Gryczynski, J., Johnson, J. L., & Caldwell, D. (2012). Historical trauma among urban American Indians: Impact on substance abuse and family cohesion. *Journal of Loss & Trauma, 17*(4), 319–336. doi:10.1080/15325024.2011.616837

Willmon-Haque, S., & Big Foot, D. (2008). Violence and the effects of trauma on American Indian and Alaska Native populations. *Journal of Emotional Abuse, 8*(1/2), 51–66. doi: 10.1080/10926790801982410

Yoder, K. A., Whitbeck, L. B., Hoyt, D. R., & LaFromboise, T. (2006). Suicide ideation among American Indian youths. *Archives of Suicide Research, 10*(2), 177–190.

10

The Utility and Practical Aspects of the Cognitive Assessment System for Professionals Working with Young Offenders with LD and ADHD

From Theory to Practice

Louise Anderson-Pawlina *and* Denise Ledi[9]

Although young offenders (YOs) are a heterogeneous population, many experience comorbid difficulties including mental health, educational, psychosocial, and behavioral problems, as well as language and communication deficits (Games, Curran, & Porter, 2012; Gregory & Bryan, 2015; Snow & Powell, 2005), and cognitive/executive (CE) impairments (Fornells, 2015; Miura & Fuchigami, 2016; Ogilvie, Stewart, Chan, & Shum, 2011; Ross & Hoaken 2010; Starnes, 2013). CE denotes a collection of abilities that includes planning, organizing, inhibition, strategizing and thought flexibility, for instance (Kelly, 2015; Ross & Hoaken, 2010). For a significant number of YOs, these problems are exacerbated by diagnosed learning disabilities (LD) or, more often, previously uniden-

9. Louise Anderson-Pawlina, Alberta Health Services; Denise Ledi, Intensive Services Alberta Hospital Edmonton. Correspondence concerning this article should be addressed to Louise Anderson-Pawlina, Alberta Health Services, 43- 20120 - Twp 515, Beaver County AB T0B 4J1. E-mail: louise.anderson@albertahealthservices.ca

tified LD and/or attention deficit hyperactivity disorder (ADHD; Harpin & Young, 2012; Maniadaki & Kakouros, 2011; Rucklidge, McLean, & Bateup, 2013). While the majority of young people with LD/ADHD do not end up in the justice system, and not all YOs suffer from LD/ADHD, the results of numerous studies indicate a noteworthy overrepresentation of both groups in the young offender population, internationally as well as in North America (Snow, Sanger, Caire, Eadie & Dinslage, 2015; Young, Moss, Sedgwick, Fridman & Hodgkins, 2015).

Some factors that likely contribute to their disproportionately large numbers in the justice system include research findings that YOs with LD/ADHD begin offending at an earlier age (Mallett, 2014; Young & Thome, 2011; Zhang, Barrett, Katsiyannis, & Yoon, 2011); commit more serious crimes (Loucks, 2007; Young, 2010; Zhang et al., 2011) and more violent offenses (Evans, Clinkinbeard, & Simi, 2015; Harpin & Young, 2012; Young, 2010); have higher rates of recidivism (Ginsberg, Långström, Larsson, & Lichtenstein, 2013; Harpin & Young, 2012); and are more persistent offenders (Gregory & Bryan, 2015; Young & Goodwin, 2010). YOs involved in early and persistent delinquency and offending have also been identified as experiencing the most severe cognitive/executive impairments (Lansing et al., 2014; Moffitt, 2003) and language/communication deficits (Gregory & Bryan, 2015; Snow & Powell, 2011).

Unsurprisingly, based on the severity of comorbid deficits and impairments experienced by many of these YOs, their behaviors while in institutional settings consist of seemingly persistent misconduct (Harpin &Young, 2012; McDougall, Campbell, & Santor, 2013; Miller, 2014; Young, Misch, Collins, & Gudjonsson, 2011), including institutional disturbances (such as violent outbursts, involvement in critical incidences, and assaults on staff and other prisoners; Harpin & Young, 2012; Young et al., 2015). In addition, their survival time in the community is considerably shorter than YOs without disabilities (Mishna & Muskat, 2002; Zhang, et al., 2011). These YOs have also been documented as responsible for the majority of juvenile crimes although they account for only 5% or so of the overall YO population (Mulder, 2010; Skeem, Scott, & Mulvey, 2014; Steinberg, 2009).

Given the above finding, it is understandable that these YOs are seen as some of the most problematic, challenging, and expensive individuals in the correctional system (Ginsberg et al., 2013; Harpin & Young, 2012; Lansing et al., 2014). Best practice demands for these individuals that assessment and treatment are informed through the use of standardized instruments (Barton, Jarjoura, & Rosay, 2012). There is a growing consensus of the critical importance of assessing and treating LD and ADHD (Eme, 2008; Rucklidge et al., 2013), in addition to language, communication, literacy and cognitive/executive functioning (Caire, 2013; Colenutt & Toye, 2012; Lansing et al., 2014; Miura & Fuchigami, 2016; National Association for the Care and Rehabilitation of Offenders (NACRO), 2011; O'Cummings, Bardack, & Gonsoulin, 2011; Ross & Hoaken, 2010; Zhang et al., 2011) as essential factors of best practice and for reducing recidivism.

Laudable is the call for best practices to inform assessment and treatment needs and to identify individual strengths and weaknesses of YOs with LD/ADHD, language, and/or communication impairments, as a means of reducing recidivism and ensuring successful interventions. However, the results of the methods utilized to date have been less than adequate in view of the costs and challenges associated with incarcerating and/or treating YOs in the correctional system. Attesting to that fact is the continued overrepresentation of YOs with LD/ADHD in the juvenile justice (JJ) system (Mallett, 2014; Miller, 2014; Snow et al., 2015; Young et al., 2015). Moreover, the problematic behaviors and recidivism rates of this small subset of the YO population appear to have remained elevated and constant over time (Lambie & Randell, 2013; Thompson & Morris, 2013).

The purpose of this paper is to provide insight into how the Cognitive Assessment System (CAS), while adhering to the principles of best practice, can effectively assess the CE processes and functioning as well as the language skills of YOs with LD/ADHD. CAS is also designed to provide diagnoses. Although a diagnostic label such as LD or ADHD provides a list of observable symptoms that can be useful in many instances (Bishop, 2004), it does not appear to have been beneficial when working with these YOs. Findings indicate that YOs identified as experiencing the most severe cognitive/executive impairments and language and communication deficits are involved in early and persistent delinquency and offending, as are YOs with LD/AHDH. Therefore, it would seem sensible to focus on understanding the processes that drive behavior rather than continuing to respond to the symptoms, as frequently seems to occur with this population. In addition, LD and ADHD are often comorbid due to the interrelationship and overlap among these areas. As such, they are currently understood to be disorders resulting from language based impairments (Brown, 2013; Cortiella, & Horowitz, 2014; Forgan, & Richey, 2015; Helland, Lundervold, Heimann, & Posserud, 2014; Meltzer, 2011), rather than as a result of learning or behavioral impairments, per se.

Focusing on processes and skills rather than behavioral symptoms is essential with this population (Attention Deficit Disorder Association and its ADHD Correctional Health/Justice Work Group, 2014; Harpin & Young, 2012; Lansing et al., 2014; Meservey & Skowyra, 2015; Miller, 2014; Nakanishi, 2015; Pollastri, Epstein, Heath, & Ablon, 2013; Ross & Hoaken, 2010; Scott & Cooper, 2013; Snow et al., 2015; Sprague et al., 2013). Understanding these processes—including recognition of the fact that they are interdependent and that prior knowledge influences all current processing and output (a major theoretical tenet of the CAS)—is also crucial when dealing with these individuals.

This degree of detail and information is necessary to more fully understand how and why language and CE processes, their function, and the inherent skill sets they encompass, can have such an influence on the behavior YOs with disabilities. This knowledge is indispensable, especially for frontline staff, in providing adequate care for YOs who persist in their offending and to enable YOs to develop the adaptive skills needed to reduce their chronic maladaptive behaviors and perpetual recidivism.

Cognitive Assessment System

CAS is a contemporary, empirically and theoretically determined, norm-referenced neuropsychological test, which conforms to the principles of best practice, and can assess CE processes and functioning, as well as attention and information processing. CAS is based on the PASS theory (Planning, Attention, Simultaneous and Successive information processing), originally proposed by J. P. Das and built upon the earlier work of Soviet neuropsychologist, Alexander Luria (Das, 1999). "The four processes included in the PASS theory represent a fusion of cognitive and neuropsychological constructs such as executive functioning (Planning), selective attention (Attention), visual–spatial tasks (Simultaneous), and serial features of language and memory (Successive)" (Naglieri, Conway, & Goldstein, 2009, p. 786). More detailed information about the cognitive measures according to the PASS theory is outlined in Table 1.

Luria's (1966) research was instrumental in conceptualizing and documenting the connection between executive function and problem-solving (Aberson, 2014; Naglieri & Otero 2014; Purdy, 2014), a concept that can be assessed using the Planning scale of the CAS. According to Naglieri, and Goldstein (2011),

> the CAS is the only test that provides a measure of this neuopsychologically derived ability that is critical to all activities where the person has to determine how to solve a problem; the activities include self monitoring and impulse control and generation, evaluation, and execution of strategies. . . .That is, . . . difficulty with planning and anticipation, organization, development and use of organizational strategies, and self-regulation . . . can be assessed using the Planning scale of the CAS. (p. 152)

Luria's research also included the study of language within cognition. "With a variety of tasks he showed that communication of thought involves cognition, namely attention-arousal, motivation, planning, and processing of information. The study of language cannot, then, be accomplished independently. It must be tied to a theory of cognition" (Bournot-Trites, Jarman, & Das, 1995, p. 126). This is a concept that is increasingly being adopted in current research (Tomasello, 2014; Zlatev, Andrén, Johansson Falck, & Lundmark, 2009). According to Luria (1981), the development of human cognitive processes and consciousness is achievable as a result of the essential role of language. He believed that it is because of language that individuals are able to explore the fundamental nature of things, go beyond the limits of direct impression, manage their planned behavior, and make sense of intricate associations and relationships which are not readily available to direct perception. Luria held that language made possible complex forms of logic and thinking, the major types of individual creative rational intellectual activity.

The CAS measures multidimensional aspects of cognitive processing—psychological processes that are the basic blocks of intellectual functioning and activities (Naglieri, 1999). Planning (located in the prefrontal cortex) consists of programming, regulation, and verification of behaviors and functions under the supervision of the attention system. Attention (located in the brain stem regions) is considered a basic component of intelligent behavior involving allocation of resources and effort. Simultaneous and successive information processing (located in the occipital, temporal, and parietal lobes) are different methods of operating on incoming information. Together these "basic building blocks" form a hierarchical inter-related system of cognitive processes (Luria, 1973) that interact with an individual's base of knowledge and skills, and subsequently alter this base of knowledge (Naglieri & Das, 1997). Rooted in neuropsychology, two main tenets of the PASS theory of cognition are that "no part of the brain works by itself" (Das, 1999, p. 109), and that a knowledge base developed through both formal and informal learning underlies cognitive processing at any point in time.

The PASS theory of intelligence has been instrumental in redefining intelligence from a neuropsychological perspective (Naglieri & Otero, 2012). The PASS emphasizes basic cognitive processes from the perspectives of information processing, cognitive processing, neuropsychological functioning, psychometric theory, and development, providing a model for conceptualizing human intellectual activities (Dash & Dash, 2011; Keat & Ismail, 2011; Naglieri et al., 2009), rather than the general intelligence model (Naglieri, 2003), as assessed by the WISC for instance. "The CAS uses a theory-based view of cognitive processing that puts emphasis on basic psychological processes that are related to performance, rather than a general intelligence verbal/non-verbal IQ model" (Naglieri, 2003, p.6).

Traditional IQ tests measure general verbal and perceptual reasoning ability, with verbal abilities measured by questions "associated with general factual knowledge, vocabulary, memory, abstract thinking, social comprehension, and judgment" (Corrado & Freedman, 2011, p.7). As such, IQ tests do not appear to measure the cognitive deficits experienced by individuals with learning or attention disorders (Naglieri & Goldstein, 2011), or aspects of information or language processing. It appears that what traditional IQ tests measure are many of the verbal abilities that YOs with disabilities struggle with, which helps to explain why so many YOs are identified as having a low IQ. In actuality, individuals with LD/ADHD, including YOs, are known to typically have at least average, or even above average intelligence (Haubner, 2010; Schuck, & Crinella, 2005; Silverman, 2004; Thapar, Cooper, Eyre, & Langley, 2013), albeit with patterns of uneven abilities.

CAS subtests, on the other hand, do not require language knowledge such as vocabulary, or other verbal abilities making them more appropriate for children with a history of school difficulties, and for minorities with linguistically and culturally diverse backgrounds. The CAS assessment yields scale scores for the four cognitive processes, in addition to a Full Scale score (an index of an individual's cognitive functioning overall; Naglieri & Das, 1997). The assessment results of the four basic psychological processes can be used to better understand how individuals think, process information, determine their strengths and needs, and can subsequently be utilized to guide diagnosis, develop appropriate instruction, and design effective interventions (Naglieri, 2003) and treatment based on realistic expectations of success (Goldstein, & Naglieri, 2008). The Full Scale score is essential to qualify for disability funding. Although CAS has not been validated with the YO population, it has been used in school setting for many years. As well, "it has now been used in neuropsychological assessment contexts for both children and adults" (McCrea, 2009, p.59).

Detailed information regarding the CAS, including an overview, development, and standardization of the CAS, its reliability, validity, and fairness across minorities, use, applications, interpretation and implications for intervention, is available in the *Cognitive Assessment System Interpretive Handbook* (Naglieri & Das, 1997). Essentials of CAS Assessments (Naglieri, 1999) also provides an overview of the CAS, as well as a discussion of its strengths and weaknesses and clinical applications. Scoring and interpretation of CAS results can easily be accomplished with the "Rapid Score Software," a scoring and interpretive software that provides a written description of the results and suggested remediation (Naglieri & Goldstein, 2009). For more in-depth information on assessments of intelligence and cognition, see Sparrow and Davis (2000).

Language, Executive Functioning and Behavior

Understanding the connection between language CE functioning and CAS is essential to appreciate the utility and practical aspects of CAS. The relationship between language, cognitive/executive processes and functions and behavior is complex, multifaceted, ongoing and evolving, and certainly beyond the scope of this chapter. In addition, these concepts are viewed and defined somewhat differently by those involved in research, policy, or practice, for instance. In the interest of clarity, what is presented here is not meant to be definitive, or the best set of terms or categorical organization, but rather a brief and selective sampling of how these concepts and ideas interrelate and overlap to produce the outcomes presented. As such, the language and definitions offered are not meant to be all encompassing, but rather informative and based on the relationship and commonalities among these concepts. The basic information provided should facilitate a cursory understanding of the fundamental elements and possible mechanisms involved in this triad (language, CE processes/functions, and behavior).

Language is a remarkable endeavor that is readily acquired and occurs naturally and predictably for most individuals. As such, it is easily taken for granted, and the complexity of this phenomenon is routinely overlooked (Kryza, 2014). The main elements of language use germane to this discussion are receptive, expressive and pragmatic language skills. Receptive language refers to the ability to comprehend language "input" and includes an understanding of words and written language (verbal and visual input), vocabulary skills, an accurate interpreting of concepts and complex grammar, questions, directions, and non-verbal communication, for example. These skills begin to develop during a child's first year of life and consequently form the basis expressive language abilities. Expressive language skills refer to the effective use of language "output" and include one's ability to put thoughts into words, sentences, and paragraphs in a way that makes sense and is grammatically accurate, as well as effectively expressing emotions, wants and needs. Pragmatic language skills generally refer to the use of eye contact, facial expressions, gestures, tone of voice, and posture and form an essential part of social skills acquisition, along with paying attention, turn taking, appropriate responses in given situations, personal space, and gauging others' reactions to us—"those subtle, complex codes of conduct we apply, often subconsciously, in our interactions with others" (Reiff, 2000, p.1).

Receptive, expressive and pragmatic language skills form an essential part of how we communicate and therefore are influential in an individual's behavior and ability to form close and complex relationships (Cozolino, 2014). The necessary components of language relevant to the development and use of communication skills and to understanding the role of language in behavior are: information processing, cognitive/executive processes and functions, self-regulation and self-talk. Although these concepts and those in the previous paragraph are addressed separately for ease of understanding, in reality they are inseparable.

Information processing refers to how information is received through the senses, perceived, recognized, attended to, processed, classified and organized, associated, encoded and decoded, stored in memory, retrieved, and utilized or expressed (Cortiella & Horowitz, 2014; Massaro, 2014; Swanson, 1987; Verhoeven, & van Balkom, 2004). As such, information processing is a dynamic developmental process that is altered as a result of prior knowledge and experience (Bournot-Trites et al., 1995; Lansford, Malone, Dodge, Pettit, & Bates, 2010), which in turn influences all current processing and output (Bournot-Trites et al., 1995, p. 126). Put simply, input comes through the senses, and processing involves sorting, analysing, and interpreting all the input. Output is the action that occurs as a result (Bournot-Trites et al., 1995).

Information processing also "involves sub-aspects such as selective and nonselective attention, discrimination, [and] memory" (Verhoeven & van Balkom, 2004, p. 9). According to Gillam, Hoffman, Verhoeven, & van Balkom, (2004), there is a dynamic relationship between language and information processing, as "information processing is essential for language, and the development of more complex language increases the efficiency and capacity of information processing" (p. 155). Information processing then provides the necessary foundation for successful language attainment and proficiency to occur (Newport, 1990). As language continues to develop and evolve, it provides the necessary base for successful information processing efficiency and capacity to continue evolving, with each dependent on a dynamic relationship with the other.

Executive functioning (EF) is a neuropsychological term that refers to higher cognitive processes involved in the regulation of complex thought and self-directed goal-oriented behaviors, as well as emotions (Carlson & Beck, 2009; Ezrine, 2010; Ogilvie et al., 2011). Although these processes have been "linked to neural systems involving the prefrontal cortex" (Müller et al., 2009, p. 53), EF is better viewed as a group of "multifaceted, related but separate, set of cognitive abilities that are subserved by numerous neurological systems distributed throughout the brain" (Ogilvie et al., 2011, p. 1065).

EF, then, is best understood as a resulting in a functional outcome, rather than simply seen as a descriptive construct (Müller et al., 2009, p. 57). The function of EF is integration, not coordination of an individual's experiences and language (Meltzer, 2011). Unsurprisingly, language in general has been assigned a significant role in descriptions of EF development (Carlson & Beck, 2009; Müller, et al., 2009), as it is understood to serve "as a critical bridge of the divide between internal states or representations and overt behavior" (Carlson, & Beck, 2009, p. 164). Language ability has also been associated with attention regulation, delay of gratification, and self-regulation (Petersen et al., 2013; Winsler, Fernyhough, & Montero, 2009).

Self-regulation refers to a proactive process whereby individuals control or direct their own behavior, and inner processes, their thoughts, feelings, emotions, impulses, and motivation (Tzuriel & Trabelsi, 2014; Watson & Tharp, 2013; Winsler et al., 2009). Therefore, self-regulation is dynamic, adaptive, goal-oriented, and includes the capacity for flexibility, self-control and self-monitoring, self-modification, self-evaluation, and behavioral adaptation (Bridgett, Oddi, Laake, Murdock & Bachmann, 2013; Ezrine, 2010; Fahy, 2014; Singer & Bashir, 1999). A significant role has been attributed to language in the development of self-regulation (Ezrine, 2010; Winsler et al., 2009), especially as it pertains to problem solving and self-regulation of behavior (Fahy, 2014; Petersen, Bates, & Staples, 2015). As children's language and self-regulatory abilities develop, so does their ability to organize and plan more functional, detailed, purposeful, and intentional behaviors, as well as solutions to future tasks and operations (Winsler et al., 2009). In addition to language ability, the development of self-regulation skills is subject to the interplay of development, individual processes, environmental influences, one's own experiences (Ezrine, 2010; Singer & Bashir, 1999), and self-talk (Fahy, 2014; Winsler et al., 2009).

Self-talk, also known as private/inner speech, or self-directed speech, refers to overt speech not addressed to any particular individual, or silent internal verbal thought when one is in effect talking to oneself inside of his/her head (Carlson & Beck, 2009; Winsler et al., 2009). Self-talk, especially inner speech, is used as a tool for thinking, self-guidance, self-organization, planning, and therefore has an adaption role in the self-regulation of behavior (Carlson & Beck, 2009; Deniz, 2009; Fahy, 2014; Winsler et al., 2009). Adequate language is a factor in children's ability to utilize self-talk in the service of self-regulation (Ezrine, 2010; Petersen et al., 2015), because "it is the conscious use of language in self-directed speech that allows children to exercise control over their thoughts, actions, and emotions" (Müller et al., 2009, p. 57).

Recent empirical findings have provided further support for the association between language and behavior as both utilize the same awareness and interpretation of sensory input, and the temporal integration/

sequencing across time is essentially identical in the two (Fuster, 2008). Correlation analysis also confirmed the close relationship that exists between language (more so receptive vocabulary), knowledge of emotions, facial emotion recognition, and awareness of mixed emotions because of the common factor associated with language and emotional competencies (Beck, Kumschick, Eid, & Klann-Delius, 2012). Current findings also point to the synergy between language development, basic reading skills and literacy (Kamhi & Catts, 2012).

Children's language develops "via social interactions and functional communication" (Goorhuis-Brouwer, Coster, Nakken, & lutje Spelberg, 2004, p. 159) with their parents, other adults, and their peers (Allen & Kelly, 2015; Roskos, Tabors, & Lenhart, 2009). Language development, in essence, opens the door for the development of other CE processes, educational, and social abilities (Goldin-Meadow et al., 2014), and life-long adaptive functioning (Allen & Kelly, 2015; Edwards, Sheridan, & Knoche, 2008). However, some children struggle with specific language impairments (SLI) (speech, language and communication needs), which refers to children whose development is normal, with the exception of language development which is atypical for no apparent reason, and with no other handicapping condition that could explain this difficulty (Bishop, 2006). For children with SLI who do not receive adequate and actively mediated individual interventions (Siqueira & Gurgel-Giannetti, 2011), "regular education is virtually inaccessible" (Verhoeven, & van Balkom, 2004, p. 5).

This is understandable as these individuals would be unlikely to have developed language skills to the degree necessary to control their behavior, acquire basic reading skills, literacy, and social skills. These are all proficiencies essential to academic success. This can go a long way towards explaining why YOs with SLI experience ongoing difficulties with learning and performance in school, while involved with the JJ system, and with life in general (Bryan, Freer, & Furlong, 2007; Cortiella & Horowitz, 2014; Rucklidge et al., 2013). For the majority of YOs this can lead to chronic delinquency (NACRO, 2011; Sherwood, 2015; Snow & Powell, 2011; SCARC, 2014) and lifelong maladaptive functioning (Gonsoulin, Griller, & Rankin, 2015; Kamhi & Catts, 2012; O'Cummings et al., 2010).

Individuals with SLI are further disadvantaged because of a lack of an obvious reason for their difficulties, as they can produce sounds and their speech can be understood (Mountstephen, 2012; Norbury, Tomblin,

& Bishop, 2008), even if their overall language abilities are impaired. For this reason, SLI are often referred to as an "invisible" handicap (Cross, 2011; Helland et al., 2014; Karande & Kulkarni 2005; Mountstephen, 2012; Snow et al., 2015). According to Snow (2013), "language deficits are not only invisible, but tend to masquerade as low IQ, or as behavioural phenomena such as rudeness, disinterest or poor motivation" (p. 17), a view shared by other authors as well (Cross, 2011; Kvarfordt, Purcell, & Shannon, 2005; Pollastri et al., 2013). SLI are heterogeneous in nature, complex, and vary in degree and intensity (Bishop, 2004) as well as reasons for limitations. As such, SLI may involve any or all aspects of receptive, expressive and pragmatic skills.

However, initially all language depends on information processing for successful implementation. Evidence reviewed by Gillam et al. (2004) led them to conclude that a variety of factors could be responsible for inadequate information processing. Difficulties could be due to general limitations in information processing (Bishop, 2014). Processing difficulties could also occur at different stages, or to differing degrees (Bernstein & Waber, 2007). They could also be the result of difficulties with co-ordinating or proper allocation of attention and processing resources (Im-Bolter, Johnson, & Pascual-Leone, 2006; Tropper, Marton, Russo-Victorino, Shafer, Schwartz, 2008).

There is also considerable evidence that difficulties could be the result of impairments in processing certain types of information, or due to overdependence on one type of processing. This view is based on studies involving children with reading disabilities assessed by CAS and who performed satisfactorily on all subtests except for successive information processing. This finding is consistent with the idea that deficits in sequencing/successive information processing result in reading impairments (Naglieri et al., 2009). It would not be unheard of for individuals with successive processing deficits to rely greatly on simultaneous processing as a means of coping and adapting (Sword & Director, 2000). Information processing impairment at any stage, but especially at an early stage, would be debilitating and affect all subsequent processing, due to a lack of adequate input (Bernstein & Waber, 2007; Bishop, 2014). Although individuals with SLI process information, the manner in which it is processed is not as efficient or effective as individuals without language impairments.

Language is a developmental process and therefore all future learning is predicated on current and past learning. It is not difficult to understand, then, that children with information processing deficits, regardless of where or why the impairments occur, would incur cumulative deficits. Consequently, they would likely experience considerable difficulty developing the cognitive tools upon which to build adequate and adaptive language skills, which would impact their vocabulary learning, grammar, and subsequent reading ability (Bishop, 2014). This language cascade could have a deleterious effect "on the elaboration of higher-order executive and regulatory capacities" (Bernstein & Waber, 2007, p. 49). Learning development under these circumstances would likely be protracted and laborious, given the dynamic relationship between language, information processing, CE functioning, and regulatory capacities, including attention, memory and ability to categorize, as previously mentioned.

Deficits in receptive, expressive, and pragmatic language commonly overlap, and all have been linked to behavioral problems (Hollo, Wehby, & Oliver, 2014). However, as receptive language development begins in the first year of life and involves the ability to understand language input, it is likely to be the language ability most affected by information processing impairments and, therefore, to have a significant impact on expressive and pragmatic skills. Results reported by Conti-Ramsden, Mok, Pickles, and Durkin (2013), which are consistent with earlier findings, indicated that receptive language deficits were a significant predictor of struggle with hyperactivity, social and emotional difficulties, relationships and behavior problems. In addition, the more difficulty individuals had in understanding receptive language, the more likely they were to report having difficulties in these areas.

Other findings indicated that individuals with receptive language impairments were perceived as less likable by their peers (Hartas, 2011). According to Benner, Nelson, and Epstein (2002), these individuals are at a substantially higher risk for reading problems, and at higher risk for antisocial behavior. They were also rated as the most antisocial and depressed by parents, the most aggressive by teachers, and clearly showed more severe challenging behavior. Aggressive individuals also used less verbal communication and more direct physical actions to solve interpersonal problems. They were likely more prone to noncompliance due to receptive language impairments that undermine their ability to understand and comply with recurring cautions or verbal cues (p.48–49). The profile of young people with receptive language disorders appears remarkably similar to the description of YOs with LD/ADHD. As such, it is likely that many of these same impairments would undermine the ability of YO with LD/ADHD to understand or benefit from verbally mediated instructions, intervention, and therapies (Conti-Ramsden, et al., 2013; Cross, 2011; Helland, et al., 2014; Hollo et al., 2014; Lansing, et al., 2014; Snow, et al., 2015), an essential component in JJ rehabilitation efforts.

For instance, the profile of YOs with SLI will likely show various aspects of strengths in simultaneous information processing, as well as in areas of need in successive information processing as assessed by CAS. Generally, individuals with this profile are visual learners who see the big picture but experience significant difficulties with verbal concepts. They would likely be unable to tell the difference between "The lost man's wallet" and "The man who lost his wallet." Therefore, verbal interactions, instructions, and intervention would be difficult for YOs to benefit from and likely seriously disadvantage them, unless they were simple, direct, concrete, and involved behavioral support to ensure comprehension and follow through (AboutKidsHealth & TeachADHD, 2013; Williams, 2005).

In order to capitalize on the strengths of these YOs, utilizing various visual formats would be essential and greatly increase their chances of successful intervention. Being provided with opportunities to apply learning, skills and interests to personal and meaningful activities would be invaluable as motivation to learn for these young people (Armstrong, 2012; Barton et al., 2012; Willis, 2011). It would also be indispensable in helping them reframe a future for themselves, utilizing their strengths and skills to visualize a life where they can be useful, productive, and find success and acceptance. Seeing it from this perspective reinforces the fact that individuals with disabilities also have areas of strengths, talents, and abilities (Armstrong, 2012). For more information on strength-based practices, see also Barton et al. (2012).

Summary

The basic building blocks of the PASS theory form a hierarchical interrelated system of cognitive processes, where no part of the brain works by itself. The prefrontal cortex (CE functions) is not a separate entity, but rather dependent on input from the brainstem (attention), and the occipital, parietal, and temporal lobes (simultaneous and successive information processing), for successful functioning. These processes interact with an individual's base of knowledge and skills, and subsequently alter this base of knowledge, which developed through both formal and informal learning. The PASS theory also highlights the importance of studying cognition and language together because of their interdependence. This helps to make clear the fact that CE functioning is dependent on language to a much greater degree than it is on IQ or general intelligence, per se (Ezrine, 2010; Schuck & Crinella, 2005).

The CAS assesses CE processes and functioning, attention, and visual and verbal information processing, all necessary components of successful language acquisition, use, and adaptive behavior. The assessment results of these basic psychological processes can be used to better understand how individual thinks, processes information, determines their strengths and needs, and can subsequently be utilized to guide diagnosis, if need be, develop appropriate instruction, and design effective interventions and treatments that are based on strengths and needs and, as such, have a realistic expectation of success.

CAS is appropriate to assess the strengths and cognitive deficits of children with a history of academic difficulties, minorities, and individuals with learning or attention disorders, for instance. CAS is also helpful in explaining areas of strengths and needs in a non-threatening manner to both YOs and their parents, as they are often unaware of the connection between disabilities, language, and problematic behaviors (Smith, Esposito, & Gregg, 2002; The PACER Center, Inc. 2000). This can also be helpful in strengthening relationships between YOs and their parents, as well as various service providers. The information provided is theoretically driven, and the assessment results are at once useful and practical in application for professionals charged with meeting the needs of YOs with SLI disabilities.

There is little doubt that in addition to the information provided by the CAS, knowledge and in-depth training pertaining to YOs with SLI are necessary (Durcan Saunders, Gadsby, & Hazard, 2014; Gregory & Bryan, 2015; Hughes, Huw, Chitsabesan, Davies & Mounce, 2012; Williams, 2005). However, this will not be sufficient to elicit the changes that service providers require to meet the needs of the most challenging, demanding, and expensive YOs in the system. These YOs are, more often than not, perceived as incorrigible (Skeem et al., 2014; Williams, 2005) and "lacking in socialization, intellect and worth" (Emdin, 2016, p. 5). Perceptions (beliefs and attitudes) have a strong impact on expectations and actions. Consequently, perceptions either implicit or explicit exert a far greater influence on behavior than knowledge does.

Given the interplay between these variables, decision makers can have a significant impact on the interaction, supervision experiences, and interventions made available to YOs with disabilities (Detchon, 2006; PBS Learning Institute, 2014; Thomas, 2014; Williams, 2005). Receiving extensive training and education on the topic of SLI, the merits of a strength-based approach, and the power of perceptions, will be necessary in order for staff to respond to the maladaptive behavior of these YOs in a healthier and more successful manner. Training and education will also be necessary to eliminate what often amounts to coercive interactions between staff and these YOs (Sprague et al., 2013).

Conclusion

CAS provides a single comprehensive assessment instrument that identifies strengths and needs across various domains, including language and CE processes and functions. This information is essential in addressing the specific needs of individual YOs, while focusing on their strengths. These are needs that must be met in order for them to begin to realize their full potential. CAS also provides an alternate way of viewing the behaviors of these YOs from willful opposition to a lack of personal resources. Understanding the behaviors of YOs does not excuse what they have done but can be influential in how they are perceived and the interventions available to them.

While it is acknowledged that many variables other than language are involved in delinquent behaviors, and that certain aspects may not always be the initial cause of significant impairments, it is always a factor in the outcome (The Senate Community Affairs References Committee, 2014). Understanding the role of language in behavior provides invaluable information needed to assist YOs in acquiring the skills necessary to move beyond maladaptive behaviors and become more productive and socially able individuals, which is after all the goal of rehabilitation.

"There is now general agreement that so long as outdated policies and practices are in place that have been demonstrated to harm children and fail to produce public safety results, lasting change remain out of reach" (Nellis, 2015, p.2). We cannot continue to punish YOs with disabilities, especially when the system charged with their care and rehabilitation is in many ways unwittingly contributing to the ongoing financial and social cost of persistent recidivism and victimization (Allen & Kelly, 2015). The "costs of unsuccessful intervention are high in terms of human suffering and finance, we can and must do better in devising solutions to criminal justice problems" (Welsh & Harris, 2016, p. viii), especially as it pertains to YOs with disabilities.

Recommendations for Practice and Research

Although the following recommendations would be suitable for all YOs, starting where the need is the greatest seems sensible.

- The file of each individual YO should contain basic CAS assessment results (or equivalent assessment results), especially as it pertains to Simultaneous (visual) and Successive (auditory) information processing strengths and deficits. This is information that should be considered as essential as their rap sheet, medical needs, etc. This would hopefully ensure that the disabilities of persistent YOs were recognized and addressed from the start of their incarceration, if not identified earlier in their offending.
- Service providers should receive specific and intensive training in dealing with disabilities, related issues, adolescent development, and the influence of perceptions. They should also receive considerable supports in obtaining, maintaining, and updating competencies (Allen & Kelly, 2015; PBS Learning Institute, 2014).
- Based on ongoing policy and reforms aimed at ameliorating outcomes for YOs with disabilities and enhancing the implementation of evidence-based practices, researchers, policy makers, and administrators should be aware of the hurdle that service providers' perceptions can create. As such, they should regard both as possible contributors to the ongoing gap between research and practice, especially as it pertains to persisting YOs (PBS Learning Institute, 2014; Thomas, 2014).

- The JJ system should draw on research findings, expertise, and experience from other disciplines dealing with individuals with SLI disabilities, as a way of obtaining different perspectives and supportive methods of dealing with this population.
- A pilot project should be established to assess and monitor the utility of CAS with YOs with disabilities. Although its use has not been validated with this population, it has been used in neuropsychological assessment contexts for both children and adults.

Table 1.

Description of Cognitive Assessment Scales and Subtests (Naglieri & Das, 1997)

Planning Scale

Planning consists of programming, regulation, and verification of behaviors and functions under the supervision of the attention system. Planning processes provide control, and these processes utilized in conjunction with prior knowledge, intentionality, and self-regulation enable an individual to establish, decide upon, utilize, and assess the chosen response to a specific problem (ability to utilize feedback).

Subtests were designed to require a child to create a plan of action, apply the plan, verify that an action conforms to the original goal, and modify the plan as needed.

Matching Numbers is a four-page paper and pencil timed task, composed of eight rows of numbers with six numbers per row. The individual is asked to underline the two numbers in each row that are the same.

Purpose To measure a child's efficiency; also provides an overview of strategies used to complete the task.

Planned Codes is a timed task that contains two items, each with its own set of codes and particular arrangements of rows and columns. A legend at the top of each page shows a correspondence of letters to specific codes (for example, A, B, C, D to OX, XX, OO, XO, respectively). Individuals are asked to fill in the corresponding codes in the empty boxes beneath each letter.

Purpose The same as with the previous task.

Planned Connections contains eight items. The first six items require children to connect numbers in sequential order. The last two items require individuals to connect both numbers and letters in sequential order in an alternating manner (for example, 1-A-2-B-3-C).

Purpose The same as with the previous task, although this subtest is the best measure of efficiency.

Attention Scale

Attention is considered a basic component of intelligent behavior involving allocation of resources and effort. Attentional processes provide focus, and selective sustained ability, over time, to resist distraction when engaged in cognitive activities. Varying amounts of attention are required for successful solutions, depending on the complexity of the problems.

Subtests require the focus of cognitive activity, detection of a particular stimulus, and inhibition of responses to irrelevant competing stimuli.

Expressive Attention contains different versions for individuals age five to seven and those eight years of age and older. Older individuals are asked to read 40 words from a stimulus page. In the final item the words BLUE, YELLOW, GREEN, and RED are printed in a different color ink that the colors the words name. The individual is instructed to name the color ink the word is printed in, rather than to read the word.

Purpose To measure selectivity and ability to shift attention.

Number Detection contains a page of numbers and individuals are asked to underline specific numbers that appear at the top of the page. In each item a condition is set whereby children are required to find a particular stimulus on a page containing many distractors.

Purpose To measure selectivity, ability to shift attention, and resistance to distraction.

Receptive Attention is a paper and pencil subtest that contains different versions for individuals age five to seven and those eight years of age and older. Older individuals are presented with two conditions, one that utilizes a physical comparison and one that uses a lexical comparison. The letters are first matched according to physical similarities (t and t) and later on the basis of lexical similarity (t and T). Thus the individual is required to underline, row by row, all the pairs of letters (t,T; b,B; r,R; e,E; n,N; a,A) that are physically the same (for example T, or t, but not N t).

Purpose To measure selectivity, ability to shift attention, and resistance to distraction.

Simultaneous Processing Scale

Simultaneous processing is a means of operating on incoming information.

Simultaneous processing arranges incoming information into a holistic pattern, to be surveyed in its entirety, as a gestalt, and units can interrelate in different ways. Requires comprehension that (meaning is obtain based on all the information provided (e.g., the meaning of a paragraph is derived from the combined sentences included).

Subtests require the synthesis of separate elements into an interrelated group using both verbal and nonverbal content.

Nonverbal Matrices is a 33-item multiple choice task. Each item utilizes shapes and geometric elements that are interrelated through spatial or logical organization. Items are composed of a variety of formats including completion of geometric patterns, reasoning

by analogy, and spatial visualization. Children are required to decode the relationship among parts of an item and respond by choosing the best of six options.

Purpose To assess the individual's ability to appreciate the relationship among all components of the item.

Verbal-Spatial Relations is composed of 27 items that require the comprehension of logical and grammatical descriptions of spatial relationships. The subject is shown six illustrations and asked to point to the picture that shows, for example, "the ball in the basket on the table" or "the woman pointing to the ruler with a pencil."

Purpose To assess the ability to evaluate logical grammatical relationships.

Figure Memory is a 27-item paper-and-pencil subtest. The individual is shown a page that contains a two- or three-dimensional geometric figure for five seconds. The individual is presented with a response page that contains the original design that is embedded within the larger figure. In the copying version, a recognizable geometric design is reproduced by the individual.

Purpose To assess the individual's ability to accurately identify all portions of a figure simultaneously.

Successive Processing Scale

Successive processing is a means of operating on incoming information.

Successive processing consists of coding information in a discrete, serial order where the sequential presentation of a narrative drives the meaning and each part is only related to preceding parts (stimuli are only sequentially related). This involves both the perception of stimuli in sequence and the formation of sounds and movement in order.

Subtests require the individual to deal with information that is presented in a specific order and for which the order drives the meaning.

Word Series consists of nine single syllable words, e.g., Book, Car, Cow, Dog, Girl, Key, Man, Show, Wall. The subtest has 27 items that the examiner reads aloud to each individual. Each series ranges in length from two to nine words, read at a rate of one word per second. The individual is required to repeat the words in the same order as presented.

Purpose To assess an individual's ability to reproduce the entire word series in the order presented.

Sentence Repetition consists of 20 sentences that are read to an individual. Each sentence is composed of color words (for example, "The blue is yellowing"). The individual is required to repeat the sentence exactly as it was presented. Color words are utilized so that the sentences contain little meaning to help reduce the influence of simultaneous processing.

Purpose A measure of syntactic structure that is based on the serial relationship among the words.

Sentence Question is a 21-item subtest that uses the same type of sentence as those in Sentence Repetition. An individual is read a sentence and then asked a

question about the sentence. For example, the individual is read a sentence, "The blue is yellowing," and the individual is asked the following question: "Who is yellowing?" (The correct answer is "The blue.")

Purpose A measure of syntax comprehension that is based on the serial relationship among words.

References

Aberson, B. (2014). Building executive functioning in children through problem solving. In S. Goldstein, & J. A. Naglieri, (Eds.), *Handbook of executive functioning.* (pp. 509–521). New York, NY: Springer.

AboutKidsHealth & TeachADHD (2013). *Rethinking ADHD from a cognitive perspective.* Retrieved from http://www.teachadhd.ca/abcs-of-adhd/Pages/Rethinking-ADHD-from-a-Cognitive-Perspective.aspx

Allen, L., & Kelly, B. B. (Eds.). (2015). *Transforming the workforce for children birth through age 8: a unifying foundation.* Washington, DC: National Academies Press.

Armstrong, T. (2012). *Neurodiversity in the classroom: Strength-based strategies to help students with special needs succeed in school and life.* Alexandria, VA: ASCD.

Attention Deficit Disorder Association (ADDA) and Its ADHD Correctional Health/Justice Work Group (2014). Diagnosis and treatment of persons with attention deficit hyperactivity disorder within the jails and juvenile facilities of the United States criminal justice system: Why it matters: executive summary of an expert white paper. Retrieved from http://www.ncchc.org/other-resources

Barton, W. H., Jarjoura, G. R., & Rosay, A. B. (2012). Applying a developmental lens to juvenile reentry and reintegration. *Journal of Juvenile Justice, 1*(2), 95–112.

Beck, L., Kumschick, I. R., Eid, M., & Klann-Delius, G. (2012). Relationship between language competence and emotional competence in middle childhood. *Emotion, 12*(3), 503–516. doi: https://doi.org/10.1037/a0026320

Benner, G. J., Nelson, J. R., & Epstein, M. H. (2002). Language skills of children with EBD: A literature review. *Journal of Emotional and Behavioral Disorders, 10*(1), 43–56. doi: https://doi.org/10.1177/106342660201000105

Bernstein, J. H., & Waber, D. P. (2007). Executive capacities from a developmental perspective. In L. Meltzer, L.(Ed). *Executive function in education: From theory to practice*, p. 39–54. New York, NY: Guilford Publications.

Bishop, D. (2014). *Uncommon Understanding (Classic Edition): Development and disorders of language comprehension in children.* New York, NY: Psychology Press.

Bishop, D. V. (2006). What causes specific language impairment in children? *Current Directions in Psychological Science, 15*(5), 217–221. doi: https://doi.org/10.1111/j.1467-8721.2006.00439.x

Bishop, D. V. (2004). Specific language impairment: Diagnostic dilemmas. *Classification of developmental language disorders:* In L. Verhoeven, L & H. van Balkom, (Eds.). *Classification of developmental language disorders: Theoretical issues and clinical implications,* p. 309–326. Mahwah, New Jersey: Lawrence Erlbaum Associates Publishers.

Bournot-Trites, M., Jarman, R. F., & Das, J. P. (1995). Luria's language theory within a cognitive theory: A Canadian perspective. *Aphasiology,* 9(2), 123–135. doi: https://doi.org/10.1080/02687039508248699

Bridgett, D. J., Oddi, K. B., Laake, L. M., Murdock, K. W., & Bachmann, M. N. (2013). Integrating and differentiating aspects of self-regulation: Effortful control, executive functioning, and links to negative affectivity. *Emotion, 13*(1), 47. doi: https://doi.org/10.1037/a0029536

Brown, T. E. (2013). *A new understanding of ADHD in children and adults: Executive function impairments.* New York, NY: Routledge.

Bryan, K., & Gregory, J. (2013). Perceptions of staff on embedding speech and language therapy within a youth offending team. *Child Language Teaching and Therapy, 29*(3), 359–371. doi: https://doi.org/10.1177/0265659013482930

Bryan, K., Freer, J., & Furlong, C. (2007). Language and communication difficulties in juvenile offenders. *International Journal of Language & Communication Disorders,* 42(5), 505–520. doi: https://doi.org/10.1080/13682820601053977

Caire, L. (2013) *Speech pathology in youth (justice) custodial education project report,*Melbourne, AU: The Speech Pathology Association of Australia Limited.

Carlson, S. M., & Beck, D. M. (2009). Symbols as tools in the development of executive function. In A.Winsler, C. Fernyhough, & I. Montero (Eds.), *Private speech, executive functioning, and the development of verbal self-regulation* (pp. 163–175). New York, NY: Cambridge University Press.

Colenutt, A., & Toye, M. A. (2012). *Critical crossroads: youth, criminal justice and literacy: Discussion paper.* Retrieved from www.frontiercollege.ca/About-Us/Background-Research

Conti-Ramsden, G., Mok, P. L., Pickles, A., & Durkin, K. (2013). Adolescents with a history of specific language impairment (SLI): Strengths and difficulties in social, emotional and behavioral functioning. *Research in Developmental Disabilities,* 34(11), 4161–4169. doi: https://doi.org/10.1016/j.ridd.2013.08.043

Corrado, R., & Freedman, L. F. (2011). *Youth at-risk of serious and life-course offending: Risk profiles, trajectories and interventions.* National Crime Prevention Centre. Retrieved from: https://www.publicsafety.gc.ca/cnt/rsrcs/pblctns/lf-crs-ffndng/index-en.aspx

Cortiella, C., & Horowitz, S. H. (2014). *The state of learning disabilities: Facts, trends and emerging issues.* New York, NY: National Center for Learning Disabilities.

Cozolino, L. (2014). *The neuroscience of human relationships: attachment and the developing social brain.* New York, NY: WW Norton & Company

Cross, M. (2011). *Children with social, emotional and behavioural difficulties and communication problems: There is always a reason.* Philadelphia, PA: Jessica Kingsley Publishers.

Das, J. P. (1999). A neo-Lurian approach to assessment and remediation. *Neuropsychology Review,* 9(2), 107–116.

Dash, M., & Dash, U. N. (2011). Cognitive processing strategies in reading. *Journal of Education and Practice,* 2(4), 79–86.

Deniz, C. B. (2009). Early childhood teachers′ awareness beliefs and practices toward children′ s private speech. In A. Winsler, C. Fernyhough, & I. Montero, *Private speech, executive functioning, and the development of verbal self-regulation*, (pp. 236–246). New York, NY: Cambridge University Press.

Detchon, M. J. D. (2006). *Teacher Beliefs, Attitudes, and Expectations Towards Students with Attention Disorders in Three Schools in the United Kingdom's Independent School System*. Retrieved from: http://search.proquest.com/docview/304940735.

Durcan, G., Saunders, A., Gadsby, B., & Hazard, A. (2014). *The Bradley report five years on. An independent review of progress to date and priorities for further development*. London, UK: Centre for Mental Health.

Emdin, C. (2016). *For white folks who teach in the hood. . . and the rest of y'all too: Reality pedagogy and urban education*. Boston, MA: Beacon Press.

Edwards, C. P., Sheridan, S. M. D., & Knoche, L. (2008). Parent engagement and school readiness: Parent-child relationships in early learning. *Faculty Publications, Department of Child, Youth, and Family Studies*, 60. http://digitalcommons.unl.edu/famconfacpub/60

Eme, R. F. (2008). Attention-deficit/hyperactivity disorder and the juvenile justice system. *Journal of Forensic Psychology Practice*, *8*(2), 174–185.

Evans, M. K., Clinkinbeard, S. S., & Simi, P. (2015). Learning disabilities and delinquent behaviors among adolescents: A comparison of those with and without comorbidity. *Deviant Behavior*, *36*(3), 200–220. doi: https://doi.org/10.1080/01639625.2014.924361

Ezrine, G. A. (2010). Effects of language on the development of executive functions in preschool children. Atlanta, GA: *Counseling and Psychological Services Dissertations*. Paper 41.

Fahy, J. K. (2014). Language and executive functions: Self-talk for self-regulation. *Perspectives on Language Learning and Education*, *21*(2), 61–71. doi: https://doi.org/10.1044/lle21.2.61

Forgan, J., & Richey, M. A. (2015). *The Impulsive, Disorganized Child: Solutions for Parenting Kids with Executive Functioning Difficulties*. Waco, TX: Prufrock Press Inc

Fornells, A. (2015). Neurophysiological correlates of cognitive flexibility and feedback processing in violent juvenile offenders. *Brain Research*, *1610*, 98–109.

Fuster, J. M. (2008). *The prefrontal cortex* (4th ed.). Beijing *China: Elsevier*.

Games, F., Curran, A., & Porter, S. (2012). A small-scale pilot study into language difficulties in children who offend. *Educational Psychology in Practice*, *28*(2), 127–140. doi: https://doi.org/10.1080/02667363.2012.665355

Gillam, R. B., Hoffman, L. M., Verhoeven, L., & van Balkom, H. (2004). Information processing in children with specific language impairment. In L. Verhoeven, &H. van Balkom, H. (Eds.). *Classification of developmental language disorders: Theoretical issues and clinical implications*, p. 137–157. Mahwah, NJ: Lawrence Erlbaum Associates Publishers

Ginsberg, Y., Långström, N., Larsson, H., & Lichtenstein, P. (2013). ADHD and criminality: could treatment benefit prisoners with ADHD who are at higher risk of reoffending? *Expert Review of Neurotherapeutics*, *13*, 345–8

Goldin-Meadow, S., Levine, S. C., Hedges, L. V., Huttenlocher, J., Raudenbush, S. W., & Small, S. L. (2014). New evidence about language and cognitive development based on a longitudinal study: Hypotheses for intervention. *American Psychologist*, *69*(6), 588–599.

Goldstein, S., & Naglieri, J. A. (2008). The school neuropsychology of ADHD: Theory, assessment, and intervention. *Psychology in the Schools, 45*(9), 859–874.

Gonsoulin, S., Griller Clark, H., & Rankin, V. E. (2015). *Quality education services are critical for youth involved with the juvenile justice and child welfare systems.* Washington, DC: National Evaluation and Technical Assistance Center for Children and Youth Who Are Neglected, Delinquent, or At-Risk

Goorhuis-Brouwer, S., Coster, F., Nakken, H., & lutje Spelberg, H. (2004). Environmental factors in developmental language disorders. In Verhoeven, L., & van Balkom, H. (Eds.). *Classification of developmental language disorders: Theoretical issues and clinical implications,* p. 159–172. Mahwah, NJ: Lawrence Erlbaum Associates Publishers

Gregory, J., & Bryan, K. (2015). Speech and language therapy intervention with a group of persistent and prolific young offenders in a non-custodial setting with previously undiagnosed speech, language and communication difficulties. *International Journal of Language & Communication Disorders,* 1–14.

Harpin, V., & Young, S. (2012). The challenge of ADHD and youth offending. *Cutting Edge Psychiatry in Practice, 1,* 138–143.

Hartas, D. (2011). Children's language and behavioural, social and emotional difficulties and prosocial behaviour during the toddler years and at school entry. *British Journal of Special Education, 38*(2), 83–91.

Haubner, P. (2010). New poll reveals dangerous confusion about children with learning disabilities. Retrieved from: http://www.ldao.ca/new-poll-reveals-dangerous-confusion-about-children-with-learning-disabilities/

Helland, W. A., Helland, T., & Heimann, M. (2014). Language profiles and mental health problems in children with specific language impairment and children with ADHD. *Journal of Attention Disorders, 18*(3), 226–235.

Helland, W. A., Lundervold, A. J., Heimann, M., Posserud, M. B. (2014). Stable associations between behavioral problems and language impairments across childhood- the importance of pragmatic language problems. *Research in Developmental Disabilities, (35)*5, 943–951.

Hollo, A., Wehby, J. H., & Oliver, R. M. (2014). Unidentified language deficits in children withemotional and behavioral disorders: a meta-analysis. *Exceptional Children, 80*(2), 169–186.

Hughes, N., Huw, W., Chitsabesan, P., Davies, R., Mounce, L. (2012). *Nobody Made the Connection: The Prevalence of Neurodisability in Young People Who Offend.* Retrieved from: http://www.childrenscommissioner.gov.uk/publications/nobody-made-connection-prevalence-neurodisability-young-people-who-offend

Im-Bolter, N., Johnson, J., & Pascual-Leone, J. (2006). Processing limitations in children with specific language impairment: The role of executive function. *Child Development, 77*(6), 1822–1841.

Kamhi, A. G., & Catts, H. W. (2013). *Language and Reading Disabilities: Pearson New International Edition.* New York, NY: Pearson Higher Ed.

Karande S, Kulkarni M. (2005). Specific learning disability: the invisible handicap. *Indian Pediatrics, 42,* 315–9.

Keat, O. B. & Ismail, K.H. (2011). PASS cognitive processing: Comparison between normal readers and children with reading difficulties. *International Journal of Humanities and Social Science, 1,* 53–60.

Kelly, W. R. (2015). *Criminal Justice at the Crossroads: Transforming Crime and Punishment.* New York, NY: Columbia University Press.

Kryza, K. (2014). Practical strategies for developing executive functioning skills for all learners in the differentiated classroom. In Goldstein, S., & Naglieri, J. A. (Eds.), (pp. 523–554). New York, NY: Springer.

Kvarfordt, C. L., Purcell, P., & Shannon, P. (2005). Youth with learning disabilities in the juvenile justice system: A training needs assessment of detention and court services personnel. *Child and Youth Care Forum, 34(1),* 27–42. doi: https://doi.org/10.1007/s10566-004-0880-x

Lambie, I., & Randell, I. (2013). The impact of incarceration on juvenile offenders. *Clinical Psychology Review, 33*(3), 448–459. doi: https://doi.org/10.1016/j.cpr.2013.01.007

Lansford, J. E., Malone, P. S., Dodge, K. A., Pettit, G. S., & Bates, J. E. (2010). Developmental cascades of peer rejection, social information processing biases, and aggression during middle childhood. *Development and psychopathology, 22*(03), 593–602.

Lansing, A. E., Washburn, J. J., Abram, K. M., Thomas, U. C., Welty, L. J., & Teplin, L. A. (2014). Cognitive and academic functioning of juvenile detainees implications for correctional populations and public health. *Journal of Correctional Health Care, 20*(1), 18–30. doi: https://doi.org/10.1177/1078345813505450

Larson, K. A., & Turner, K. D. (2002). Best practices for serving court involved youth with learning, attention and behavioral disabilities. *Center for Effective Collaboration and Practice, American Institutes for Research, 19,* 1–54.

Loucks, N. (2006) *No one knows: Offenders with learning difficulties and learning disabilities. review of prevalence and associated needs.* London, England: Prison Reform Trust.

Luria, A. R. (1966). *Human brain and psychological processes.* New York, NY: Harper & Row.

Luria, A. R. (1973). *The working brain: An introduction to neuropsychology.* New York, NY: Basic Books.

Luria, A. R. (1981). *Language and cognition.* New York, NY: Wiley.

Mallett, C. A. (2014). The "learning disabilities to juvenile detention" pipeline: a case study. *Children & Schools.* doi: 10.1093/cs/cdu010

Maniadaki, K., & Kakouros, E. (2011). Attention problems and learning disabilities in young offenders in detention in Greece. *Psychology,* 2(1), 53–59.

Massaro, D. W. (Ed.). (2014). *Understanding language: An information-processing analysis of speech perception, reading, and psycholinguistics.* New York, NY: Academic Press.

McCrea, S. M. (2009). A review and empirical study of the composite scales of the Das-Naglieri cognitive assessment system. *Psychology Research and Behavior Management,* 2, 59–79. doi: https://doi.org/10.2147/prbm.s5074

McDougall, A., Campbell, M. A., & Santor, D. A. (2013). Institutional offense patterns in adolescent offenders the role of antisocial and mental health indicators. *Youth Violence and Juvenile Justice, 11*(2), 99–114. doi: https://doi.org/10.1177/1541204012457960

Meltzer, L. (Ed.). (2011). *Executive function in education: From theory to practice.* New York, NY: Guilford Press

Meservey, F., & Skowyra, L. K. R. (2015). *Caring for Youth with Mental Health Needs in the Juvenile Justice System: Improving Knowledge and Skills.* Retrieved from http://www.ncmhjj.com/resources/caring-youth-mental-health-needs-juvenile-justice-system-improving-knowledge-skills/

Miller, L. (2014). Juvenile crime and juvenile justice: Patterns, models, and implications for clinical and legal practice. *Aggression and Violent Behavior, 19*(2), 122–137. doi: https://doi.org/10.1016/j.avb.2014.01.005

Mishna, F., & Muskat, B. (2002). Social group work for young offenders with learning disabilities. *Social Work with Groups, 24*(3–4), 11–31 doi: https://doi.org/10.1300/j009v24n03_03

Miura, H., & Fuchigami, Y. (2016). Impaired executive function in 14-to 16-year-old boys with conduct disorders is related to recidivism: A prospective longitudinal study. *Criminal Behavior and Mental Health*. Retrieved from: (wileyonlinelibrary.com). doi: 10.1002/cbm.193

Moffitt, T. E. (2003). Life-course-persistent and adolescence-limited antisocial behavior: a 10-year research review and a research agenda. In B. B. Lahey, T. E. Moffitt, & A. Caspi, (2003). *Causes of conduct disorder and juvenile delinquency,* (pp.49–75). New York, NY: Guilford Press.

Mountstephen, M. (2012). *Meeting special needs: A practical guide to support children with speech, language and communication needs (SLCN).* London, England: Practical Pre-School Books

Mulder, E. (2010). *Unraveling serious juvenile delinquency: Risk and needs assessment by classification into subgroups.* Doctoral dissertation, Erasmus MC: University Medical Center Rotterdam.

Müller, U., Jacques, S., Brocki, K., & Zelazo, P. D. (2009). The executive functions of language on preschool children. In A. Winsler, C. Fernyhough, C., & I. Montero (Eds,), *Private speech, executive functioning, and the development of verbal self-regulation* (pp. 53–68). New York, NY: Cambridge University Press.

National Association for the Care and Rehabilitation of Offenders (NACRO). (2011). *Speech, language and communication difficulties: young people in trouble with the law.* London, England: NACRO.

Naglieri, J. A. (1999). *Essentials of CAS assessment*, (Vol. 2). New York, NY: John Wiley & Sons.

Naglieri, J.A., Conway, C., & Goldstein, S. (2009). Using the Planning, attention, Simultaneous, Successive (PASS) Theory. In C. R. Reynolds, & E. Fletcher-Janzen, (Eds.). *Handbook of clinical child neuropsychology, (783–800).* New York, NY: Springer. Retrieved from: http://link.springer.com

Naglieri, J.A., & Das, J. P., (1997). *Cognitive assessment system interpretive handbook.* Itasca, IL: Riverside.

Naglieri, J. A., & Goldstein, S. (2011). *Assessment of cognitive and neuropsychological processes. Understanding and managing learning disabilities and ADHD in late adolescence and adulthood (2nd ed.).* New York, NY: Wiley.

Naglieri, J. A., & Otero, T. M. (2014). The Assessment of Executive Function Using the Cognitive Assessment System. In S. Goldstein, & J. A. Naglieri (Eds.), *Handbook of executive functioning* (pp. 191–208). New York, NY: Springer.

Naglieri, J. A. (2003). Current advances in assessment and intervention for children with learning disabilities. *Advances in Learning and Behavioral Disabilities, 16*, 163–190. doi: https://doi.org/10.1016/s0735–004x(03)16005–3

Naglieri, J. A., & Otero, T. M. (2012). The cognitive assessment system: From theory to practice. In D. P. Flanagan & P. L. Harrison (Eds.), *Contemporary intellectual assessment: Theories, tests, and issues* (pp. 376–399). New York, NY: Guilford.

Naglieri, J. A., & Goldstein, S. (2009). Understanding the strengths and weaknesses of intelligence and achievement tests. In J. Naglieri & S. Goldstein (Eds.), *Practitioner's guide to assessing intelligence and achievement* (pp. 3–10). Hoboken, NJ: Wiley.

Nakanishi, K. (2015). *Reintegrative education for students in conflict with the law* (Doctoral dissertation, University of Toronto).

National Association for the Care and Rehabilitation of Offenders (NACRO). (2011). *Speech, language and communication difficulties: Young people in trouble with the law.* London, England: NACRO.

Nellis, A. (2015). *A Return to justice: Rethinking our approach to juveniles in the system.* Lanham, MD: Rowman & Littlefield.

Newport, E. L. (1990). Maturational constraints on language learning. *Cognitive Science, 14*(1), 11–28.

Norbury, C. F. (2014). Practitioner review: Social (pragmatic) communication disorder conceptualization, evidence and clinical implications. *Journal of Child Psychology and Psychiatry, 55*(3), 204–216. doi: https://doi.org/10.1111/jcpp.12154

O'Cummings, M., Bardack, S., & Gonsoulin, S. (2010). *Issue brief: The importance of literacy for youth involved in the juvenile justice system.* Washington, DC: The National Evaluation and Technical Assistance Center for the Education of Children and Youth Who Are Neglected, Delinquent, or At Risk NDTAC). Available online: http://www. *neglecteddelinquent. org/nd/docs/literacy_brief_20100120*

Ogilvie, J. M., Stewart, A. L., Chan, R. C., & Shum, D. H. (2011). Neuropsychological measures of executive function and antisocial behavior: A meta-analysis. *Criminology, 49*(4), 1063–1107. doi: https://doi.org/10.1111/j.1745-9125.2011.00252.x

PBS Learning Institute, (2014). Performance-based standards: staff perceptions. Retrieved from pbstandards.org/cjcaresources/158/StaffPerceptions_2014.pdf

Petersen, I. T., Bates, J. E., & Staples, A. D. (2015). The role of language ability and self-regulation in the development of inattentive-hyperactive behavior problems. *Development and Psychopathology, 27*(1), 221–237. doi: https://doi.org/10.1017/s0954579414000698

Petersen, I. T., Bates, J. E., D'Onofrio, B. M., Coyne, C. A., Lansford, J. E., Dodge, K. A., Pettit, G.S., & Van Hulle, C. A. (2013). Language ability predicts the development of behavior problems in children. *Journal of Abnormal Psychology, 122*(2), 542.

Pollastri, A. R., Epstein, L. D., Heath, G. H., & Ablon, J. S. (2013). The collaborative problem-solving approach: Outcomes across settings. *Harvard Review of Psychiatry, 21*(4), 188–199.

Purdy, M. H. (2014). Executive functions: Theory, assessment, and treatment. In L. M. Kimbarow, *Cognitive Communication Disorders*, 77–93 San Diego, CA: Plural Publishing.

Reiff, H. B. (2000). Social skills and adults with learning disabilities. *Linkages, 2*(2), 1–3.

Roskos, K. A., Tabors, P. O., & Lenhart, L. A. (2009). *Oral Language and early literacy in preschool: Talking, reading, and writing (2nd ed.).* Newark, NJ: International Reading Association Inc.

Ross, E. H., & Hoaken, P. N. (2010). Correctional remediation meets neuropsychological rehabilitation: How brain injury and schizophrenia research can improve offender programming. *Criminal Justice and Behavior, 37*(6), 656–677. doi: https://doi.org/10.1177/0093854810363104

Rucklidge, J. J., McLean, A. P., & Bateup, P. (2013). Criminal offending and learning disabilities in New Zealand youth does reading comprehension predict recidivism? *Crime & Delinquency*, *59*(8), 1263–1286. doi: https://doi.org/10.1177/0011128709336945

The Senate Community Affairs References Committee. (2014). *Prevalence of different types of speech, language and communication disorders and speech pathology services in Australia*. Retrieved from: www.aph.gov.au/Parliamentary_Business/Committees/. . ./Speech_Pathology/Report

Schuck, S. E., & Crinella, F. M. (2005). Why children with ADHD do not have low IQs. *Journal of Learning Disabilities*, *38*(3), 262–280. doi: https://doi.org/10.1177/00222194050380030701

Scott, T. M., & Cooper, J. (2013). Tertiary-tier PBIS in alternative, residential and correctional school settings: Considering intensity in the delivery of evidence-based practice. *Education and Treatment of Children*, *36*(3), 101–119. doi: https://doi.org/10.1353/etc.2013.0029

Sherwood, K. N. (2015). *stuck in detention–the connection between disengaging from school and youth offending in New Zealand*. Retrieved from www.otago.ac.nz/law/research/journals/otago451226.pdf

Silverman, L. K. (2004). At-risk youth and the creative process. In *ARTernatives for At-Risk Youth Conference, May* (14). Retrieved from http://giftedhomeschoolers.org/resources/parent-and-professional-resources/articles/issues-in-gifted-education/at-risk-youth-and-the-creative-process/

Singer, B. D., & Bashir, A. S. (1999). What are executive functions and self-regulation and what do they have to do with language-learning disorders? *Language, Speech, and Hearing Services in Schools*, *30*(3), 265–273. doi: https://doi.org/10.1044/0161-1461.3003.265

Siqueira, C. M., & Gurgel-Giannetti, J. (2011). Poor school performance: an updated review. *Revista da Associação Médica Brasileira*, *57*(1), 78–87 doi: https://doi.org/10.1016/s0104-4230(11)70021-5

Skeem, J. L., Scott, E. S., & Mulvey, E. P. (2014). Justice policy reform for high-risk juveniles: Using science to achieve large-scale crime reduction. *Annual Review of Clinical Psychology*, *10*, 709–739. doi: https://doi.org/10.2139/ssrn.2386959

Smith, C., Esposito, J., & Gregg, S. (2002). *Advocating for children with behavioral and cognitive disabilities in the juvenile justice system*. Retrieved from www.edjj.org/Publications/AdvocatingChildren.pdf

Snow, P. C., & Powell, M. B. (2011). Oral language competence in incarcerated young offenders: Links with offending severity. *International Journal of Speech-Language Pathology*, *13*(6), 480–489.

Snow P C, and Powell M B. (2005) What's the story? An exploration of narrative language abilities in male juvenile offenders. *Psychology, Crime and Law*, 11, 239–253

Snow, P. (2013). Language competence: a hidden disability in antisocial behaviour. *InPsych: The Bulletin of the Australian Psychological Society Ltd*, *35*(3), 16.

Snow, P. C., Sanger, D. D., Caire, L. M., Eadie, P. A., & Dinslage, T. (2015). Improving communication outcomes for young offenders: a proposed response to intervention framework. *International Journal of Language & Communication Disorders*, *50*(1), 1–13.

Sprague, J. R., Scheuermann, B., Wang, E., Nelson, C. M., Jolivette, K., & Vincent, C. (2013). Adopting and adapting PBIS for secure juvenile justice settings: Lessons learned. *Education and Treatment of Children*, *36*(3), 121–134.

Steinberg, L. (2009). Adolescent development and juvenile justice. *Annual Review of Clinical Psychology, (5)*, 459–485.

Steinberg, L., Cauffman, E., & Monahan, K. C. (2015). *Psychosocial maturity and desistance from crime in a sample of serious juvenile offenders* (75). Washington, DC: Office of Juvenile Justice and Delinquency Prevention.

Swanson, H. L. (1987). Information processing theory and learning disabilities a commentary and future perspective. *Journal of Learning Disabilities, 20*(3), 155–166.

Sword, L., & Director, G. (2000). I think in pictures, you teach in words: The gifted visual spatial learner. *Gifted, 114*(1), 27–30.

Thapar, A., Cooper, M., Eyre, O., & Langley, K. (2013). Practitioner review: what have we learnt about the causes of ADHD? *Journal of Child Psychology and Psychiatry, 54*(1), 3–16.

The PACER Center, Inc. (2000). *Reaching Out to Parents of Youth With Disabilities in the Juvenile Justice System.* Minneapolis, MN: Author

The Senate Community Affairs References Committee. (2014). *Prevalence of different types of speech, language and communication disorders and speech pathology services in Australia.* Retrieved from: www.aph.gov.au/Parliamentary_Business/Committees/. . ./Speech_Pathology/Report

Thomas, C. N. (2014). Considering the impact of preservice teacher beliefs on future practice. *Intervention in School and Clinic, 49*(4), 230–236.

Thompson, K. C., & Morris, R. J. (2013). Predicting recidivism among juvenile delinquents: Comparison of risk factors for male and female offenders. *Journal of Juvenile Justice,* 3(1), 36.

Tomasello, M. (2014). *The new psychology of language: Cognitive and functional approaches to language structure.* New York, NY: Psychology Press.

Tropper, B., Marton, K., Russo-Victorino, K., Shafer, V., & Schwartz, R.G. (2008, November). Research on executive functions in children with SLI. *Neurobiological Determinants of Human Communication: Prematurity & Early Childhood.* Symposium presented at the American Speech-Language-Hearing Association Convention, Chicago, IL.

Tzuriel, D., & Trabelsi, G. (2014). The effects of the Seria-Think Program (STP) on planning, self-regulation and math achievements among Grade 3 Children with attention deficit hyperactivity disorder (ADHD). In T. Papadopoulos, R.K. Parrila, & J.R. Kirby (Eds.), *Cognition, intelligence, and achievement: A tribute to JP Das* (p.345–367). New York, NY: Elsevier/Academic Press.

Verhoeven, L., & van Balkom, H. (Eds.). (2004). *Classification of developmental language disorders: Theoretical issues and clinical implications.* Mahwah, NJ: Lawrence Erlbaum Associates Publishers.

Vila-Ballo, A., Cunillera, T., Rostan, C., Hdez-Lafuente, P., Fuentemilla, L., & Rodriguez-Fornells, A. (2015). Neurophysiological correlates of cognitive flexibility and feedback processing in violent juvenile offenders. *Brain Research, 16*(10), 98–109.

Watson, D., & Tharp, R. (2013). *Self-directed behavior: Self-modification for personal adjustment.* Boston, Mass: Cengage Learning.

Welsh, W. N., & Harris, P. W. (2016). *Criminal Justice Policy and Planning: Planned Change.* 5th ED. New York, NY: Routledge.

Williams, A. C. (2005). Promoting appropriate responses toward disabilities in juvenile justice settings: Applying disability studies' perspectives to practice. *Journal for Juvenile Justice Services, 20*(1), 7–23.

Willis, J. (2011). *Three brain-based teaching strategies to build executive function in students. Edutopia*. Retrieved from http://www. edutopia. org/blog/brain-based-teaching-strategies-judy-willis.

Winsler, A., Fernyhough, C., & Montero, I. (2009). *Private speech, executive functioning, and the development of verbal self-regulation*. New York, NY: Cambridge University Press.

Young, S., & Goodwin, E. (2010). Attention-deficit/hyperactivity disorder in persistent criminal offenders: The need for specialist treatment programs. *Expert review of Neurotherapeutics*, *10*(10), 1497–1500.

Young, S., Moss, D., Sedgwick, O., Fridman, M., & Hodgkins, P. (2015). A meta-analysis of the prevalence of attention deficit hyperactivity disorder in incarcerated populations. *Psychological Medicine*, *45*(02), 247–258.

Young, S., & Thome, J. (2011). ADHD and offenders. *The World Journal of Biological Psychiatry*, *12*(1), 124–128.

Young, J. (2010). ADHD and crime: Considering the connections. *Medscape Education Psychiatry and Mental Health*. Retrieved from www.medscape.org/viewarticle/719862

Young, S., Misch, P., Collins, P., & Gudjonsson, G. (2011). Predictors of institutional behavioural disturbance and offending in the community among young offenders. *The Journal of Forensic Psychiatry & Psychology*, *22*(1), 72–86.

Zhang, D., Barrett, D. E., Katsiyannis, A., & Yoon, M. (2011). Juvenile offenders with and without disabilities: Risks and patterns of recidivism. *Learning and Individual Differences*, *21*(1), 12–18.

Zlatev, J., Andrén, M., Johansson Falck, M., & Lundmark, C. (2009) Bringing language and cognition back together again. In Zlatev, J., Andrén, M., Johansson Falck, M., & Lundmark, C. (eds.) *Studies in Language and Cognition*, p. 1–17. Newcastle, UK: Cambridge Scholars Publishing.

11

Spiritual Transcendence, Religious Affiliation, and Anorexia Symptoms

Juleen K. Buser *and* Terry L. Pertuit[10]

Individuals who struggle with anorexia symptomatology may experience their behavior as an addiction (Godier & Park, 2015). Specifically, authors have framed disordered eating patterns as process/behavioral addictions (Hagedorn, 2009; Van Wormer & Davis, 2018) and have noted the comparable symptomatology between those who struggle with an addiction to a substance, such as alcohol or heroin, and those who struggle with symptoms of anorexia, such as self-starvation activities (Barbarich-Marstellar, Foltin, & Walsh, 2011; Godier & Park, 2015). For example, in a qualitative study of 40 participants struggling with anorexia symptoms, Godier and Park (2015) noted that participants reported elements of their anorexia symptoms that aligned with substance use disorder criteria. Specifically, participants reported a lack of control over their behavior, such as being unable to reduce anorexia symptomatology. Participants also reported the all-consuming nature of anorexia symptoms, such that these symptoms adversely affected other life domains. Moreover, despite

10. Juleen K. Buser and Terry L. Pertuit, Department of Graduate Education, Leadership, and Counseling, Rider University. Correspondence concerning this article should be addressed to Juleen K. Buser, Department of Graduation Education, Leadership, and Counseling, 202 Memorial Hall, Rider University, 2083 Lawrenceville Road, Lawrenceville, NJ 08648. E-mail: jbuser@rider.edu.

the admittedly harmful psychological impact of symptoms, participants persisted in anorexia symptoms. Finally, participants reported tolerance and withdrawal in relation to anorexia symptomatology.

In the literature on the addictive symptomology of disordered eating, researchers have examined the ways in which spirituality and/or religion intersect with disordered eating attitudes and behaviors (Buser, 2013; Buser & Bernard, 2013; Buser & Gibson, 2016; Forthun, Pidcock, & Fischer, 2003, Homan & Boyatzis, 2010; Latzer et al., 2014; Rider, Terrell, Sisemore, & Hecht, 2014). Research on disordered eating, spirituality, and religion represents a growing area of study, but one that is still relatively small (Akrawi, Bartrop, Potter, & Touyz, 2015; Boyatzis & Quinlan, 2008). In general, several additional areas of investigation are warranted in this area. Akrawi and colleagues (2015) recommended additional research on the ability for religion and/or spirituality to serve protective functions in relation to disordered eating. In addition, while researchers have investigated the relationship between disordered eating and faith beliefs from Judeo-Christian traditions (Buser, 2013; Buser & Bernard, 2013; Author 2016; Homan & Boyatzis, 2010; Latzer et al., 2014; Rider et al., 2014), less is known about the link between disordered eating and non-Judeo-Christian beliefs. In the present study, we added to this developing research in three areas: (a) extending inquiry into the protective potential of spiritual and/or religious beliefs, (b) examining spiritual and/or religious beliefs that include a variety of faith traditions, and (c) studying the outcome of anorexia symptoms in relation to spirituality and/or religion.

Anorexia Symptoms

The *Diagnostic and Statistical Manual of Mental Disorders* (5th edition; *DSM-5;* American Psychiatric Association [APA], 2013) explicates the symptomatology of clinical eating disorders, such as Anorexia Nervosa (AN) and Bulimia Nervosa (BN). Self-starvation behaviors and low body weight characterize the symptom presentation of individuals struggling with AN. In the present study, we focused exclusively on anorexia symptoms. Anorexia symptoms are distinct from other disordered eating attitudes and behaviors, such as bulimia symptoms, and it is thus important to assess types of eating disorder symptoms separately in research, versus using scales that combine anorexia and bulimia symptomatology (Stice, 2002).

Individuals may struggle with clinical symptoms of AN or may exhibit symptoms of AN that do not meet criteria for a clinical diagnosis. Symptoms of subclinical anorexia may include fasting, dieting, and portrayal of control over eating habits (e.g., Anderson & Petrie, 2012; Celio et al., 2006; Fayet, Petocz, & Samman, 2012; Neumark-Sztainer et al., 2011; Tylka and Subich, 2002). In this study, *anorexia symptoms* are defined as clinical and subclinical symptoms of anorexia. *Disordered eating* and *eating disorder symptoms* refer to symptoms of both anorexia and bulimia.

Prevalence of Anorexia Symptoms

Among females, Hudson, Hiripi, Pope and Kessler (2007) reported the prevalence rate of clinical AN as 0.9%. This prevalence rate, however, was not determined by using diagnostic criteria from the *DSM*-5 (APA, 2013), but rather an earlier version of the manual. Mancuso et al. (2015) reported that diagnoses of clinical AN (among participants seeking outpatient treatment) increased when participants were assessed via *DSM*-5 criteria.

As expected, rates of subclinical anorexia symptoms, such as detrimental dieting habits, are higher than rates of clinical AN. For example, Neumark-Sztainer and colleagues (2011) reported that among 419 young adult females, 20.4% reported weight loss activities characterized as extreme, such as taking diet pills. Similarly, Celio et al. (2006) reported that 32.4% of college women in their study used at least one diet aid, such as a diet pill, in the last year. Fayet, Petocz, and Samman (2012) documented that 57.1% of college female participants engaged in restrictive eating behavior. Among female college athletes, 13.9% of gymnasts and 10% of swimmers reported excessive dieting or fasting 2–3 times in the last year (Anderson & Petrie, 2012). In addition, Tylka and Subich (2002) presented data indicating that 36.7% of college age and high school female participants reported eating less than 1200 calories a day, and 15.7% used appetite suppressants.

Etiology of Anorexia Symptoms

To explain why certain individuals develop eating disorder symptoms, authors have discussed sociocultural models of eating disorder etiology, wherein family, peers, and media messages may pressure women to desire and seek a thin body ideal (Stice, 1994; Thompson & Stice, 2001). Pressure to meet a certain body ideal can lead to an *internalization of this ideal*, such that an individual accepts the socially prescribed standards of beauty (Thompson & Stice, 2001). Thompson, van den Berg, Roehrig, Guarda, and Heinberg (2004) defined internalization as the "incorporation of specific values to the point that they become guiding principles" (p. 294). Internalization of the thin-ideal has been discussed as a risk factor for disordered eating behavior (Culbert, Racine, & Klump, 2015; Stice, 2002; Thompson & Stice, 2001), and Homan (2010) documented a link between thin-ideal internalization and symptoms of anorexia.

Thompson and Stice (2001) highlighted the need to identify variables that may attenuate the negative influence of thin-ideal internalization. Moderating variables help explain why, for example, some women who accept the thin-ideal of beauty do not develop symptoms of anorexia, while other women who ascribe to this attractiveness ideal develop disordered eating patterns (Frazier, Tix, & Barron, 2004). Stice (2001) identified body dissatisfaction as a risk factor for anorexia symptomatology, and researchers have identified moderating variables in the link between body dissatisfaction and anorexia symptomatology (Buser & Gibson, 2017; Tylka, 2004; Brannan & Petrie, 2008). Markedly less is known about moderating factors relevant to the link between thin-ideal internalization and anorexia symptomatology; thus, there is need for research in this area.

Spirituality, Religion, and Anorexia Symptoms

Hill et al. (2000) discussed a prominent trend of distinguishing between religion and spirituality. Specifically, these authors noted that religion has been associated with institutional forms of faith, and spirituality has been tied to a more personal experience of faith. Despite this distinction, authors have acknowledged the ways in which spirituality and religion are connected, discussing how both constructs are concerned with the meaningful, sacred, holy elements of life (Hill et al., 2000; Pargament, 1999). Cashwell and Young (2011) noted that clients may distinguish between these terms, such as eschewing an identity of being religious and embracing a spiritual identity, or may reject a distinction between these identifies and view themselves as spiritual and religious. In the present study, we use the term *spirituality and/or religion* in order to denote the potential distinctions and commonalities of these constructs. When reviewing extant literature, we followed the terms used by study authors.

Researchers have explored the link between spirituality and/or religion and the genesis and maintenance of anorexia symptoms (Buser, 2013; Buser & Bernard, 2013; Buser & Gibson, 2016; Forthun, et al., 2003, Homan & Boyatzis, 2010; Latzer et al., 2014; Rider et al., 2014). In the following section, we focus on research that assessed anorexia symptoms separately from bulimia symptoms. We did not review studies that used combined measures of eating disorder symptomatology or combined participants with anorexia and bulimia diagnoses. As noted previously, Stice (2002) advocated for the discrete measurement of anorexia and bulimia symptoms; moreover, authors have reported different results for participants struggling with anorexia versus bulimia symptoms (Brannan & Petrie, 2008; Tylka, 2004). We also focused on studies that measured spiritual and/or religious beliefs, rather than broad constructs such as religious affiliation or devotion, in order to be able to understand the specific content of faith beliefs.

Forthun and colleagues (2003) provided evidence for the beneficial influence of spirituality and/or religion in relation to anorexia symptoms. Among 876 college women, these authors found that the construct of intrinsic religiosity buffered the impact of parental eating disorder history on symptoms of anorexia. Allport (1966) defined intrinsic religiosity as an internalization of faith principles and an inner commitment to faith.

Alternately, authors have reported the negative impacts of spiritual and/or religious beliefs (Gates & Pritchard, 2009; Homan & Boyatzis, 2010; Kim. 2006; Latzer et al., 2014; Rider et al., 2014). Rider et al. (2014) reported that 22 participants with subclinical levels of anorexia symptoms reported higher levels of negative religious coping than the levels of negative religious coping reported by individuals with no anorexia symptoms (n = 88). These authors used a scale that referred to an individual's personal beliefs about God in relation to coping, such as a belief in being punished or abandoned by God in times of stress (Pargament,

Smith, Koenig, & Perez, 1998). Latzer et al. (2014) examined anorexia symptomatology among 102 females (ages 17–18) identifying as Modern Orthodox Jewish; these researchers reported links between negative religious coping and increased anorexia symptoms. Kim (2006) also found negative religious coping to be associated with increased dieting among 353 women from the community. Homan and Boyatzis (2010) found that, among 231 college female participants, an insecure attachment to God was associated with increased dieting behavior. This insecure spiritual attachment referred to worry about being abandoned by God and feeling unloved by God (Beck & McDonald, 2004). Gates and Pritchard (2009) reported that higher levels of religious angst, which was assessed via questions about feeling isolated in one's spiritual life, was associated with increased anorexia symptoms among 330 college men and women.

Boyatzis and McConnell (2006) reported null findings when examining the impact of spirituality and/or religion on anorexia symptoms. These authors reported that quest spiritual orientation, which refers to spiritual beliefs about the value of doubting, existential inquiry, and change in faith beliefs, was not linked with anorexia symptoms among 125 college women. In sum, the research on spirituality/religion and anorexia symptoms is mixed, with researchers indicating a beneficial, detrimental, or null relationship. Additional research is needed to better understand this relationship—specifically using constructs not studied before in this literature.

Spiritual Transcendence

As many researchers investigating disordered eating and anorexia symptoms used measures rooted in a Judeo-Christian belief system (Buser 2013; Buser & Bernard, 2013; Buser & Gibson, 2016; Homan and Boyatzis, 2010; Latzer et al., 204; Rider et al., 2014), examination of the construct of spiritual transcendence in relation to anorexia symptoms has the potential to add to existing research. Spiritual transcendence is a construct that references beliefs relevant to multiple spiritual traditions, such as Buddhism, Hinduism, Quakerism, Lutheranism, Catholicism, and Judaism (Piedmont, 2005, 1999). Spiritual transcendence is "a motivational construct that reflects an individual's efforts to create a broad sense of personal meaning for his/her life" (Piedmont, 2005, p. 4). Individuals with elevated levels of spiritual transcendence "are able to find a larger sense of meaning and purpose to life that goes beyond their immediate sense of time and place. . . . and feel an attachment to nature and communities" (Piedmont, 2012, p. 105). Alternately, scales of faith-based coping (Pargament, Koenig, & Perez, 2000) and faith-based attachment (Beck & McDonald, 2004) refer to a participant's belief in God; such language could exclude those with faith beliefs that do not include God or a higher power. Moreover, spiritual transcendence has not been explored as a moderator in the association between thin-ideal internalization and anorexia symptoms.

Researchers have documented that spiritual transcendence is beneficial in relation to other mental health issues. For example, Piedmont (2004) reported that spiritual transcendence was associated with increases in global well-being and improved coping among 56 individuals who completed substance abuse treatment. In addition, using a version of this scale translated into the Filipino language of Tagalog, Piedmont (2007) documented a link between spiritual transcendence and increased positive affect and decreased negative affect among 654 participants. Katsogianni and Kleftaras (2015) established further support for spiritual transcendence as favorable in relation to mental health. These researchers reported that, among 300 individuals struggling with addiction, higher spiritual transcendence was associated with decreased depression. Moreover, researchers have suggested that the construct of spiritual transcendence may serve as a protective variable. For example, Bamonti et al. (2016) investigated a construct with conceptual similarity to spiritual transcendence; these authors assessed spirituality (as operationalized by the Spiritual Transcendence Index). Bamonti and colleagues (2016) found that spirituality buffered the relationship between depression and life meaning. Specifically, participants who reported high levels of depression and high spirituality had increased life meaning compared to participants who reported high level of depression and low spirituality.

The Current Study

In this study, we investigated the relationship between spiritual transcendence and anorexia symptoms. Authors have conceptualized individuals' struggles with anorexia symptoms as a period of spiritual vacancy and search for meaning (Berrett, Hardman, O'Grady, & Richards, 2007; Garrett, 1996; Hardman, Berrett, & Richards, 2003; Lewica, 1999). Recovery, on the other hand, has been understood as a movement toward spiritual meaning and connection (Berrett et al., 2007; Garrett, 1996; Lewica, 1999; Marsden, Karagianni, & Morgan, 2007). For example, in a qualitative study with 32 participants, Garrett (1996) documented that participants understood their recovery from anorexia as being related to an increased spirituality. As this author explained, participant spirituality involved connection with self, others, and the greater natural world. This description of spirituality is conceptually similar to Piedmont's (2005, 2012) definition of spiritual transcendence. These authors' findings and hypotheses about spirituality and the process of recovery suggest a potential link between spiritual transcendence and anorexia symptoms.

Given the empirical support for the construct of spiritual transcendence as beneficial in regard to mental health outcomes and its potential association with anorexia symptoms, additional investigations are merited. To date, the relationship between spiritual transcendence and anorexia symptoms has not been studied. In the present study, we extended the research by exploring the link between spiritual transcendence and anorexia symptoms. We examined three hypotheses: (a) increased spiritual transcendence will be correlated with reduced anorexia symptoms in a bivariate analysis; (b) after accounting for thin-ideal internalization, higher levels of spiritual transcendence will be associated with lower levels of anorexia symptoms; and (c) spiritual transcendence will buffer the relationship between thin-ideal internalization and anorexia symptoms.

Method

Procedures

After receiving Institutional Review Board approval, we recruited 476 college women for the present study in 2007. We used a private northeastern university directory to randomly select 2,858 female college students who had recently completed their first, sophomore, and junior years. We emailed these potential participants the survey via the web-based tool SurveyMonkey©. We gave students the choice to opt-out of receiving reminder emails and provided an incentive to participate. Respondents were eligible to enter a drawing to win one of two $200 VISA© gift cards. Castle (2009) also reported findings from this data collection effort and examined attachment and facets of wellness in relation to disordered eating among college women.

Participants

Participants self-reported the following academic classes: freshmen (*n* = 3; 0.6%), sophomores (*n* =145; 30.5%), juniors (*n* =185; 38.9%), seniors (*n* = 138; 29%), and graduate students (*n* = 5; 1.1%). Participants ranged in age from 18–25, with a mean age of 20.3 (*SD* = 1.1). Participants mainly identified as Caucasian (*n* = 384; 80.7%); the remainder identified as follows: Asian/Pacific Islander (*n* = 32; 6.7%), Hispanic/Latina (*n* = 28; 5.9%), African American (*n* = 23; 4.8%), Native American/Alaskan Native (*n* = 2; 0.4%), and international students (*n* = 5; 1.1%), and 2 participants chose not to answer. Also, 10.3% (*n* = 49) of participants self-identified as biracial, and 1 participant chose not to answer. The majority of the participants (*n* = 455; 95.6%) self-identified as heterosexual, 0.4% (*n* = 2) self-identified as lesbian, 3.6% (*n* = 17) self-identified as bisexual, and 2 participants chose not to answer. Participants reported a mean body mass index (BMI) of 23.3 (*SD* = 4.1). We calculated BMI based on participant self-reported height and weight. Based on the Centers for Disease Control and Prevention (2018) benchmarks, this average body mass index is in the normal/healthy range. While participant self-reported height and weight may not be completely accurate, particularly among women and those with higher BMIs (Gunnare, Silliman, & Morris, 2013), we followed precedent in the eating disorder literature in terms of the inclusion of this variable and its measurement via self-report (Buser & Gibson, 2017; Brannan & Petrie, 2008, 2011; Cheng, 2014).

In terms of religious affiliation, 35.9% (*n* = 171) self-identified as Catholic, 17.9% (*n* = 85) as Protestant, 10.3% (*n* = 49) as Jewish, 5.5% (*n* = 26) as Agnostic, 2.3% (*n* = 11) as Atheist, 1.9% (*n* = 9) as Buddhist, 0.2% (*n* = 1) as Hindu, 0.8% (*n* = 4) as Unitarian, 0.4% (*n* = 2) as Mormon, 0.2% (*n* = 1) as Muslim, 9% (*n* = 43) as Other Faith/Religious Tradition, 15.1% (*n* = 72) as No Religious Affiliation, and 2 participants chose not to answer. For economic class, 11.3% (*n* = 54) self-identified as lower middle class, 43.1% (n = 205) as middle class, 41.6% (n = 198) as upper middle class, 2.7% (n = 13) as upper class, and 6 participants chose not to answer.

Instruments

Participants completed demographic questions for the purposes of the present study, to assess characteristic such as economic background, age, and religious affiliation. In addition, participants completed three instruments. We used instruments that assessed thin-ideal internalization, spiritual transcendence, and anorexia symptomatology.

Thin-ideal internalization. We operationalized internalization of the thin-ideal with a subscale from the Sociocultural Attitudes Toward Appearance Questionaire-3 (SATAQ-3; Thompson et al., 2004). The Internalization-General scale is a 9-item subscale that measures the degree to which one accepts the media body ideal. Participants answer items on a 5-point Likert-type scale *(definitely disagree, mostly disagree, neither agree nor disagree, mostly agree, definitely agree).* Higher scores indicate higher thin-ideal internalization. Thompson et al. (2004) reported sufficient reliability (a = .92) for this subscale and documented convergent validity. Reliability of scores from current participants was a = .93.

Spiritual transcendence. Our hypothesized moderating variable was spiritual transcendence, and we operationalized this construct through the Spiritual Transcendence Scale, which is included in the Assessment of Spirituality and Religious Sentiments (ASPIRES; Piedmont, 2005). The Spiritual Transcendence Scale contains 23 items, and the total score comprises the construct of spiritual transcendence. The scale is scored with a 5-point Likert-type scale *(strongly disagree, disagree, neutral, agree, strongly agree).* Higher scores are indicative of higher spiritual transcendence. Piedmont (2012) reported adequate reliability (a = .89) and convergent and discriminant validity for this scale. The reliability for scores from the current study participants was a= .91.

Anorexia symptoms. Symptoms of anorexia served as the outcome variable in this study. Participants completed the Eating Attitudes Test-26 (EAT-26; Garner, Olmstead, Bohr, & Garfinkel, 1982), a 26-item instrument, which has been conceptualized as a screening instrument for disordered eating and has been reported to correlate with symptoms of eating pathology (Garner et al., 1982). This scale is comprised of three subscales (i.e., dieting, oral control, and bulimia and food preoccupation); two of these subscales specifically tap into anorexia symptomatology. The dieting subscale taps into a "pathological avoidance of fattening foods and shape preoccupation," and the oral control subscale measures an individual's self-control around food (Garner et al., 1982, p. 877). Following the precedent of previous researchers (Buser & Gibson, 2017; Brannan & Petrie, 2008), the dieting (13 items) and oral control (7 items) subscales were combined and used to assess symptoms of anorexia. These subscales are scored on a Likert-type scale of 0, 0, 0, 1, 2, 3 *(never, rarely, sometimes, often, usually, always).* Garner et al. (1982) reported evidence for convergent and discriminant validity for these subscales. When the dieting and oral control subscales are combined to assess anorexia symptoms, researchers reported reliability coefficients of a = .86 (Brannan & Petrie, 2008) and a = .84 (Buser & Gibson, 2017). Among current study participants, the combined dieting and oral control subscales had a reliability of a = .79.

Results

We visually assessed the continuous variables and determined that these data approximated a normal curve. None of the continuous variables had problematic skew or kurtosis values, according to the guidelines specified by Miles and Shevlin (2006). We completed analyses to determine the association between demographic variables and anorexia symptoms. In a bivariate correlation, age was significantly associated with anorexia symptoms, $r = -.12$, $p < .05$, such that younger participants reported higher levels of anorexia symptoms. BMI was also significantly related to anorexia, such that higher BMI was associated with increased symptoms, $r = .11$, $p < .05$.

We conducted Kruskal-Wallis and Mann-*U* Whitney tests to assess the relationship between anorexia symptoms and the remaining categorical demographic variables, due to the uneven cell sizes (Tabachnik & Fidell, 2007). The only significant finding was a link between religious affiliation and anorexia symptoms. A Kruskal-Wallis test indicated a significant relationship between anorexia symptoms and religious affiliation, $x2$ (11, $n = 474$) = 24.74, $p < .05$. To understand the nature of this relationship, we carried out six follow-up Mann-Whitney *U* tests. Pallant (2007) recommended selecting a small number of follow-up tests after a significant Kruskal-Wallis test. We did not compare affiliation categories that had less than 40 participants. We also applied a Holm-Bonferroni correction to the alpha level, in order to account for the multiple follow-up tests (Holm, 1979; Gaetano, 2013). We compared participants identifying as Protestant, Catholic, and Jewish to participants who identified as having an "other" faith/ religious tradition and those who identified as having no religious affiliation. These follow-up Mann-*U* Whitney tests revealed that Catholic participants ($Md = 5$; $n = 171$) reported higher levels of anorexia symptoms, compared to participants with an "other" faith/religious tradition ($Md = 3$; $n = 43$), $U = 2773.5$, $z = -2.5$, $p < .05$. This was a small effect, $r = .14$ (Cohen, 1992). Catholic participants ($Md = 5$; $n = 171$) also reported higher levels of anorexia symptoms, compared to participants with no religious affiliation ($Md = 4$; $n = 72$), $U = 5111.5$, $z = -2.1$, $p < .05$. This was a small effect, $r = .13$ (Cohen, 1992).

The means, standard deviations, ranges and Pearson correlations for thin-ideal internalization, spirituality, and eating attitudes are shown in Table 1. We found a statistically significant positive correlation between thin-ideal internalization and anorexia symptoms ($r = .44$, $p < .001$). Spiritual transcendence was not significantly correlated with thin-ideal internalization ($r = -0.01$, *ns*) or anorexia symptoms ($r = -0.02$, *ns*). We did not find support for the first hypothesis.

Next, we carried out a regression analysis to determine the relationship between thin-ideal internalization, spirituality, and disordered eating. An *a priori* power analysis indicated that, in a regression with six predictors, our sample size was sufficient for appropriate study power (Soper, 2017). This calculation was based on an estimate of a small effect size of $f2 = .06$, which was projected from other research on spirituality/ religion and disordered eating (Buser, 2013; Buser & Gibson, 2016).

We carried out a hierarchical regression, using the procedures described by Frazier et al. (2004). Age, BMI, and religious affiliation were included as control variables in the regression. Anorexia symptoms served as the dependent variable. We entered data in three steps in the regression, and the two predictor variables (thin-ideal internalization and spiritual transcendence) were centered, as recommended by Frazier et al. (2004) for moderation analyses. Variables entered at each step of the regression were as follows: (a) age, BMI, and religious affiliation;

(b) internalization of the thin-ideal and spiritual transcendence; (c) the interaction term (internalization x spiritual transcendence). Despite the nonsignificant correlation between spiritual transcendence and anorexia symptoms, we still carried out a regression due to the potential for suppressor influences (Tabachnick & Fidell, 2007). In the first step of the regression, age, BMI, and religious affiliation together accounted for 3.2% of the variance in anorexia symptoms, DF (3, 470) = 5.24, $p < .01$. In the second step, thin-ideal internalization and spiritual transcendence accounted for an additional 20.4% of the variance in anorexia symptoms, DF (2, 468) = 62.53, $p < .001$. While the beta value for thin-ideal internalization was statistically significant (b = -.45, $p < .001$), the beta value for spiritual transcendence was not statistically significant (b = -.03, $p = .50$, *ns*). This indicated that spiritual transcendence did not contribute any unique variance to the outcome of anorexia symptoms. In step three, the interaction term was not significant, indicating that a moderation effect for spiritual transcendence was not detected (change R2 = .00). We did not find support for the second and third hypotheses.

Discussion

In this study, we explored the empirical association between spiritual transcendence, thin-ideal internalization, and anorexia symptoms among college female participants. Thin-ideal internalization was significantly associated with anorexia symptoms, confirming a base of research documenting a relationship between internalization of a thin body ideal and disordered eating (Homan, 2010; Stice, 2002; Thompson & Stice, 2001). However, we did not find support for the posited link between spiritual transcendence and anorexia symptoms. Specifically, spiritual transcendence did not explain additional significant variance in the outcome variable or moderate the link between thin-ideal internalization and disordered eating. This was a rigorous initial test of the link between spiritual transcendence and anorexia symptoms.

Several potential explanations for this nonsignificant result exist. First, the construct of spiritual transcendence is a broad construct that measures an individual's sense of meaning and connection (Piedmont, 1999; Piedmont, 2005, Piedmont, 2012). This construct may not have been specific enough to identify the aspects of an individual's faith that are beneficial. In particular, the construct of spiritual transcendence may have tapped into both the positive and negative aspects of spirituality and/or religion, thus explaining the null findings. In support of this explanation, Forthun et al. (2003) documented that the construct of religious orientation had helpful and damaging aspects in relation to disordered eating. These authors reported that an intrinsic religious orientation, wherein participants identify an inner desire to live out their faith practices (Allport, 1966), was protective in relation to disordered eating. Alternately, an extrinsic religious orientation, wherein participants identify external motivations for their beliefs and practices (Allport, 1966), was detrimental in relation to disordered eating. The construct of spiritual transcendence may have failed to distinguish between participants' intrinsic and extrinsic orientations. Specifically, participants who were internally motivated to live in harmony with their faith (i.e., intrinsic religiosity) may have endorsed spiritual transcendence at the same level as individuals who viewed their faith as "utilitarian" (i.e., extrinsic religiosity; Allport, 1966, p. 455).

Offering further support for this interpretation of the null findings, researchers have reported significant links among the use of certain religious coping strategies, faith-based attachment styles, and eating disorder symptomatology (Buser, 2013; Buser & Bernard, 2013; Authors 2016; Rider et al., 2014; Kim, 2006). Specifically, these researchers found beliefs that God/Higher Power abandoned or was punishing an individual were linked to increased bulimia (Buser, 2013; Buser & Bernard, 2013) and anorexia symptoms (Kim, 2006; Rider et al., 2014), while a belief that God/Higher Power partnered with an individual was linked with decreased bulimia symptoms (Buser & Bernard, 2013). In addition, individuals with an insecure spiritual attachment style had increased rates of anorexia symptoms (Homan & Boyatzis, 2010) and bulimia symptoms (Buser & Gibson, 2016). Therefore, future research in this area may want to focus on scales of religion and spirituality that measure both potentially positive and negative elements of faith, such intrinsic and extrinsic religiosity (Allport, 1966), positive and negative religious coping (Pargament et al., 2000), or secure and insecure spiritual attachment styles (Beck & McDonald, 2004) in determining the relationship with spiritual beliefs and anorexia symptoms.

Furthermore, the nonsignificant findings of the current study suggest that, in examining the link between spiritual beliefs and anorexia symptoms, broad scales of spiritual and/or religious beliefs that include diverse beliefs may not be the most useful. Rather, scales that focus on a specific faith tradition may be more informative. For example, scales that assess the nature of one's relationship with God or a Higher Power in the Judeo-Christian tradition (e.g., feeling supported or ignored by God/Higher Power) may be more informative than scales such as the Spiritual Transcendence Scale, which does not reference qualities of a divine relationship relevant to a specific faith. Boyatzis and McConnell (2006) also reported null findings when using a scale of quest religious orientation, which was a broad measure of faith rather than one referencing a specific theology. But, given the need to expand the scope of the inquiry in this area to faith beliefs outside of Judeo-Christian traditions, the use of scales that are specific to faith traditions outside of Judeo-Christian theology may represent the next step in this line of inquiry.

Demographic Findings

In the initial demographic analyses in the present study, younger participants and those with a higher BMI reported increased anorexia symptoms. We therefore controlled for these demographic variables in our multivariate analysis. These findings support extant research on age of onset for AN (Volpe et al., 2016) and the association between self-reported BMI and anorexia symptoms (Brannan & Petrie, 2008). In addition, participants identifying as Catholic were found to have significantly more anorexia symptoms than participants with no religious affiliation or those endorsing an "other" faith/religious tradition. We also controlled for religious affiliation in the regression analysis. This aligns with prior findings that the religious affiliation of individuals with eating disorder symptoms was different than that of individuals without eating disorder symptoms. Specifically, Sykes et al. (1986) found that a higher proportion of individuals with an eating disorder identified as Catholic compared to the proportion in the general population who identified as Catholic. Gates and Pritchard (2009) found that college students identifying as Catholic had higher levels of anorexia symptoms than those identifying as LDS, no affiliation, and "other" affiliation.

Researchers have also documented that participants identifying with other Judeo-Christian religious affiliations reported higher levels of disordered eating. For example, Sykes et al. (1986) documented higher rates of a Jewish religious affiliation among participants with eating disorder symptoms compared to participants in the general population. Pinhas, Heinmaa, Bryden, Bradley, and Toner (2008) reported that participants with a Jewish religious affiliation had higher rates of anorexia symptoms than those with a non-Jewish religious affiliation. In addition, Wilbur and Colligan (1981) reported that females with AN had higher levels of religious fundamentalism than a matched control group.

In attempting to understand these results, authors have suggested that issues such as religious asceticism could rationalize dietary restriction and a low body weight (Joughin, Crisp, Halek, and Humphrey, 1992). Associated with notions of sacrifice and a disdain for physical pleasures and desires (James, 1902/2002; Vandereycken & Van Deth, 1994), asceticism has been primarily discussed as a facet of Judeo-Christian religions, such as Catholicism and Christian fundamentalism (Rampling, 1985; Marsden, 1980). Authors have provided case examples of individuals who defined their disordered eating in terms of ascetic practices (e.g., spiritual practices providing sustenance and striving to discipline the physical body; Banks, 1992).

Our finding that Catholic participants reported higher levels of anorexia symptoms than participants with no religious affiliation or an "other" faith/religious tradition may support literature on the potential relationship between religious fasting, principles of asceticism, and disordered eating (e.g., Huline-Dickens, 2000; Rampling, 1985). Asceticism and beliefs about sin and punishment have been discussed as being a part of some Catholic theological principles (Rampling, 1985; Marsden, 1980). Yet, religious affiliation is an inexact construct. The content of Catholic participants' faith beliefs in unknown. We did not assess participants' beliefs about sin and punishment and, thus, the mechanisms by which Catholic religious affiliation and anorexia symptoms are related remain unclear and need additional research attention.

Also, in contrast with prior research, participants identifying as Jewish and Protestant did not report increased symptoms of anorexia. As noted previously, researchers have found increased rates of eating disorder symptomatology among Jewish participants (Pinhas et al., 2008; Sykes et al., 1986) and among individuals with higher religious fundamentalism (Wilbur & Colligan, 1981). Yet, in a likely indication of the crude measure of faith provided by religious affiliation, authors have also reported lower rates of disordered eating among Orthodox Jewish participants compared to secular Jewish participants (Gluck & Geliebter, 2002). As we did not assess the content of Jewish and Protestant participants' religious beliefs in this study, the interpretation of the result is unclear. Possibly, beliefs such as asceticism and punishment for sin may not have been a salient part of participants' faith principles. In addition, other faith beliefs may have been relevant in explaining this result.

Implications for Counseling Practice

Symptoms of anorexia are a common concern among college women (Celio et al., 2006; Fayet et al., 2012; Tylka & Subich, 2002) and thin-ideal internalization is documented as a risk factor for disordered eating (Thompson & Stice, 2001). In the current study, we supported this base of research and reported a link between thin-ideal internalization and anorexia symptoms. Counselors who lead prevention programs may want to target thin-ideal internalization. Researchers have reported that dissonance prevention programs diminished levels of thin-ideal internalization among participants (e.g., Stice, Chase, Stormer, & Appel, 2001; Stice, Mazotti, Weibel, & Agras, 2000). Such programs help women deconstruct media messages about thin-ideal internalization and become aware of the detriments of such a body ideal (Stice et al., 2001; Stice et al., 2000).

Although this study did not support a connection between spiritual transcendence and anorexia symptoms, the nonsignificant finding may have important implications for counseling assessment and treatment planning. The construct of spiritual transcendence was potentially too broad to adequately measure the protective characteristics of participants' spiritual/religious beliefs. However, as noted previously, researchers have provided support for intrinsic religiosity (Forthun et al., 2003), positive spiritual coping (Buser, 2013; Authors 2013b), and a secure attachment to God/Higher Power (Buser & Gibson, 2016) as beneficial factors in relation to disordered eating. Thus, the null findings in the present study potentially accentuate the importance of specific assessment of clients' spiritual and/or religious beliefs. When working with clients who struggle with anorexia symptoms, counselors may want to consider an assessment of spirituality and/or religion that includes detailed and extensive questions. Moreira-Almeida, Koenig, and Lucchetti (2014) summarized several assessments related to mental health and spirituality and highlighted the Royal College of Psychiatrists Assessment (RCPA; Culliford & Powell, 2006) as an assessment targeting mental health and spirituality concerns. As Moreira-Almeida et al. (2014) summarized, the RCPA assesses issues such as a client's childhood faith, how a client uses faith to manage stressors, and a client's religious/spiritual community affiliation. This assessment tool also encourages the clinician to delve into how issues related to spirituality/religion impact a client's past, present, and future. For example, a counselor can ask a client to reflect on past losses and discuss ways of dealing with those losses. Moreira-Almeida et al. (2014) stressed the importance of clinical exploration of multiple facets of client faith and noted that in-depth questioning and discussion of specific faith content may be valuable. For example, asking clients about disagreements or struggles they have in relation to spiritual/religious doctrines could be useful, in addition to inquiring about tension clients have had with spiritual/religious communities. These authors also accentuated the import of inquiries into: a client's method of spiritual/religious coping; the characteristics of a client's relationship with the divine; potential spiritual difficulties a client might experience, such as blaming a Higher Power for problems; and a client's faith development over time, including childhood experiences, hurtful spiritual/religious incidents, role of the client's parents in their faith, and shifts in the client's relationship to spiritual/religious teachings.

Moreover, one area of inquiry on the RCPA involves asking clients to share their thoughts on the relevance of spiritual beliefs to their presenting concern. Thus, counselors can ask clients to consider how spiritual and/or religious beliefs have served as protective and/or detrimental functions in relation to anorexia symptoms. By engaging in such a detailed and direct assessment, counselors can identify faith beliefs such as asceticism, which could be damaging and foster anorexia symptoms.

In addition, we found that Catholic participants evidenced higher rates of anorexia symptoms than participants with no religious affiliation or an "other" faith/religious tradition. Our findings related to participants' Catholic religious affiliation should be interpreted with caution. The mechanism by which Catholic religious affiliation was associated with anorexia symptoms is unknown. While our present investigation indicates that that there may be something about a Catholic religious affiliation associated with increased anorexia symptoms, we do not know the specific beliefs that may explain this link. Moreover, authors have found that institutionalized religion moderated the damaging influence of depression on physical health (Wink, Dillon, & Larsen, 2005); thus, we want to caution over-interpretation of our findings.

Possibly, individuals who identify with a Catholic religious affiliation ascribe to beliefs (e.g., beliefs about fasting and asceticism) that may promote and/or perpetuate symptoms of anorexia (Banks, 1992; James, 1902/2002; Joughin, et al., 1992; Marsden, 1980; Rampling, 1985; Vandereycken & Van Deth, 1994). Counselors might consider exploring and discussing specific religious practices in this tradition, such as fasting, and clients' related beliefs. In addition, asking clients how they feel about and relate to their physical versus spiritual self may be informative, such as steps they take for self-care both physically and spiritually. Clients who ascribe to an ascetic mindset may prioritize caring for and nourishing their spiritual selves over their physical body. In general, however, mental health professionals will want to approach a client's spiritual and/or religious belief system and religious affiliation in an open manner; faith beliefs could have positive or negative influences.

Strengths, Limitations, and Future Research

In the present study, we contributed to the research by reporting the nonsignificant association between spiritual transcendence and anorexia symptoms. Prior researchers have examined spiritual and/or religious beliefs that reference Judeo-Christian principles, and we endeavored to fill a gap by using a scale inclusive of multiple spiritual and/or religious beliefs. However, spiritual transcendence was not related to anorexia symptoms among participants. The inclusive nature of this measure may explain the null findings. We may have captured beneficial and detrimental elements of faith and failed to assess beliefs associated with a specific theology that are relevant to anorexia symptoms. To expand the literature beyond Judeo-Christian beliefs, future researchers may want to choose instruments that assess beliefs pertinent to a particular spiritual and/or religious tradition. For example, Tarakeshwar, Pargament, and Mahoney (2003) created a measure of Hindu religious coping; instruments such as this one may be more salient in relation to anorexia symptoms than broad spirituality measures.

Our study was also limited in specific ways. Our participants reported minimal diversity in demographic characteristics such as racial/ethnic background, age, and sexual identity. This lack of diversity impacts the generalizability of study results, which would be limited to similar participants. The current results are based on data collected in 2007, which should be considered in understanding our findings. This may be a limitation, as, for example, levels of anorexia symptoms among college females may have shifted since data collection. However, in recent research, authors continue to identify anorexia symptomatology as a concerning issue among adolescent and young adult women (Loth, MacLehose, Bucchianeri, Crow, & Neumark-Sztainer, 2014). Another study limitation is related to our use of self-report data. As noted previously, self-reported BMI may not be accurate (Gunnare et al., 2013), and our measurement of other variables may be similarly limited by self-report data. Other researchers studying anorexia symptomatology have controlled for social desirability (Brannan & Petrie, 2008), which would be an improvement to this study.

Also, we did not explicitly measure religious attitudes such as asceticism or participants' level of dedication to the Catholic faith. Therefore, it is unclear as to the specific mechanisms by which anorexia symptoms and Catholic religious affiliation were correlated. Given these preliminary findings, future research could study the mechanisms through which religious affiliation is associated with anorexia symptoms. Measuring constructs such as punishment for sin and ascetic beliefs may reveal specific types of spiritual and/or religious beliefs that correlate with anorexia symptoms.

Table 1

Means, Standard Deviations, Ranges, and Pearson Correlations (n=476)

Variable	M	SD	Range	1	2	3
Anorexia Symptoms	4.98	4.02	0–20			
Thin-Ideal Internalization	29.35	8.54	9–45	.44*		
Spiritual Transcendence	76.75	14.65	37–112	-.02	-.01	

Note. Anorexia Symptoms as measured by Dieting and Oral Control subscales on the EAT-26; Thin-Ideal Internalization as measured by the Internalization-General scale on the SATAQ-3; Spiritual Transcendence as measured by the ASPIRES. * = $p < .001$.

References

Akrawi, D., Bartrop, R., Potter, U., & Touyz, S. (2015). Religiosity, spirituality in relation to disordered eating and body image concerns: A systematic review. *Journal of Eating Disorders, 3*(29), 1–24. doi:10.1186/s40337-015-0064-0

Allport, G. W. (1966). The religious context of prejudice. *Journal for the Scientific Study of Religion, 5*(3), 447–457. doi:10.2307/1384172

American Psychiatric Association (2015) *Diagnostic and statistical manual of mental disorders* (5th ed.). Washington, DC: Author.

Anderson, C., & Petrie, T. A. (2012). Prevalence of disordered eating and pathogenic weight control behaviors among NCAA division I female collegiate gymnasts and swimmers. *Research Quarterly for Exercise and Sport, 83*(1), 120–124. doi:10.1080/02701367.2012.10599833

Banks, C. G. (1992). 'Culture' in culture-bound syndromes: The case of anorexia nervosa. *Social Science and Medicine, 34*(8), 867–884. doi:10.1016/0277-9536(92)90256-P

Bamonti, P., Lombardi, S., Duberstein, P. R., King, D. A., & Van Orden, K. A. (2016). Spirituality attenuates the association between depression symptom severity and meaning in life. *Aging & Mental Health, 20*(5), 494–499. doi:10.1080/13607863.2015.1021752

Barbarich-Marsteller, N. C., Foltin, R. W., & Walsh, B. T. (2011). Does anorexia nervosa resemble an addiction?. *Current Drug Abuse Reviews, 4*(3), 197–200. doi:10.2174/1874473711104030197

Beck, R. & McDonald., A. (2004). Attachment to God: The Attachment to God Inventory, tests of working model correspondence and an exploration of faith group differences. *Journal of Psychology and Theology, 32,* 92–103. doi:10.1177/009164710403200202

Berrett, M., Hardman, R., O'Grady, K., & Richards, P. (2007). The role of spirituality in the treatment of trauma and eating disorders: recommendations for clinical practice. *Eating Disorders, 15*(4), 373–389. doi:10.1080/10640260701454394

Boyatzis, C. J., & McConnell, K. M. (2006). Quest orientation in young women: Age trendsduring emerging adulthood and relations to body image and disordered eating. *International Journal for the Psychology of Religion, 16*(3), 197–207. doi:10.1207/s15327582ijpr1603_4

Boyatzis, C. J., & Quinlan, K. B. (2008). Women's body image, disordered eating, and religion:A critical review of the literature. *Research in the Social Scientific Study of Religion, 19,* 183–208. doi:10.1163/ej.9789004166462.i-299.61

Brannan, M. E., & Petrie, T. A. (2008). Moderators of the body dissatisfaction-eating disorder symptomatology relationship: Replication and extension. *Journal of Counseling Psychology, 55*(2), 263–275. doi:10.1037/0022-0167.55.2.263

Buser, J. K. (2013). Stress, spiritual coping, and bulimia: Feeling punished by God/Higher Power. *Journal of Mental Health Counseling, 35*(2), 154–171. doi: 10.17744/mehc.35.2.g57871267wg641r2

Buser, J. K., & Bernard, J. M. (2013). Religious coping, body dissatisfaction, and bulimic symptomatology. *Counseling & Values, 58*(2), 158–176. doi:10.1002/j.2161-007X.2013.00031.x

Buser, J. K., & Gibson, S. (2016). Attachment to God/Higher Power and bulimic symptoms among college females. *Journal of College Counseling, 19*(2), 124–137. doi:10.1002/jocc.12036

Buser, J. K., & Gibson, S. (2017). Protecting women from the negative effects of body dissatisfaction: The role of differentiation of self. *Women & Therapy.* Advance online publication. doi:10.1080/02703149.2017.1352277

Cashwell, C. S., & Young, J. S., Eds. (2011). *Integrating spirituality and religion into counseling: a guide to competent practice* (2nd ed). Alexandria, VA: American Counseling Association.

Castle, K. S. (2009). Attachment, wellness, and disordered eating in college women. *Dissertation Abstracts International Section A, 70*, 99.

Celio, C. I., Luce, K. H., Bryson, S. W., Winzelberg, A. J., Cunning, D., Rockwell, R., et al. (2006). Use of diet pills and other dieting aids in a college population with high weight and shape concerns. *International Journal of Eating Disorders, 39*, 492–497. doi:10.1002/eat.20254

Centers for Disease Control and Prevention (2018). *About Adult BMI.* Retrieved from https://www.cdc.gov/healthyweight/assessing/bmi/adult_bmi/index.html

Cheng, H. (2014). Disordered eating among Asian/Asian American women: Racial and cultural factors as correlates. *The Counseling Psychologist, 42*(6), 821–851. doi:10.1177/0011000014535472

Cohen, J. (1992). A power primer. *Psychological Bulletin, 112*, 155–159. doi:10.1037/0033-2909.112.1.155

Culbert, K. M., Racine, S. E., & Klump, K. L. (2015). Research review: What we have learned about the causes of eating disorders—A synthesis of sociocultural, psychological, and biological research. *Journal of Child Psychology and Psychiatry, 56*(11), 1141–1164. doi:10.1111/jcpp.12441

Culliford. L., & Powell, A. (2006). *Spirituality and mental health.* Retrieved from: http://www.rcpsych.ac.uk/mentalhealthinformation/therapies/spiritualityandmentalhealth.aspx

Fayet, F., Petocz, P., & Samman, S. (2012). Prevalence and correlates of dieting in college women: a cross sectional study. *International Journal of Women's Health, 4*, 405–411. doi:10.2147/ijwh.s33920

Forthun, L. F., Pidcock, B. W., & Fischer, J. L. (2003). Religiousness and disordered eating: Does religiousness modify family risk? *Eating Behaviors, 4*, 7–26. doi:10.1016/S1471–0153(02)00099–5

Frazier, P. A., Tix, A. P., & Barron, K. E. (2004). Testing moderator and mediator effects in counseling psychology research. *Journal of Counseling Psychology, 51*(1), 115–134. doi:10.1037/0022–0167.51.1.115

Gaetano J. (2013). *Holm-Bonferroni sequential correction: An EXCEL calculator (1.2)* [Microsoft Excel workbook]. Retrieved from https://www.researchgate.net/publication/242331583_Holm-Bonferroni_Sequential_Correction_An_EXCEL_Calculator_-_Ver._1.2 . doi:10.13140/RG.2.1.3920.0481

Garner, D. M., Olmstead, M. P., Bohr, Y., & Garfinkel, P. E. (1982). The eating attitudes test: Psychometric features and clinical correlates. *Psychological Medicine, 12*, 871–878. doi:10.1017/S0033291700049163

Garrett, C. (1996). Recovery from anorexia nervosa: a Durkheimian interpretation. *Social Science & Medicine, 43*(10), 1489–1506. doi:10.1016/0277–9536(96)00088–3

Gates, K., & Pritchard, M. (2009). The relationships among religious affiliation, religious angst, and disordered eating. *Eating & Weight Disorders, 14*(1), e11–5. doi:10.1007/bf03354622

Gluck, M., & Geliebter, A. (2002). Body image and eating behaviors in orthodox and secular Jewish women. *Journal of Gender-Specific Medicine, 5*(1), 19–24.

Godier, L. R.., & Park, R. J. (2015). Does compulsive behaviour in Anorexia Nervosa resemblean addiction? A qualitative investigation. *Frontiers in Psychology, 6*, doi:10.3389/fpsyg.2015.01608/full

Gunnare, N. A., Silliman, K., & Morris, M. N. (2013). Accuracy of self-reported weight and role of gender, body mass index, weight satisfaction, weighing behavior, and physical activity among rural college students. *Body Image, 10*(3), 406–410. doi:10.1016/j.bodyim.2013.01.006

Hagedorn, W. B. (2009). The call for a new Diagnostic and Statistical Manual of Mental Disorders diagnosis: Addictive disorders. *Journal of Addictions & Offender Counseling, 29*(2), 110–127. doi:10.1002/j.2161–1874.2009.

Hardman, R. K., Berrett, M. E., & Richards, P. S. (2003). Spirituality and ten false beliefs and pursuits of women with eating disorders: Implications for counselors. *Counseling & Values, 48*(1), 67–78. doi:10.1002/j.2161–007x.2003.tb00276.x

Hill, P. C., Pargament, K. I., Hood, R. W., McCullough, M. E., Swyers, J. P., Larson, D. B., & Zinnabauer, J.B. (2000). Conceptualizing religion and spirituality: Points of commonality, points of departure. *Journal for the Theory of Social Behavior, 30*(1), 51–77. doi:10.1111/1468–5914.00119

Holm, S. (1979). A simple sequential rejective method procedure. *Scandinavian Journal of Statistics, 6*, 65–70.

Homan, K. (2010). Athletic-ideal and thin-ideal internalization as prospective predictors of body dissatisfaction, dieting, and compulsive exercise. *Body Image, 7*, 240–245. doi:10.1016/j.bodyim.2010.02.004

Homan, K., & Boyatzis, C. (2010). The protective role of attachment to God against eating disorder risk factors: concurrent and prospective evidence. *Eating Disorders, 18*(3), 239–258. doi:10.1080/10640261003719534

Huline-Dickens, S. H. (2000). Anorexia nervosa: Some connections with the religious attitude. *British Journal of Medical Psychology, 73*, 67–76. doi:10.1348/000711200160309

Hudson, J. I., Hiripi, E., Pope, H. R., & Kessler, R. C. (2007). The prevalence and correlates of eating disorders in the national comorbidity survey replication. *Biological Psychiatry, 61*(3), 348–358. doi:10.1016/j.biopsych.2006.03.040

James, W. (1902/2002). *The varieties of religious experience: A study in human nature.* New York, NY: The Modern Library.

Joughin, N., Crisp, A. H., Halek, C., & Humphrey, J. (1992). Religious belief and anorexia nervosa. *International Journal of Eating Disorders, 12*(4), 397–406. doi:10.1002/1098–108X(199212)12:4<397::AID-EAT2260120407>3.0.CO;2–2

Katsogianni, I. V., & Kleftaras, G. (2015). Spirituality, meaning in life, and depressive symptomatology in drug addiction. *International Journal of Religion & Spirituality in Society, 5*(2), 11–24. doi:10.18848/2154–8633/cgp/v05i02/51104

Kim, K. H. (2006). Religion, body satisfaction and dieting. *Appetite, 46*(3), 285–296. doi:10.1016/j.appet.2006.01.006

Latzer, Y., Weinberger-Litman, S. L., Gerson, B., Rosch, A., Mischel, R., Hinden, T., & . . . Silver, J. (2015). Negative religious coping predicts disordered eating pathology among Orthodox Jewish adolescent girls. *Journal of Religion and Health, 54*(5), 1760–1771. doi:10.1007/s10943–014-9927-y

Lewica, M. M. (1999). *Starving for salvation: The spiritual dimensions of eating problems among American girls and women.* New York, NY: Oxford University Press.

Loth, K. A., MacLehose, R., Bucchianeri, M., Crow, S., & Neumark-Sztainer, D. (2014). Predictors of dieting and disordered eating behaviors from adolescence to young adulthood. *Journal of Adolescent Health, 55*(5), 705–712. doi:10.1016/j.jadohealth.2014.04.016

Marsden, G. M. (1980). *Fundamentalism and American culture: The shaping of twentieth century evangelicalism:* 1870–1925. New York, NY: Oxford University Press

Marsden, P., Karagianni, E., & Morgan, J. (2007). Spirituality and clinical care in eating disorders: a qualitative study. *International Journal of Eating Disorders, 40*(1), 7–12. doi:10.1002/eat.20333

Mancuso, S. G., Newton, J. R., Bosanac, P., Rossell, S. L., Nesci, J. B., & Castle, D. J. (2015). Classification of eating disorders: comparison of relative prevalence rates using DSM-IV and DSM-5 criteria. *British Journal of Psychiatry, 206*(6), 519–520. doi:10.1192/bjp.bp.113.143461

Miles, J., & Shevlin, M. (2006). *Applying regression and correlation.* London: Sage.

Moreira-Almeida, A., Koenig, H. G., & Lucchetti, G. (2014). Clinical implications of spirituality to mental health: review of evidence and practical guidelines. *Revista Brasileira De Psiquiatria, 36*(2), 176–182. doi:10.1590/1516–4446-2013–1255).

Neumark-Sztainer, D., Wall, M., Larson, N. I., Eisenberg, M. E., & Loth, K. (2011). Dieting and disordered eating behaviors from adolescence to young adulthood: Findings from a 10-year longitudinal study. *Journal of The American Dietetic Association, 111*(7), 1004–1011. doi:10.1016/j.jada.2011.04.012

Pallant, J. (2007). *SPSS survival manual* (3rd ed.). New York, NY: McGraw Hill.

Pargament, K. I. (1999). The psychology of religion and spirituality? Yes and no. *International Journal for the Psychology of Religion, 9*(1), 3–16. doi:10.1207/s15327582ijpr0901_2

Pargament, K. I., Koenig, H. G., & Perez, L. M. (2000). The many methods of religious coping: Development and initial validation of the RCOPE. *Journal of Clinical Psychology, 56*(4), 519–543. doi: 10.1002/(SICI)1097–4679(200004)56:4<519::AID-JCLP6>3.0.CO;2–1

Pargament, K. I., Smith, B. W., Koenig, H. G., & Perez, L. (1998). Patterns of positive and negative religious coping with major life stressors. *Journal for the Scientific Study of Religion, 37*, 710–724. doi:10.2307/1388152

Piedmont, R. L. (1999). Does spirituality represent the sixth factor of personality? Spiritual transcendence and the five-factor model. *Journal of Personality, 67*(6), 987–1013. doi:10.1111/1467–6494.00080

Piedmont, R. L. (2004). Spiritual transcendence as a predictor of psychosocial outcome from an outpatient substance abuse program. *Psychology of Addictive Behaviors, 18*(3), 213–222. doi:10.1037/0893–164X.18.3.213

Piedmont, R. L. (2005). *Assessment of Spirituality and Religious Sentiments.* Technical Manual. Baltimore, MD: Author.

Piedmont, R. (2007). Cross-cultural generalizability of the Spiritual Transcendence Scale to the Philippines: Spirituality as a human universal. *Mental Health, Religion & Culture, 10*(2), 89–107. doi:10.1080/13694670500275494

Piedmont, R. L. (2012). Overview and development of a trait-based measure of numinous constructs: The Assessment of Spirituality and Religious Sentiments (ASPIRES) Scale. In L. Miller (Ed). *The Oxford Handbook of Psychology and Spirituality.* New York, NY: Oxford University Press.

Pinhas, L., Heinmaa, M., Bryden, P., Bradley, S., & Toner, B. (2008). Disordered eating in Jewish adolescent girls. *The Canadian Journal of Psychiatry / La Revue Canadienne De Psychiatrie, 53*(9), 601–608. doi:10.1177/070674370805300907

Rampling, D. (1985). Ascetic ideals and anorexia nervosa. *Journal of Psychiatric Research, 19*(2/3), 89–94. doi:10.1016/0022-3956(85)90003-2

Rider, K. A., Terrell, D. J., Sisemore, T. A., & Hecht, J. E. (2014). Religious coping style as a predictor of the severity of anorectic symptomology. *Eating Disorders: The Journal of Treatment & Prevention, 22*, 163–179. doi:10.1080/10640266.2013.864890

Soper, D. (2017). A-priori sample size calculator for hierarchical multiple regression. In *Free Statistics Calculators.* Retrieved from: http://www.danielsoper.com/statcalc3/calc.aspx?id=16

Stice, E. (1994). Review of the evidence for a sociocultural model of bulimia nervosa and an exploration of the mechanisms of action. *Clinical Psychology Review, 14*(7), 633–661. doi:10.1016/0272-7358(94)90002-7

Stice, E. (2002). Risk and maintenance factors for eating pathology: A meta-analytic review. *Psychological Bulletin, 128*(5), 828–848. doi:10.1037/0033-2909.128.5.825

Stice, E., Chase, A., Stormer, S., & Appel, A. (2001). A randomized trial of a dissonance-based eating disorder prevention program. *International Journal of Eating Disorders, 29*, 247–262. doi:10.1002/eat.1016

Stice, E., Mazotti, L., Weibel, D., & Agras. W. S. (2000). Dissonance prevention program decreases thin-ideal internalization, body dissatisfaction, dieting, negative affect, and bulimic symptoms: A preliminary experiment. *International Journal of Eating Disorders, 27*, 206–217. doi:10.1002/(SICI)1098-108X(200003)27:2<206::AID-EAT9>3.0.CO;2-D

Sykes, D. K., Gross, M., & Subishin, S. (1986). Preliminary findings of demographic variables in patients suffering from anorexia nervosa and bulimia. *International Journal of Psychosomatics, 34*(1), 27–30.

Tabachnick, B. G., & Fidell, L. S. (2007). *Using multivariate statistics* (5th ed.). New York, NY: Pearson.

Tarakeshwar, N., Pargament, K. I., & Mahoney, A. (2003). Initial development of a measure of religious coping among Hindus. *Journal of Community Psychology, 31*(6), 607. doi:10.1002/jcop.10071

Thompson, J. K., & Stice, E. (2001). Thin-ideal internalization: Mounting evidence for a new risk factor for body-image disturbance and eating pathology. *Current Directions in Psychological Science*, 181–183. doi:10.1111/1467-8721.00144

Thompson, J. K., van den Berg, P., Roehrig, M., Guaurda, A. S., & Heinberg, L. J. (2004). The sociocultural attitudes toward appearance scale-3 (SATAQ-3): Development and validation. *The International Journal of Eating Disorders, 35*, 293–304. doi:10.1002/eat.10257

Tylka, T. L. (2004). The relation between body dissatisfaction and eating disorder symptomatology: An analysis of moderating variables. *Journal of Counseling Psychology, 51*, 178–191. doi:10.1037/0022-0167.51.2.178

Tylka, T. L., & Subich, L., M. (2002). Exploring young women's perceptions of the effectiveness and safety of maladaptive weight control techniques. *Journal of Counseling & Development, 80*, 101–110. doi:10.1002/j.1556-6678.2002.tb00172.x

Van Wormer, K. & Davis, D. R. (2018). *Addiction treatment: A strengths perspective* (4th ed.). Belmont, CA: Brooks/Cole.

Vandereycken, W., & Van Deth, R. (1994). *From fasting saints to anorexic girls: The history of self starvation.* New York, NY: University Press.

Volpe, U., Tortorella, A., Manchia, M., Monteleone, A. M., Albert, U., & Monteleone, P. (2016). Eating disorders: What age at onset?. *Psychiatry Research*, 238225–227. doi:10.1016/j.psychres.2016.02.048

Wilbur, C.J. & Colligan, R. C. (1981). Psychologic and behavioral correlates of anorexia nervosa. *Developmental and Behavioral Pediatrics*, 2(3), 89–92. doi:10.1097/00004703–198109000-00005

Wink, P., Dillon, M., & Larsen, B. (2005). Religion as a moderator of the depression-health connection: Findings from a longitudinal study. *Research on Aging*, 27(2), 197–220. doi:10.1177/0164027504270483

The *Annual Review of Addictions and Offender Counseling, Volume IV: Best Practices* is the fourth volume in a series of peer-reviewed edited books sponsored by the International Association of Addiction and Offender Counselors (IAAOC), a division of the American Counseling Association (ACA). Continuing the mission of past volumes, this volume provides a forum for publications addressing a broad array of topics in the field of addictions and offender counseling. Experts in the profession present innovative strategies and recommendations for best practices in drug education, intervention strategies, multicultural considerations, and counselor education.

Dr. Trevor J. Buser is an Associate Professor at Naropa University, where he teaches coursework in the Mindfulness-Based Transpersonal Counseling program. His research centers on cognitive predictors of nonsuicidal self-injury. He also brings a dedicated focus on addictions counseling and is former editor of the *Journal of Addictions and Offender Counseling*. Dr. Buser is a licensed professional counselor, certified school counselor, and approved clinical supervisor. He also served as President of IAAOC.

Dr. Pamela S. Lassiter is a Professor of Counseling in the Department of Counseling at the University of North Carolina at Charlotte. She has over 30 years of work experience in substance abuse treatment and community mental health. Dr. Lassiter holds credentials as a Licensed Professional Counselor, a Licensed Marriage & Family Therapist, and as a Licensed Clinical Addiction Specialist. She serves as Director of the Addictions Program at UNC Charlotte and teaches graduate courses in addiction and mental health counseling. She is also a Past-President of IAAOC and currently the Editor of the *Journal of Addiction and Offender Counseling.*

Dr. Kathleen Brown-Rice is an Associate Professor and Chair of the Department of Counselor Education at Sam Houston State University. Her clinical work is focused on clients with trauma and co-morbid substance use and mental health concerns. Dr. Rice holds credentials as a Licensed Professional Counselor, Licensed Clinical Addiction Specialist, National Certified Counselor, and Approved Clinical Supervisor. She is currently the Associate Editor of the *Journal of Addiction and Offender Counseling.*

IAAOC

International Association of Addictions & Offender Counselors

The International Association of Addictions and Offender Counselors (IAAOC) is an organization of professional substance abuse/addictions counselors, corrections counselors, students, and counselor educators who are concerned with improving the lives of individuals exhibiting addictive and/or criminal behaviors. Our mission is to provide leadership in and advancement of the professions of addiction and offender counseling. IAAOC is a division of the American Counseling Association.

Made in the USA
Columbia, SC
15 May 2020